WHERE THE RUBBER MEETS THE ROAD

The Bridgestone/Firestone Conspiracy of Death & Destruction

WHERE THE RUBBER MEETS THE ROAD

The Bridgestone/Firestone Conspiracy of Death & Destruction

A True Story

"A Company that Literally has Blood on its Hands"

Joseph Louis Lisoni
and
Gail Landtbom Lisoni

Mill City Press

Mill City Press, Inc.
2301 Lucien Way #415
Maitland, FL 32751
407.339.4217
www.millcitypress.net

© 2019 by Joseph Louis Lisoni and Gail Landtbom Lisoni

All rights reserved. No part of this publication may be reproduced, stored in a retrieval system, or transmitted, in any form or by any means, electronic, mechanical, photocopying, recording, or otherwise, without the prior written permission of the author.

Printed in the United States of America

ISBN-13: 978-1-54565-596-2

DEDICATION

We dedicate this book to the victims of the Bridgestone/Firestone "Steeltex" tire failures and to all the work the surviving victims have voluntarily done to collect the body of evidence that resulted in the February 2004 recall of 490,000 defective Firestone "Steeltex" tires. They were manufactured at the Bridgestone/Firestone plant in Joliette, Canada. Statistics rank this devastating incident as the third largest tire recall in U.S. history.

IN MEMORY OF OUR PARENTS
Patsy & Bill Landtbom
and
Frances & Joe Lisoni

FOREWORD

In the 1960s and 70s, a few pioneering attorneys changed the entire world of auto manufacturing. David Harney's exposure of the defective Corvair Monza, Ralph Nader's book, *Unsafe at Any Speed* and Mark Robinson's elimination of the defective Ford Pinto immortalized the doctrine of "crashworthiness" product liability in the field of motor vehicle safety.

The automotive community of the world owes these pioneers a huge debt of gratitude for the development of safer automobiles. Their efforts forced the entire world of automobile manufacturers and sub-component part suppliers to design, manufacture and market reasonably safe motor vehicles. Engineers were restricted in their efforts to design safe automobiles by board room directives or greed-based, cost cutting-conspiracies that pursue profits at the expense of safety. The vehicles we drive today are safer than any others manufactured since the invention of the wheel.

While *Where the Rubber Meets the Road* has been dedicated to others, the safety campaign it describes was motivated by the past efforts of these three aforementioned great Americans. The streets and highways of the world are safer now because they devoted the best years of their lives using hand-made sling slots and self-procured rocks to defeat the forces of a modern-day "Goliath." These men battled corporate greed, corruption, and all those who do not dream for a wonderful world that is a secure place for people to pursue a life free of unnecessary defective automobiles, needless bodily injury, and excessive air pollution.

Black's Law Dictionary defines a *conspiracy* as a "Combination of two or more persons or corporations acting in concert for an unlawful purpose."

"A defective product is an imperfection that has a manufacturing or design defect or is faulty because of inadequate instructions or warnings. A product is in a defective condition if it is unreasonably dangerous to the user or consumer who purchases the program and then causes damage."

This is the story of two attorneys exposing the deadly cover-up which led to the Bridgestone/Firestone Conspiracy of Death and Destruction.

TABLE OF CONTENTS

I. Background of Joe & Gail Lisoni 17
"A Pair to Draw To"

II. Background of Other Main Characters 21
"The Whole is Equal to the Sum of the Parts"

III. Attitude 24
"A Job Worth Doing is Worth Doing Well"

IV. Bridgestone/Firestone, Inc. 34
"Passion for Profits" Replaces "Passion for Excellence"

V. The Conspiracy Begins 44
"A Journey of a Thousand Miles Begins with a Single Step"

VI. The <u>One</u> Tire that Destroyed 10 Lives 50
"One Bad Apple Can Destroy the Whole Barrel"

VII. The Firestone Steeltex National Class Action to Remove the Defective Steeltex Tires from the Roads & Highways of the U.S. 75
"Bad acts give birth to drastic remedies"

VIII.	Petition NHTSA to re-open its investigation of the Steeltex line of tires	94

"If at first you don't succeed, try try again."

IX.	Documentation of the Litigation of the Nationwide Class Action	116

"The Nature of the Medium is the Nature of the Message"

X.	Direct Mail Investigation and Public Information Campaign	118

"Knowledge is Power"

XI.	Lobby the House & Senate, Attorneys General and Governors for a Congressional Investigation	126

"Not Influence Peddling, but Peddling Influence"

XII.	File Personal Injury Cases Nationwide to Compensate Victims of Steeltex Failures	130

"Eat the Elephant One Bite at a Time"

XIII.	File Insurance Company Property Damage and Personal Injury Subrogation Cases	133

"The Enemy of My Enemy is My Friend"

XIV.	Lobby the United Nations Regarding the Designed-In Defects of Steeltex Tires	135

"International Cooperation Equals International Safety"

XV.	Cooperate With the Illinois Federal Grand Jury Investigation	138

"Best Intentions Do Not Always Produce the Best Results"

Foreword

XVI.	Promote Dialogue with Stock Analysts and Encourage Institutional Shareholders to Liquidate Bridgestone/Firestone Holdings	140
	"Buy Low, Sell High – Damage Control"	
XVII.	Bridgestone/Firestone Concealed the Defective Tires and Then Destroyed Them	143
	"If You Can't Hide the Damning Evidence, You Must Destroy It"	
XVIII.	Lisoni & Lisoni Lobbies NHTSA and Congress	164
	"A Government of the People, by the People and for the People"	
XIX.	Motion for Class Certification	167
	"A Commonality of Wrongs Produces an Attempt at a Single Remedy"	
XX.	Bridgestone/Firestone, Inc and Bridgestone Corporation	190
	"They Were Corporations with Splendid Abilities But Were Absolutely Corrupt"	
XXI.	NHTSA	207
	"Absolute Power Corrupts Absolutely"	
XXII.	Tires Across America	224
	"The 4th of July - Independence Day"	
XXIII.	Bridgestone/Firestone: A Company that Literally has Blood on Its Hands	229
	"Slave labor equals human rights violations"	

| XXIV. | Conclusion | 234 |

"Never Have So Few Done So Much For So Many"

| XXV. | An Open Message to Bridgestone Corporation | 238 |

"Those Who Do Not Learn From History
Are Doomed to Repeat It"

| XXVI. | The Personal Toll on Lisoni & Lisoni | 241 |

"Great Victories Requires Great Sacrifices"

| XXVII. | The Players – Who They Were and What are
They Doing Now | 244 |

"All the World is a Stage"

On December 22, 2008, although it was winter, it was a sunny day in Los Angeles, California. Joe and Gail drove south on the Pasadena freeway, headed for the U.S. Bankruptcy Court in downtown Los Angeles, for our First Meeting of Creditors. Our life had suffered a catastrophic financial loss for unreimbursed expenses relating to the National Firestone Steeltex Tire Recall Campaign.

We filed for protection against our creditors pursuant to the bankruptcy laws in California. The action, In re the Bankruptcy of Lisoni & Lisoni, Case No.2:08-bk-30214-SB was filed on or about October 8, 2008, and discharged on August 5, 2010.

We were extremely anxious about our First Meeting of Creditors, as we suspected there would be people there to object to our bankruptcy.

We arrived early and parked the car, paying $26.00 to park. We went through "security". We rode the elevator up and appeared outside the large hearing room. We looked at the calendar and saw that we were No. 1 on the calendar. We did see some of our creditors there to object to our discharge, however, their objections were subsequently denied.

At 9:00 a.m., the Judge took the bench, announced that this was the First Meeting of Creditors, and called the calendar of 30 cases. He called our case and we walked up to the table and the Judge administered the oath, and then asked "So, what happened?"

Chapter I

BACKGROUND OF JOE & GAIL LISONI

"A Pair to Draw To"

We were partners in the successful law firm, Lisoni & Lisoni, of Pasadena, California. For over thirty years, we had practiced law in the field of product liability, personal injury, property damage and consumer advocacy, representing plaintiffs against large Fortune 500 companies, multinational corporations and governmental agencies.

Joseph Louis Lisoni was born in Los Angeles, in March, 1947. As an eleven year old, Joe's father built him a quarter midget racecar, in 1958, "Missfire". During the three years of racing before he out grew the car, he amassed many trophies. His quarter midget racecar, built by his father, has the first set of aluminum rims in a race car, the first midget with four-wheel suspension and had an engine built by Indianapolis legend, Carl Offenhauser. The racecar ran on alcohol fuel, which would prepare him for his legal career in product liability law and his pursuit of it as an alternate fuel source for automobiles manufactured worldwide. Today, the 1958 quarter midget racer is part of the collection of historic cars at the world famous, $120 million dollar Petersen Automotive Museum located on Wilshire Boulevard's "Miracle Mile" in Los Angeles, California.

Joe attended Junipero Serra High School in Gardena, California (1965), St. Mary's College in Moraga, California, (1969) and received his Juris Doctorate degree (1972) from the University of California, Hastings College of the Law in San Francisco, California. He passed the California State Bar Exam in 1972 on his first attempt. At Hastings Law School, he won the prestigious William Prosser Moot Court Award for outstanding appellate advocacy.

While awaiting his Bar results in 1972, Joe Lisoni was returning from an interview in downtown Los Angeles at the City Attorneys' Office when he was hit by an automobile with defective brakes. At the time, he was a pedestrian in a crosswalk, with a green light at the intersection of Spring and Temple Streets. The woman who hit him was driving a 1965 Pontiac Bonneville, which had lost its brakes due to a rupture of her right front hydraulic brake hose (a product failure) while going down the hill east bound on Temple Street. Unfortunately, Joe was a fast walker and was ahead of the pack of pedestrians in the crosswalk when the woman driving the Bonneville hit him in the crosswalk—going thirty-five miles per hour. He fractured his left femur, suffered internal injuries and sustained a concussion which caused him to spend almost six weeks in California Hospital, in traction, and nine months on crutches and a wheel chair.

A police officer was standing on the corner of Temple & Spring Streets and witnessed the accident and he immediately called the paramedics, who saved Joe's life by stabilizing his left leg preventing a laceration of his left femoral artery. The paramedics testified that he remembered Joe because he kept going in and out of consciousness, and kept saying "I'm a lawyer! I have insurance! Take me to a good hospital!" The City Attorney's Office called Joe while he was in the hospital in Los Angeles to offer him a job, but he had to decline due to his severe injuries.

Gail Marie Landtbom Lisoni was born in San Francisco, California in March, 1949. She, is one of seven children, born to William and Patsy Landtbom, and has a twin brother, Greg Landtbom, with whom she is very close. Her father, William Landtbom, a graduate of the University of San Francisco Law School, was an attorney, had been appointed by J. Edgar Hoover

Background of Joe & Gail Lisoni

in 1940 to the Federal Bureau of Investigation. After he completed his basic training at Quantico, Virginia, he was assigned to the FBI office in San Francisco, California where he was instrumental in breaking the Japanese code during World War II.

Gail graduated from St. Rose Academy High School in San Francisco, California (1967) and Dominican College (now Dominican University of San Rafael, California (1971). She met Joe Lisoni in her senior year, and immediately embarked on an exclusive relationship, culminating in their marriage in March, 1984, at Holy Angeles Catholic Church, in Arcadia, California.

She received her Juris Doctorate degree in 1978 from the University of West Los Angeles, School of Law. She attended law school at night, and worked as a law librarian for a large Century City law firm, Mitchell Silberberg & Knupp, during the day. She also worked as a paralegal during the day for the Housing Authority of the City of Los Angeles to pay her living expenses and law school tuition.

Joe and Gail practiced law together as Lisoni & Lisoni, A Law Corporation, first in Los Angeles, California and then in Pasadena, California. Lisoni & Lisoni handled several multi-million dollar personal injury cases involving defective products. They had sued many of the largest manufacturing corporations in the United States and abroad, and therefore, were not intimidated at all by the size of the defendant, Bridgestone/Firestone, the largest tire manufacturer of the world.

Joe Lisoni believed in the National Football League Legend, John Madden's philosophy, "I don't care if the horses are blind, load the wagons". John Madden was the head coach of the Oakland Raiders Super Bowl Champions and an Emmy Award winning television football commentator. Joe had the "can do" spirit, especially if he was told by others that he could not accomplish his goal.

Joe developed a "can do" attitude towards the challenges of life that began with his application to various law schools in his senior year of college at St. Mary's College of California, where he maintained a 3.0 Grade Point Average (GPA), as a political science major and a minor in speech and debate. He applied to the UCLA School of Law, but his application was summarily denied by the admissions office. When Joe had a meeting with the Dean of Admissions at UCLA to appeal his admissions denial he was told, "The law is not for everyone," and "Why don't you go to graduate school and get a masters and PhD in your undergraduate major of political science and become a University Professor?" Not deterred by his rejection by UCLA, Joe applied to the prestigious University of California Hastings College of the Law in San Francisco. His application again was summarily denied.

Joseph Alioto was the Mayor of San Francisco at the time and he was a graduate of St. Mary's. His three sons had also graduated from St. Mary's, one of them—Tom Alioto—was in Joe's class. Joe asked him if he could arrange a meeting with the Mayor to seek his assistance in being admitted to Hastings Law School. The meeting was arranged and the mayor agreed to call the Hastings Dean of Admissions, asking him to re-evaluate Joe's application. Three days before graduating from St. Mary's College, Joe received a letter from Hastings Law School advising him his name had been removed from the school's admissions waiting list and he was accepted to be admitted as a first-year student in the 1969-70 academic year – the class of 1972.

Chapter II
BACKGROUND OF OTHER MAIN CHARACTERS

"The Whole is Equal to the Sum of the Parts"

In the early 1940s, the Japanese government killed thousands of Chinese people. They kidnapped and separated many Chinese families and sent the able-bodied Chinese men and women away to farming work camps. The parents of our legal assistant, Jiang Ping, were married in 1940, and were then separated by the Chinese Communist government for eight years in different work camps. They believed that they would never see each other again.

However, as fate would have it, they found each other again and Jian Ping Zhang was the product of their reunification. She had grown up in Dalien, on the north east coast of China. During the 1960's in China, under the Communist rule of Mao, many Chinese men and women were taken from their homes and family at the age of eighteen, and were sent to the "country" to farm, and were required to spend at least eight years in the country. Jian Ping Zhang was sent to the country in 1968 and was relieved of these duties in 1976. She went to work for a Chinese printing company located in California, and so was able to come to the United States.

After completing her work for the Chinese company in the United States, she settled in Los Angeles, and began working for a criminal defense attorney, Fred Witherspoon, Esq. in Alhambra,

When The Rubber Meets The Road

California. We had known Fred Witherspoon, Esq. over the years and he had referred several cases to us.

Firestone Tire & Rubber Co. was an American company, built by Harvey Firestone in 1900. It was purchased by Bridgestone Corporation of Japan in 1988 and in 1990 it became Bridgestone/Firestone, Inc., a wholly owned subsidiary of Bridgestone Corporation of Japan. Firestone was purchased because of its massive manufacturing infrastructure, which the Bridgestone Corporation of Japan needed so that they could "corner the market" on tire sales in China, the world's last frontier for tire sales. Times were changing and the millions of people who rode bicycles in China would soon be driving cars, which would require four tires and a spare.

In the 1990's, Bridgestone Corporation began quietly building production plants and retail sales outlets in China. The Japanese intended to exploit the Chinese people once again. It planned to use Firestone's huge manufacturing capacity to enable it to make tires to sell in China while it finished building manufacturing tire plants in China.

During this same period of time in Ningbo, China, on the southeast coast of China, ten Chinese individuals, born in the 50's, were also sent to the "country" to be farmers. After eight years they were released. They attended college, graduated, went on to medical school, and then completed their internship and residency. They began practicing medicine for the Chinese Communist government, and eventually they worked their way up to prestigious medical positions of substantial authority in the Chinese Communist government. The eight doctors and two hospital administrators each have their own personal stories of the courage and bravery they demonstrated throughout this a period of adversity.

In 1976, in Lavergne, Tennessee, William (Bill) Orr, a decorated combat veteran of the 101st airborne division serving in Vietnam, went to work for Firestone Tire & Rubber in Lavergne, Tennessee. He worked for Bridgestone/Firestone for a total of twenty-five years; twelve years in production and another thirteen years in quality control where he was trained by Bridgestone/Firestone in the art and science of tire failure analysis.

Background of Other Main Characters

All of these individuals came together tragically in 2000 to correct a serious injustice resulting from the implementation of the Bridgestone/Firestone cost-cutting program, "C-95," memorialized in a written memorandum from the CEO of Bridgestone in Japan (Mr. Masatoshi Ono) directed to the CEO of Bridgestone/Firestone (Mr. John Lampe), all in furtherance of the Bridgestone/Firestone Conspiracy of Death & Destruction.

Chapter III

ATTITUDE

"A Job Worth Doing is Worth Doing Well"

Our preparation and pathway to attempt an endeavor such as a national tire recall campaign of over 30 million tires began like this:

After being released from the hospital, Joe got his first job as an attorney. He used his entire salary of $750.00 per month to pay for a taxi to take him to and from his first job as an attorney at Ibold & Anderson in 1973, in Los Angeles, California.

Joe talked to several attorneys about suing General Motors for damages for product liability. It was a relatively new field of law and all of them told him that he could not sue General Motors for the defective brake hose and win. At the time, General Motors was the Number one automobile manufacturer in the world, the largest publicly held corporation in the world and was very powerful.

Consequently, he decided to represent himself, in conjunction with Gail, who was a paralegal and in law school at the time. Together, they filed a lawsuit against General Motors for damages for product liability.

They researched the facts of the accident and found that the brake failure was the result of a defect in the front hydraulic brake hoses General Motors was installing in the 1965 Pontiac Bonneville. They were using cotton instead of nylon in their construction, which caused them to rupture as the cotton deteriorated after a long period of use. He went to several junk yards in the Los Angeles area, looking for any 1965 Pontiac Bonnevilles with front end damage, resulting from brake hose failures. He found thirty-three ruptured hoses from 1965 Pontiac Bonnevilles with front end damage and purchased the vehicles' broken brake hoses from the auto wrecking yards, and he kept them in a large, orange crate. It was produced several months later at his deposition taken by General Motors defense attorney, Eugene Genson, Esq. of Spray, Gould & Bowers and General Motors General Counsel Charles Bennett, Esq.

We litigated the case and would send General Motors weekly discovery demands, described as "the treat of the week," the likes of which the defense attorneys were not used to and did not want to answer. We filed motions in court against General Motors to compel compliance with discovery demands and were successful every time. Gail's research produced a case in the Arkansas Appellate Court involving the exact same defect which General Motors had covered up and lied about the defect in their answers to discovery—under penalty of perjury.

We amended the complaint and alleged punitive damages against General Motors for the "Wanton, reckless, and willful disregard for the safety of the motoring public."

General Motors flew out its General Counsel, Charles Bennett, Esq. to take Joe's Deposition. Gail was the paralegal and their friend, Fred T. Ragsdale, Esq. was Joe's attorney at the deposition. During Joe's testimony, he advised GM's defense attorneys that he wanted all 1965 Pontiac Bonneville vehicles still in service to be recalled. It was important to note that Joe's testimony at the deposition established that 850,000 vehicles had been recalled for this defect by the National Highway Traffic & Safety Administration (NHTSA).

Joe settled his case in 1975, on the day of his deposition, for $90,000 tax-free, from General Motors and $15,000 from Midas Muffler, and invested the funds in his new law practice at 3701 Wilshire Boulevard, Suite 700, Los Angeles, California.

Gail had moved to Los Angeles in 1973 to attend paralegal school. She finished the course and then went on to law school at the University of West Los Angeles, attending at night. During the day, she worked as the paralegal for the Housing Authority of the City of

Los Angeles' General Counsel, Frank. M. Garcia, Esq., and worked for Joe as often as she could. After passing the Bar Examination in 1979, she worked full time as Joe's full partner.

During the time she was employed by the Housing Authority of the City of Los Angeles as the paralegal assigned to the office of the General Counsel, she came into possession of information that demonstrated that the officers of the Housing Authority were perpetrating illegal and unlawful acts during the course and scope of their employment at the Housing Authority. Michael Saltzman, Executive Director and Ida Arestead, Assistant Executive Director learned that Gail possessed this damaging information and formed an unlawful conspiracy to oust her from her job at the Housing Authority.

In an attempt to force Gail to resign her position as paralegal, they began verbally harassing her at her workplace at the Los Angeles headquarters of the Housing Authority. When their verbal harassment and workplace abuse failed, they would order Gail, on occasion, to go to the Nickerson Gardens and Jordan Downs Housing projects alone. The Housing projects had the highest crime rate in the city of Los Angeles. This tactic endangered Gail's safety—at the time, she was a young twenty-four year old Caucasian female, in the most dangerous public housing project in Los Angeles County. It exposed her to criminal assaults and much worse. When this final desperate attempt to force Gail to resign her job did not work, Michael Saltzman, Executive Director and Ida Arestead falsely charged Gail with allegedly lying on her application for employment and terminated her from her position.

Gail filed for a Grievance Hearing to defend herself against the false charges. Gail was in law school at the time and if she was found guilty of lying on her application for a job with a federally funded public entity, she could be found unfit to practice law when she applied for admission to the California State Bar.

Joe Lisoni represented to the hearing officer of the Housing Authority, Thomas Tapp, that the charge against her was fabricated and untrue. We were unsuccessful in our attempt to clear the record before the biased hearing officer, but she had satisfied her duty to exhaust her administrative remedies. We filed a Los Angeles County

Superior Court wrongful termination lawsuit against the Housing Authority employees, Michael Saltzman, Ida Arestead, and Thomas Tapp, and every member of the Board of Directors who conspired together to terminate her employment for cause.

After vigorous litigation on our part, and after receiving a one-million dollar default judgment (which was a front page story in the legal newspaper, Metropolitan News), she received a large monetary damage award but, most importantly, she received an unprecedented "Confession of Judgment" signed by all of the Directors of the Housing Authority, admitting they falsified their claims of wrongful conduct on her part to allow them to terminate her before she could go public with the damaging information. She needed a "Confession of Judgment" in order to establish her fitness for the practice of law by the State Bar of California.

Subsequent to the resolution of the case, the Los Angeles Times conducted an investigation lasting several weeks, making public the scandalous information we possessed, which lead to a Congressional investigation that resulted in a complete reorganization of the Housing Authority of the City of Los Angeles. Subsequent to the Congressional investigation ordering a complete reorganization, Gail received several telephone calls from disgruntled employees of the Housing Authority seeking advice on how to protect themselves from unmerited criticism of their job performance. Joe received several calls requesting his representation at the grievance hearings, but he declined because the cost of such litigation exceeded the value of the damages suffered by the employee victims of workplace abuse.

Joe and Gail moved in together in 1980 and married in 1984, and became the firm of Lisoni & Lisoni, a Law Corporation, in Los Angeles, California.

Joe always had a dream to run for the United States Congress. In 1979, he learned that Charles ("Chuck") Manatt, Esq. was the National Democratic Finance Chairman, the president of the National and California Bankers Associations, as well as the founder, president and chairman of the board of First Los Angeles Bank, located in the Century City District in Los Angeles, California.

In furtherance of his dream, he asked his client, Lynn Slaughter, head clerk of the bank, what would be the best way to get a meeting with Chuck Manatt to determine if he had the credentials to run for Congress. Lynn Slaughter advised Joe that the best way to develop a relationship with Chuck Manatt was to get other attorneys to open up new client trust accounts. The bank was courting attorneys for their client trust accounts in order to increase the capital base, which determined how much money it was allowed to loan its customers. Joe was very successful in his efforts to get attorneys to open up new client trust accounts at the bank.

The Bank President, Joe Digange, was so impressed with Joe's business development with regard to new client trust accounts, that he asked Joe if there was anything he could do for him to show his appreciation. Joe said yes, and he requested a lunch with Chuck Manatt to discuss his desire to be a United States Congressman.

Within a week, Joe Lisoni, Joe Digange, and Chuck Manatt were having lunch in the Il Padrino Restaurant in the Beverly Wilshire Hotel, in Beverly Hills. Joe told Chuck that it was his dream to run for Congress, but he needed to know if he "had a major league fast ball," and if not, he would go back to practicing law.

He verbally went through his resume with Chuck Manatt and Joe Digange, and then asked, "So, do you think I have a major league fast ball?" Chuck responded, "How would you like to go to President Jimmy Carter's Birthday Party on Friday in Washington, DC?" Joe said "Yes" and Chuck Manatt agreed to make all of the travel arrangements for the trip. Chuck asked Joe if he would like to become a member of the prestigious National Democratic Party Finance Committee, located in Washington, DC. Joe's reply was "Most definitely!"

During his first trip to the nation's capital—as a guest of Chuck Manatt—the day before the President's Birthday Celebration, Joe was invited to a special event party in the Senate Caucus Room where prestigious members of the United States Senate were supposed to "schmooze," with the invited, important Democratic supporters, and entice them to contribute money to President Jimmy Carter's 1980 re-election campaign.

During the event, Joe noticed that Senator Ted Kennedy was giving some of the donors the "bums rush" in his reception line. Joe felt this was because Kennedy was considering a challenge to Jimmy

Carter's nomination at the National Democratic Party Convention. Joe complained to Committee members about what he had seen, and they responded, "How can we prove it?" Joe explained that he would change his nametag to read "Joe Kopekne", and he felt that Kennedy should notice the name and stop him to talk, but probably would not notice. Sure enough, Kennedy did not notice, proving his claim against Senator Kennedy.

While Joe was standing in line with his new nametag, he was unaware that members of the National Finance Council had advised a Washington Post reporter of his plan. Joe went through Senator Kennedy's receiving line once again and Senator Kennedy did not notice his nametag. After being snubbed twice, while Joe was making a comment about it to a member of the Finance Council, a Washington Post reporter, with microphone in hand and a photographer recording the event, verbally criticized Joe for what the reporter characterized as an insulting, unethical, and unprofessional act on Joe's part in trying to discredit Senator Kennedy's fundraising efforts. The reporter said, "While I understand that you are a prominent California attorney, your conduct just now with regard to Senator Kennedy was 'unethical, insulting and very unprofessional.'" She was a strong supporter of Senator Kennedy and was very upset with Joe's antics.

Joe immediately assessed the situation and told the Washington Post reporter, with microphone in hand, "You are correct, I am a prominent California attorney, and I am also a private citizen and that I am at a private party and that if one word appears in the Washington Post about the incident, I will make the Washington Post famous for something other than Watergate." As a guest of Chuck Manatt on his first trip to Washington, he realized that his conduct could be construed by some to be inappropriate. Not wanting to embarrass Chuck Manatt, or escalate the situation, he left the party immediately. Upon his return to his hotel, he called Gail in Los Angeles and told her he thought his political career was over before it had started.

The next morning, there was nothing in the Washington Post and Joe thought he was safe. He called Gail to tell her he thought there was no damage done to his political career. He was invited to the presidential dinner that evening at the Washington Hilton Hotel and found that he was seated with President Jimmy Carter, First Lady Rosalyn Carter, Speaker of the House, Tip O'Neill, Senator Thomas Eagleton, Senator Birch Bye and Chuck Manatt. When he saw Chuck Manatt as other attendees were arriving for the dinner, he felt great apprehension as to whether or not Mr. Manatt had heard about the Kennedy incident. Chuck Manatt approached Joe, extended his hand, and welcomed Joe to the event, saying, "What's this I hear about you and Senator Kennedy at last night's fund-raiser on the hill?" Joe, realizing that Mr. Manatt had already heard of the Kennedy incident, Joe was immediately overcome with a sense of anxiety and in fact now believed his political career was over.

Joe's response was an immediate apology to Chuck Manatt, stating he hoped that he had not embarrassed the Finance Council members with the potential campaign contributors that were at the fundraising event. Chuck's response was music to Joe's ears "Joe, no apology necessary. Your first night in Washington, DC, you successfully took on Senator Kennedy and the Washington Post. That's just the kind of man that belongs in the United States Congress." To make this result even better, Chuck Manatt asked Joe if he would like to meet Walter Mondale, the Vice President. Joe replied, "It would be an honor." Chuck Manatt responded, "Well the Vice President is standing right behind you." Walter Mondale, having overheard the conversation between Joe and Chuck, extended his hand and said "Welcome to Washington, Joe, but be careful of the press, they're barracudas."

Subsequent to Joe's dinner with President Carter at his birthday celebration where his guests were entertained by the singer Diana Ross, the Democratic National Committee appointed Joe to the National House & Senate Council. This organization was composed of three representative Democrats from each of the fifty states of the U.S. All members would meet in the West Wing of the White House every 90 days to inform President Carter's Chief of Staff, Hamilton Jordan, of the issues that were most important to the citizens of each state. Joe was appointed to a position as a vehicle to begin his career in politics. In his tenure as a member of the organization representing California, Joe served with Leland Prussia, President and CEO of Bank of America as well as Lew Wasserman, President and CEO of Universal Studios, exclusive company to partner with in the pursuit of the implementation of President Carter's political agenda. Also, subsequent to the "Kennedy incident," Chuck Manatt appointed Joe to a high ranking position in the National Democratic Finance Council.

Hugh Hefner, publisher of Playboy Magazine, invited Lew Wasserman to use his Southern California Mansion for a Democratic fund-raising event. Joe and Leland Prussia co-chaired the fundraising event with Lew Wasserman. The event was very successful and raised thousands of dollars for the National Democratic Party. Most importantly, after a one-on-one conversation with Hugh Hefner at the gala event, Mr. Hefner agreed to endorse Joe in any attempt to run for public office from California.

As fate would have it, Joe's *Ted Kennedy* antics did not end his career in Democratic politics, but rather elevated him to a place where he would be recognized as a credible candidate for an elective public office. Joe Lisoni decided to run for Congress from the 26th Congressional District of California as a Democrat in 1980. He became licensed to practice law in Washington, DC; he purchased a condo near Embassy Row and opened a bank account at the prestigious Riggs National Bank on Pennsylvania Avenue, two blocks from the White House.

He was "groomed" for Washington by Charles (Chuck) Manatt, Esq., the new National Democratic Party Chairman. Joe continued on as a member of the National House & Senate Advisory Council, and he made trips to Washington, DC every ninety days for a White House briefing from Hamilton Jordan, President Carter's Chief of Staff. Gail was the Treasurer of his campaign committee, "Californians for Lisoni," and ran the law office on Wilshire Blvd. in Los Angeles, during the campaign, in addition to working on the campaign trail.

Joe had anticipated an open race since the Republican incumbent, John Rousselot, had announced he would give up his seat in Congress to run for the U.S. Senate seat against Senator Alan Cranston. Tom Mack, an engineer, and former offensive lineman for the Los Angeles Rams, was expected to be Joe's republican opposition candidate. Given Joe's professional credentials, he was not expected to have any problem defeating the former NFL football star in the November, 1980 general election. Joe's candidacy for the congressional seat representing California's 26th District was so strong that no Democrat was expected to challenge him in the Democratic primary election, however, at the last minute, the Republican incumbent, John Roussellot, decided not to run against Alan Cranston for the Senate, and stayed in his congressional race. Joe was successful in winning the Democratic nomination. Joe ran a good race, but he was out matched by the ten-year incumbent in November, 1980.

John Rousselot had represented part of California's San Gabriel Valley in Congress and was formerly an Officer of the John Birch Society. A glad-hand and energetic campaigner, Rousselot was controversial and colorful as he surfed the changing waves of political power. He first gained office in 1960 when he ousted the Democratic Congressman, George Kasem in the 25th Congressional District. But he was so outspoken in defending the right wing Birch Society, which he had just joined, that he failed to win re-election. As a result of the census and redistricting, the 25th Congressional District became the 26th Congressional District. In 1970, he was returned to Washington for one of four more terms, prior to defeating Joe in 1980.

Joe's campaign focused on rebuilding the United States Military, developing affordable housing for all U.S. citizens in fulfillment of the American dream and replacing dirty fossil fuel for the automobile with clean burning and less expensive alcohol fuel. Iran was holding dozens of American citizens hostage during Joe's year-long campaign for Congress. His campaign motto was "A nation that is energy self-sufficient cannot be held hostage economically or militarily."

Although the slogan had no "traction" in 1980—today, it is the definition of the "green economy". Joe's advanced understanding of the major challenges facing the U.S. was many years ahead of his time. Joe ran such an impressive campaign against John Rousellot that after the campaign Congressman Rousellot asked Joe to change parties and become a Republican candidate for Congress. Given the huge success of the Ronald Reagan Presidential campaign of 1980, Joe found this to be a flattering offer but, as a life-long

Italian, Catholic Democrat, he decided to turn down the offer and return to the practice of law with his wife, Gail. The loss of the campaign was a financial disaster. When John Rousellot re-entered the race for Congress, it caused all of Joe's campaign contributions to evaporate, and it took Joe and Gail until 1983 to pay off all of the campaign debts.

During the Campaign for Congress, Joe and Gail were unable to raise much money for Joe's campaign organization, *Californians for Lisoni*, after Rouselott re-entered the race. To further complicate his bid to be elected to the U.S. Congress in 1980, over 200 political action committees rejected his request for donations. He was a political unknown, given no chance of being elected in the November 1980 General Election. Consequently, Joe & Gail financed the campaign with more than $500,000 in Mastercard and Visa credit card cash advances. To add insult to injury, after the 1980 election loss, the Federal Elections Commission did not believe Joe & Gail when they filed disclosure statements saying that they had self-funded Joe's campaign. After much investigation, the Federal Elections Committee finally accepted the fact that Joe's campaign was self-funded—violating the age-old campaign strategy mandating that a candidate never use his or her own money to get elected to public office. Facing a massive debt, Joe and Gail chose not to file bankruptcy but instead worked very hard to pay off the debt.

During this period, Joe and Gail, as Lisoni & Lisoni, were major litigators and handled high profile product liability and personal injury cases. Lisoni & Lisoni sued American Motors for a defective CJ-5 Jeep fuel storage system; sued the state of California for a defective and dangerous Highway 126; sued Anheiser-Busch for a defective beer bottle; sued the Catholic Church for damages resulting in quadriplegia, due to negligent supervision; sued the Los Angeles Dodgers and Pyrotechnics, Inc. for a defective fireworks mortar; sued Mobil Oil Co. for personal injuries resulting from a refinery fire; sued several insurance companies for bad faith breach of insurance contracts, all producing multi-million dollar judgments/settlements.

Chapter IV

BRIDGESTONE/FIRESTONE, INC.

"Passion for Profits" Replaces "Passion for Excellence"

In 1900, Harvey Firestone founded Firestone Tire & Rubber Company. In 1931, Shojiro Ishibashi founded Bridgestone Corporation. Shojiro was born February 1, 1889, and died September 11, 1976. He was a Japanese businessman. The Bridgestone Corporation was named after its founder. In the Japanese language, "ishi" means "stone" and bashi (hashi) means "bridge", hence the origin of the company's name is English. It's ironic, that, given Bridgestone's current "passion for profits," which resulted in the production of millions of defective tires. His motto for Bridgestone Corporation was "To serve society with products of superior quality." The motto no longer reflects Bridgestone's quality control standards. Firestone continued to grow and diversify into new markets and developed numerous advances in tire and rubber technology. However, in 1978, Firestone suffered a major setback with the recall of fourteen-million Firestone 500 tires, due to tread separations caused by the use of sub-standard component parts, resulting in the largest recall in U.S. history by the National Highway & Traffic Safety Administration (NHTSA).

In 1983, Bridgestone Corporation of Japan purchased the Firestone Tire & Rubber Co., head quartered in Akron, Ohio, with its major production facility in Lavergne, Tennessee. In furtherance of its "Passion for Profits", Bridgestone Corporation purchased all of the assets of Firestone Tire & Rubber, Inc. in 1988 for $2.6 billion dollars, making Bridgestone Corporation of Japan the world's largest tire and rubber company.

In 1995, in an attempt to reduce its massive debt, Bridgestone Corporation authorized its wholly-owned American subsidiary, Bridgestone/Firestone Inc., to secretly implement an unprecedented tire manufacturing cost-reduction program, "C-95", which reduced production costs of their tires by 26% over four years. This conspiratorial cost reduction program was responsible for more global deaths, injuries, and property damage claims than any other tire manufacturing process since the invention of rubber tires. The cost reduction program, "C-95," was memorialized in a written memorandum from the Chief Executive Officer (CEO) of Bridgestone/Firestone, Inc., Mr. Masatoshi Ono, and directed to the Chief Executive Officer (CEO) of Bridgestone/Firestone, Inc., Mr. John Lampe. The "C-95" cost reduction program and Firestone's agreement to implement such a program was fully inspired by, accepted and approved by Bridgestone Corporation, which owned 100% of the stock of Bridgestone/Firestone, Inc, and marked the first act in the formation of the Bridgestone/Firestone Conspiracy of Death and Destruction. The New Cost Reduction Program—Project C-95, written by Masatoshi Ono, provided:

"In order to build on this success and establish a firm business foundation for the 21st century, however, we must implement further cost reduction measures. I am sure each of you understands the need to redouble our efforts, but let me present my own perspective. At present, BFS is approximately two-billion dollars in debt. This represents a massive liability – especially in view of the fact that market interest rates are expected to rise in the United States as the Federal Reserve moves to keep inflation down and correct the country's current account deficits. . .

To create a solid base as a tire manufacturer operating in North America and hold our own against the competition in the 21st century, the most critical management issues for BFS in the next four to five year are to eliminate the causes of its higher costs and establish price competitiveness...To do this, we need to lower our development and production costs dramatically, including costs for materials, conversion costs, and costs for waste and scrap...I have set goals for us to reduce Bridgestone Firestone's company-wide cost base on a year-to-year (annual improvement) basis by 5% in 1994, 7.5% in 1995, 7.5% in 1996, and an additional 7.5% in 1997. These may be considered very challenging or even extremely difficult... but Bridgestone Japan and its southeast Asian plants have been implementing similar plans since 1993 and have already achieved remarkable results...

The headquarters and staff divisions must implement their own cost reductions while supporting the planning and implementation of these measures so that the technology, production, and sales and marketing divisions can achieve their goals."

The conspiracy to design and implement the "C-95" tire manufacturing cost reduction program was a textbook example of two corrupt and profit-driven industrial giants combining their resources to perform criminal acts in violation of federal legislation (T.R.E.A.D. Act) by intentionally producing unsafe and dangerous Firestone Steeltex tires. Millions of these tires were marketed for sale to the public and put into the stream of national and international commerce. Bridgestone/Firestone concealed the defects in the tires as a result of making a "business decision" that it was less expensive to pay millions in damages to the injured victims than to spend billions to recall the defective tires. Bridgestone/Firestone, Inc. and Bridgestone Corporation of Japan knew that the intentional and premeditated conspiracy to use substandard components in the tire manufacturing process used by Bridgestone/Firestone, Inc. certainly would result in the production of dangerously defective tires that would experience sudden, unexpected, and catastrophic tread separations. In furtherance of the conspiracy, the two corrupt corporations manufactured millions of defective Firestone Steeltex tires and then concealed their criminal acts by installing the defective tires as *original equipment* on seventy-one models of vehicles in the U.S., knowing that they were not subject to further inspections by the manufacturers.

On February 4, 2000, Bridgestone Firestone, Inc. issued the following press release regarding its Radial ATX (Wilderness) tires:

> "We at Bridgestone/Firestone, Inc. take great pride in the quality and durability of our products and we stand behind all of them. We work hard every day to earn and maintain the loyalty and trust of our customers, and we have full confidence in the performance of our Firestone Radial ATX tires. Firestone has manufactured more than 12 million Radial ATX tires—nearly 6.8 million of which were original equipment on virtually all of the millions of Explorers produced by the Ford Motor Company from 1990 to 1996. The Radial ATX has proven to be a reliable workhorse for U.S. consumers. Our experience with the Radial ATX indicates high consumer satisfaction with the quality and reliability of these tires. No court or jury has ever found any deficiency in these tires."

This statement from Bridgestone/Firestone, Inc. was completely false, as history has shown. In August, 2000, as a result of the implementation of "C-95" cost reduction program, and after a Congressional investigation, co-chaired by Senator John McCain and Congressman William Tauzin, Bridgestone/Firestone Inc. suffered the second largest tire recall in U.S. history, the recall of ten-million Firestone "Wilderness" AT & ATX tires, which came as original equipment on Ford Explorers. Ford Motor Company replaced an additional eighteen-million Wilderness tires to protect the brand name integrity of the Ford Explorer. Finally, in 2005, Bridgestone/Firestone agreed to pay $240 million dollars to Ford Motor Company in settlement for its responsibility in manufacturing defective tires as a result of the "C-95" reduction program. In addition, a Ford Motor

Co. stockholders' suit resulted in a multi-million dollar settlement for tires not covered by the Congressional Order of Recall that Ford purchased to protect the Ford Explorer brand name.

While the "C-95" cost reduction program provided some relief from debt for the parent company, Bridgestone Corporation, it was seriously flawed. The fundamental assumption that a tire manufacturing company could reduce the quality of its products, eliminate company debt, and increase profits at the same time is an economist's dream, but was realistically flawed.

The reality of the implementation of the Bridgestone/Firestone manufacturing cost reduction plan, "C-95," was that its fundamental flaws began to appear almost immediately through tire failures. Tire defects caused deaths, injury accidents, and property damage to vehicles on the roads and highways of the United States and numerous foreign countries.

It is very important to note that prior to the Congressional Order of Recall of the Wilderness A/T and ATX tires that came as original factory equipment on Ford Explorers, Steve Beretsky, Chief Defect Investigator of the NHTSA wrongfully and summarily denied the Taxpayer Petition to order a government recall of the Wilderness tires. During the recall of the Wilderness At and ATX tires, the National Highway Traffic & Safety Administration (NHTSA) also investigated the "Steeltex" tire line at that time, but refused to issue a recall of that tire, secretly admitting that to implement an additional recall would force Bridgestone/Firestone out of business or into bankruptcy—it was "too big to fail." This was an incredibly irresponsible and unlawful act on the part of Steve Beretsky personally and the NHTSA generally. The Firestone Steeltex tire was used on seventy-one different model vehicles as original factory equipment. Steve Beretsky and NHTSA knew that the Firestone Steeltex tire was just the "big brother" of the Wilderness tire and it was produced with the identical flaws that had been found in the production of the Wilderness tires, in furtherance of the "C-95" Cost Reduction Program and the criminal conspiracy to implement it. Bridgestone Firestone, Inc. knew of the existence of the defects and secretly conspired with the NHTSA to attempt "damage control" and "ride out the storm."

In June, 1999, attorneys from the legal department in Akron, Ohio, came to the Lavergne, Tennessee plant and instructed Bill Orr, who knew of the "C-95" Cost Reduction Program, on writing documents and how to give testimony which would be beneficial to Bridgestone/Firestone. He was instructed *not* to use the word "defect", but to use the word "anomaly," and not to use the word "counter-measure," but to use the word "improvement." He was also instructed to destroy all technical quality and development documents over three years old. Also, he was provided with a "pocket sized" manual entitled "Bridgestone Passenger Radial Cured Tire Guard." Employees were instructed to keep this "pocket size" guide in their pocket for quick reference. This book documented substandard production anomalies/defects resulting from "C-95 Cost Reduction Program" and how to cover them up. Although Bridgestone/Firestone executives knew of the upcoming recall of the Wilderness tires in June, 1999, Bill Orr was not made aware of the recall until June, 2000.

Bill Orr was selected to serve in the Lavergne, Tennessee Technical Center because of his production experience in the tire assembly department, the curing department, and the Banbury department. His college academic degree and his widely known reputation for quality work were also factors for his selection. During August 21-25, 2000, his team went to Ontario, California and Portland, Oregon to examine the first returns of the "recall" tires. Many of the failed Wilderness tires examined in California and Oregon, and determined to be defective, were returned to the Lavergne, Tennessee factory and Bill Orr observed some of the tires being re-tested at the Lavergne plant laboratory.

For his last thirteen years with Firestone, Bill Orr was a Senior Lab Technician, in Research and Development in the Technical Center. One of his main functions was to analyze customer complaint tires which had been returned to the Technical Center in Lavergne, Tennessee. He was trained by Firestone, and considered to be one of the best experts in failure mode identification and cutting analysis by engineers, Japanese advisors, corporate quality assurance executives, sales engineers, technicians, and his department manager, Larry Elkins.

Joe first contacted Bill Orr after being referred to him by John Carr, Jr., a Steeltex tire injury victim. Joe was in Birmingham, Alabama to assist John Carr's attorney, Thomas Maxwell, at the deposition of the tire expert, retained by Maxwell to prove the existence of the defect in the Steeltex tire that exploded and caused serious injuries to Mr. Carr.

In Birmingham, after enjoying a meal at a very good Italian restaurant, selected by attorney Maxwell to please Joe's craving for Italian food, John called Bill Orr on his cell phone while in his car, still in the restaurant's parking lot. Joe introduced himself to Bill Orr, explained the purpose of the Firestone Steeltex National Recall Campaign, and requested his help as a whistle-blower to further the progress of the campaign.

Bill Orr enthusiastically granted Joe's request, on the condition that he not be paid for his expert testimony to preserve his credibility in assisting Lisoni & Lisoni in its recall campaign. His participation elevated the status of the effort to an entirely different level of credibility. Lisoni & Lisoni now had a high-ranking former employee of Bridgestone/Firestone, Inc. to support its allegations against the tire manufacturer that it was using sub-standard component parts, dictated by the "C-95" Cost Reduction Program, during which, they manufactured millions of Firestone Steeltex tires. At that time, Lisoni & Lisoni did not have a copy of the "C-95" Cost Reduction Program. Since Bill Orr had worked extensively with defective Steeltex tires made pursuant to the "C-95" Cost Reduction Program, his decision to join the Lisoni & Lisoni team was invaluable. At this time, Bill Orr had already appeared on CBS Evening News with Dan Rather and interviewed on camera by Sharyl Attkisson with regard to the reason the Wilderness tires were suffering catastrophic tread separations across the United States. Bill Orr's advantage over the Bridgestone/Firestone experts, during the Lisoni & Lisoni campaign to recall the entire line of Steeltex tires, was that he had done the "hands on" work in the factory lab. He also had vast experience in tire-cutting analysis in the Research &Development lab on failed, returned, and developmentally-defective tires.

In December, 2001, Bridgestone/Firestone, Inc. initiated a series of changes to its corporate structure. Although Bridgestone/Firestone cited "an effort to focus more effectively on its core business units," as the reason, it was abundantly clear that they were attempting to limit their liability exposure resulting from these defective Wilderness and Steeltex tires. As a "shell game scenario," the reorganized company does business in the United States under a holding company structure now known as Bridgestone Americas Holding, Inc. Bridgestone/Firestone, Inc., is now known as Bridgestone/Firestone North American Tire, LLC, and is a subsidiary of the new Bridgestone Americas Holding, Inc., a wholly owned subsidiary of Bridgestone Corporation of Japan.

> Miles Moore, Senior Correspondent for Rubber & Plastic News, reported: December 24, 2002: "Bridgestone Corporation, citing a desire to 'Build a strong, high performance corporate identity under the Bridgestone name,' will rename its American business unit Bridgestone Americas Holding, Inc., effective Jan 1.
>
> The name change comes just a year after Bridgestone announced The Bridgestone/Firestone Americas Holding, Inc. corporate organization. It won't affect other operating units, such as Bridgestone/Firestone North American Tire LLC. John Lampe will continue to serve as chairman, president and CEO of the holding company, while Mark Emkes is president, chairman, and CEO of the North American tire unit. Bridgestone said the name change will allow the individual businesses 'To build strong brand identities for their products under primarily, the Bridgestone and Firestone names.'"

Bridgestone Corporation through Bridgestone Americas Holding, Inc. had been "buying time," in order to complete the building of several new manufacturing plants in China, Brazil and other foreign countries, and before it ceased manufacturing tires in the U.S.

The United Steelworkers had recently negotiated a new contract, as reported by Bush Bernard in The Nashville Tennessean: "The union workers had been operating their plant without a contract for almost two years, and the issues were not about money. The union was concerned about the outsourcing of the production of the tires, safety in the workplace, and the union members' being forced to manufacture unsafe tires."

It was documented by the union that Bridgestone/Firestone was moving its production infrastructure to China.

As reported in The Tennessean, by Bush Bernard on June 21, 2005, Bridgestone/Firestone advised the union bargaining committee on the first day of negotiations, "Our plan is to build plants offshore and replace your production." Bridgestone Corporation, Bridgestone Americas Holding, Inc. Bridgestone/Firestone North American Tire LLC and the National Highway Traffic & Safety Administration engaged in a criminal Conspiracy of Death and Destruction, which caused many thousands of injuries, deaths, and property damage claims worldwide. In furtherance of the conspiracy, Bridgestone Corporation changed its corporate structure in an attempt to limit its liability, in the hope that it could escape the responsibility for its defective tires manufactured in the U.S.—and several foreign countries—in accordance with "C-95" and the resulting damages to innocent victims. The thousands of foreseeable tire failures caused by substandard component parts, as dictated by "C-95, directly relate to the Bridgestone/Firestone conspiracy with NHTSA to allow it to secretly reduce production costs. These actions, along with the concealing of claims on the website of NHTSA forms the foundation of the Bridgestone/Firestone and NHTSA Conspiracy of Death & Destruction.

In particular, the Chevrolet and Ford dealerships in the United States willingly granted their customers' requests to remove the Firestone Steeltex tires from their newly purchased vehicles. This was a result of Joseph Drexler (Director of Special Projects, P.A.C.E. Union) mailing notices of the "Post-Sale Duty to Warn" to every Ford and Chevrolet Dealership in the U.S. In addition, Lisoni & Lisoni issued a nationwide press release notifying the American motoring public of their rights pursuant to this positive new development in the area of automobile safety. As a direct result of the two public information campaigns (Lisoni & Lisoni and P.A.C.E.), many purchasers of Chevrolet and Ford light trucks and vans returned to the dealership that sold them their new vehicles and demanded that they replace the Firestone Steeltex tires on the vehicles with safe tires produced by other tire manufacturers.

The dealerships, in response to their replacement duties, demanded monetary credits from Bridgestone/Firestone, Inc. for the cost of the replacement tires. The tires on vehicles sold in the U.S. are the only part of an automobile that the vehicle manufacturer is not liable for damages caused by their design or manufacturing defects. The nationwide campaign designed to inform the U.S. motoring public of their rights pursuant to the new doctrine of the "post-sale duty to warn" cost Bridgestone/Firestone, Inc. millions of dollars.

The Bridgestone/Firestone flaw that is the most damaging to its future standing in the global family of multinational tire manufacturing companies, is their total disregard for quality control. In the world's consumer market, its motto "Passion for Excellence" was replaced by "Passion for Profits" as the unmistakable mission of Bridgestone/Firestone, Inc.

Chapter V

THE CONSPIRACY BEGINS

"A Journey of a Thousand Miles Begins with a Single Step"

Although Bridgestone Corporation became the largest tire manufacturer in the world, with the purchase of Firestone Tire & Rubber Co., it put Bridgestone Corporation of Japan in debt in excess of two-billion dollars. In order to reduce this debt, Bridgestone Corporation implemented the cost cutting program entitled Project "C-95", which would reduce production costs 5% in the first year, and 7.5% in each successive three years, for a total cost reduction of 26%. This massive cost reduction had the effect of de-engineering the tires, by removing all safety features, and using substandard materials, resulting in weak skim stock and under-curing the tires.

The de-engineering of these tires included, but is not limited to:

(1) Using out of "spec" pigments
(2) Using out of "spec" synthetic polymers
(3) Reducing the natural rubber content in tire compounds
(4) Using reduced-gauge calendared steel cord
(5) Reducing tire inner-liner gauge
(6) Reducing the wedge gauge
(7) Reducing curing times
(8) <u>Using World War II surplus rubber</u>

Bill Orr, as a tire-failure analyst for Bridgestone/Firestone Inc. in the late 1990's, was present the day the "C-95" program was introduced at Bridgestone/Firestone, Inc., by Larry Elkins, and he knew it was a "recipe for disaster." He immediately began to see the results of the cost-cutting program, as the number of tire failures involving the Wilderness and the Steeltex tires began to dramatically increase after the implementation of the "C-95" cost reduction program. He complained to his supervisors about the effects of "C-95" cost reductions, but his complaints fell on deaf ears.

In August, 2000, he was sent by Bridgestone/Firestone to California and Oregon to examine the early returns in the "Wilderness recall". He found the tires suffering from the same defect: weak skim stock, as a result of the implementation of "C-95". The Firestone Steeltex tires are the "big brother" of the Wilderness tires on Ford Explorers (recalled in 2000), designed to be installed as original factory equipment on larger vehicles (seventy-one different models of trucks, RVs and SUVs), including ambulances and rescue vehicles converted from Ford F-350 and F-450 chassis vehicles. Most of these Steeltex tires were manufactured in Lavergne, Tennessee, Decatur, Illinois, and Joliette, Quebec, Canada at the same time and through the same "C-95" process that the admittedly defective Wilderness tires were manufactured.

In November, 2000, Bill Orr was asked to examine some Firestone Steeltex tires which had failed on an ambulance while transporting a patient. He determined that these Steeltex tires suffered from the exact same defect as the admittedly defective Wilderness tires he had recently examined. Mr. Orr took the evidence to his boss at Bridgestone/Firestone, Inc., Larry Elkins, who ignored his concerns, and made it quite clear that there was to be "no paper trail" of the findings. In January, 2001, Bill Orr went to the Japanese advisors, visiting from Bridgestone Corporation of Japan, and advised them of the alarming number of defective tire failures as a result of the cost cutting program, "C-95," used by Bridgestone/Firestone as ordered by Bridgestone of Japan's CEO, Mr. Masatoshi Ono and John Lampe in 1995, when the conspiracy of death and destruction was first implemented.

When The Rubber Meets The Road

Bill Orr was summarily fired by Bridgestone/Firestone, immediately escorted off of the premises at gunpoint, and accused of theft—which was proven to be totally false. The letter was short and to the point: "January 30, 2001: Our investigation has revealed that you were engaged in gross misconduct through the misappropriation of funds. You have lost the trust and confidence of management. Your employment with the company is being terminated effective today."

Bridgestone/Firestone had employed extortion tactics and forced people to lie about the tires, and about Bill Orr. He was finally exonerated, and all charges against him were dismissed. However, he was completely "black-balled" in the tire industry and was forced to seek employment in other fields.

> On May 8, 2001, Miles Moore, correspondent for the Rubber & Plastic News, reported: "The attorneys generals of at least six states soon may file suit against Bridgestone/Firestone Inc. and Ford Motor Co. for alleged unfair and deceptive trade practices, according to Florida Attorney General Bob Butterworth... 'With what information we have, both Ford & Firestone knew they had a problem and yet they continued to sell a product,' Mr. Butterworth was quoted as saying in Florida newspapers. 'We believe they knew about the problem and they continued to sell the tires'... 'Firestone has these nice, fuzzy ads running, saying, "We care about the quality of your tires," he said. 'That does not make the quality of the tire on your SUV any better...In a prepared statement attributed to General Counsel Saul Solomon, BFS noted that it has cooperated with the attorneys general's investigation since its inception. 'We will continue to cooperate with them on all serious and regulatory issues.' Mr. Solomon said."

> On May 30, 2001, CBS News reporter, Sharyl Attkisson reported: "A CBS News investigation last March uncovered more than twenty complaints about Firestone tires failing on rescue vehicles, mostly Steeltex tires, which are under federal investigation...Bill Orr, who was a senior lab technician for Firestone says the company retaliated against

The Conspiracy Begins

him when he repeatedly criticized the way the truck tires were designed and manufactured at the Lavergne plant where he worked, reports CBS News Correspondent Sharyl Attkisson. He was on a Firestone survey team last fall that examined hundreds of used truck tires and allegedly found more problems than usual. 'An anomaly' is a word that we use at the factory because it's much less offensive than saying 'a factory defect,' explained Orr. When Orr told local plant managers about his worries, he says they didn't want to hear it – something he finds ironic in light of Firestone's pledge to make things right after last August's passenger tire recall..." In November, Orr went over his bosses' heads and alerted visiting Bridgestone/Firestone corporate engineers to several problems he'd identified. He says they took photos and seemed concerned. Orr doesn't know what steps they may have taken. But when they left, he began feeling the heat. Two months later, after twenty-five years at Firestone, Orr was fired – he feels in retaliation for speaking up. 'Officially? I was fired for misappropriation of funds,' said Orr. Firestone accused Orr of pocketing $7,000 from a tire vendor that should have gone to the company, and denied him unemployment benefits. But Orr appealed and won his case when the Tennessee Department of labor ruled Firestone's allegations against him 'were not substantiated.' As for Orr's claims, Firestone says when he raised questions to corporate engineers, 'The tire was taken out of production and examined.' Firestone claims those qualified to analyze the data 'find the tires in the survey performed properly.'"

Bridgestone/Firestone, Inc. immediately released a Press Release on May 30, 2001: "We take very seriously any issues about the tires produced at our plants. Our policy is to address those immediately and take appropriate action. This was no different in Mr. Orr's case. Even though Mr. Orr's job did not involve tire manufacturing, when he brought an issue with a tire in production to the attention of his managers at Bridgestone/Firestone, the tire was taken out of production and examined.

When The Rubber Meets The Road

Whenever considering allegations about our tires or anyone's tires, it is important to keep in mind the source. Mr. Orr was terminated by Bridgestone/Firestone and is currently being sued by the company to recover monies fraudulently obtained by him."

Bill Orr was completely exonerated. It has been documented that two big burly men in suits came into a Firestone tire store with a Firestone-prepared declaration stating that Bill Orr had misappropriated a check in the amount of $7000. The man was pressured and finally agreed to sign the declaration. The men handed a declaration to the owner's wife to sign, but she refused. They pressured her and she fought back, cussing at them until they left the store. She never signed the declaration. The next day, her husband immediately disavowed the declaration and told the truth about what had happened. CBS Evening News with Dan Rather reported the story and Correspondent, Sheryl Attkisson interviewed Bill Orr on camera about his findings regarding the defective Firestone Steeltex tires as a result of the implementation of the "C-95" cost-reduction program.

After an administrative hearing, the Tennessee Department of Labor & Workforce Development decided in favor of Bill Orr that he was not terminated for cause. It stated:

"William J. Orr: Conclusions of law: The Appeals Tribunal holds the claimant is eligible for benefits. The issue is whether the employer discharged the claimant for misconduct connected with the work under TCA section 50-7-303(a)(2). Misconduct is behavior that shows a willful disregard for the employer's interests, or deliberately violates or disregards the standards of behavior, which an employer has the right to expect of an employee. Even if the claimant is discharged for supposedly legitimate reasons, the employer still must prove the claimant was guilty of misconduct, before he is disqualified from unemployment benefits. The evidence establishes the employer discharged the claimant for misappropriation of funds, but provided insufficient competent evidence to show the claimant committed the acts.

The claimant is eligible for benefits, because the employer failed to prove disqualifying misconduct. The auditor for the employer testified at the hearing, however, the auditor has no personal knowledge of the claimant's misdeed. Furthermore, the witnesses to the claimant's actions did not appear at the hearing and therefore, the statements presented by the employer alleging misconduct were not substantiated. Finally, the claimant's denial could not be refuted by competent evidence. The employer's evidence was hearsay and this Tribunal cannot base a finding on hearsay alone. The Agency decision is reversed. DECISION: The claimant is eligible for unemployment benefits."

Chapter VI

THE ONE TIRE THAT DESTROYED 10 LIVES

"One Bad Apple Can Destroy the Whole Barrel"

In July, 2000, a group of eight Chinese doctors and two hospital administrators were invited to the U.S. to tour our hospital facilities, medical schools, and medical clinics. Their tour lasted two weeks and included stops in Chicago, San Francisco, and Los Angeles. While in Los Angeles, they took a side trip to Las Vegas to view and study what kind of economic development that could be achieved in a desert, similar to China's huge Kobe desert. On July 30, 2000, while returning to Los Angeles from Las Vegas, they were in a fifteen-passenger Ford Club Wagon, when the Firestone Steeltex tire suffered a catastrophic tread separation of the right rear tire, causing the driver to lose control and the vehicle to roll-over. Two of the hospital administrators were killed and three of the doctors were hospitalized for weeks at Loma Linda University Hospital, in Loma Linda, California. The other doctors were all very seriously injured and most were injured to such a degree that they could no longer practice medicine when they returned to their homes in the City of Ningbo, on the east coast of China. Many of them lost their positions with the Chinese Communist Government, because they could no longer handle the physical requirements of their jobs, due to their permanent injuries. All of their efforts in their careers were lost, and they are now unemployed. These doctors had been the "best of the best" in China, and in an instant, their lives were ruined by a single defective Firestone Steeltex tire, resulting from the Bridgestone/Firestone and the National Highway Traffic & Safety Administration's Conspiracy of Death & Destruction. The right rear tire tread separation was a direct result of the implementation of the "C-95" cost reduction program instituted by John Lampe and Matismoshi Ono.

The plaintiffs' and their respective employment positions and the value of their lost income in US dollars of the accident were:

1. Chaun Tong Lu, President, Ningbo Medical Information Institute.

Chaun Tong Lu, graduated from the best medical school in China, Shang HaiFuDan University Medical School, in August, 1985. He specialized in public health administration, and served as President of Ningbo Medical Information Institute. He directed medical and science technology information services in Ningbo, which includes documentation, indexing, procedure evaluation, medical journal review, and the examination of medical science applications (similar to the FDA).He also edited & published Modern Practical Medicine, a widely-read magazine authorized by the government. Dr. Lu returned to work in February, 2001, however, the injuries suffered in the accident severely hampered his abilities to perform his many responsibilities and, although he had staff assisting him, his employment was soon terminated. His employment was terminated during the year of 2002, he was forty-five-years old with a work expectancy of an additional twenty years.

At $400,000 per year, based on his expertise and reputation, for twenty years, with an additional 50% for his supplemental income, a reasonable value of his loss of earnings as a result of this accident was ($400,000 X 20 yrs. $8,000,000 + 50% additional income($4,000,000) = $12,000,000.

2. Kong Kang Qui (Deceased), Vice President, Medical Bureau of Ningbo.

Mr. Qui worked for the military, specializing in economic management and development administration, as Vice President of the Medical Bureau of Ningbo. The Bureau controlled all hospitals, doctors and staff (including placement) and all hospital admission authorizations. It also managed disease control (public epidemic prevention), public hygiene, hazardous waste management, as well as the organization and maintenance of medical equipment. Mr. Qui's position as Vice President, Medical Bureau of Ningbo was a very powerful position. He had at least eight more years working for the government, but then he could have, and most likely would have, gone into the private sector, making a lot more money. His salary would have been in the area of $200,000 per year for at least eight years ($1,600,000)plus an average of $300,000 to $500,000 per year in the private sector, based on his knowledge and expertise, for the additional five years until age sixty-five ($2,000,000).His outside consulting work would have been worth an additional $100,000 per year. $100,000 X 13 years ($1,300,000) The reasonable value of his loss of earnings and earning capacity as a result of his untimely death was $4,900,000.

3. He Qin Ying, (Deceased), Deputy Director of Ningbo Jiang Bei District.

Dr. Ying was Deputy Director in charge of medical and cultural education, health and civil administration of health, hygiene, cultural sports, and welfare. Her authority included budgeting, facility management, and teaching credential standards. She authorized all sports activities and related facilities as well as the construction of sports arenas and stadiums. She oversaw public health, population control, food distribution, shelter, benevolent aid, medical care, cultural education, and legal services for the impoverished citizens of the country. Dr. Ying had an additional seventeen years prior to retirement. At the time of her death, she was forty-eight and she could retire from the government at age fifty-five and pursue her career in the private sector. Her salary as Deputy Director for Ningbo Jiang Bei District Medical Bureau was worth approximately $200,000 per year for seven years ($1,400,000), plus an average of $300,000 to $500,000 per year in the private sector for an additional ten years ($5,000,000). The reasonable value of her loss of earnings and earning capacity claim as a result of her untimely death was $6,400,000.

4. Xing Rong Zhou, Division Director, Ningbo Public Health Medical Bureau

Dr. Zhou graduated from Lanzhou Medical School, Gan Su Province in 1962. In his position as Division Director, he set up programs and regulations regarding public health administration as well as hospital and clinic locations. He carried out the development plan of medical organizations in hospitals, and he controlled inspection, examination and approval of all medical organizations. Dr. Zhou was forced to retire in August 2000, due to injuries sustained in this accident. Dr. Zhou had at least an additional five years prior to retirement. Based on the salaries of a Medical Director of $187,800 per year and a Hospital Administrator, average of $400,000 per year, the reasonable value of Dr. Zhou's salary would have been approximately $300,000 per year for five years, or $1,500,000.

5. Ya Lun Mao, Vice President, Ningbo Second Hospital

Dr. Mao graduated from Zhe Jiang Medical School in 1982, and was chief administrator for nine years. Dr. Mao was Vice President of the Ningbo Branch of the China Medical Association, and President of the Infectious Disease Center at Ningbo City Hospital. He served simultaneously as Assistant Professor at Zhe Jiang Medical School, Ningbo University Medical School and Hong Zhou Pharmacology School. Dr. Mao returned to work part time in September, 2000 and returned to full time in November, 2000. As Vice

When The Rubber Meets The Road

President of Ningbo Second Hospital, Dr. Mao's salary was comparable to a Hospital Administrator for a large hospital such as Cedar Sinai of Los Angeles or $500,000 per year. ($500,000 - 52 wks = $9,615 per week) Dr. Mao was off work six weeks full time and eight weeks part time. The reasonable value of his lost earnings was $96,154.00.

6. Lin Long Wang, Associate Dean, University of Ningbo Medical School and Director of the Affiliated Hospital of Ningbo Third Hospital

In addition to his duties as a Medical School Associate Dean, Dr. Wang served as Director at the affiliated Hospital of Ningbo. Dr. Wang did not take any time off from work due to his injuries, because he was too busy.

7. Jian Hua Xie, Deputy Director of Ningbo Women & Children's Hospital & Chief Physician for OB/GYN Department

Dr. Xie graduated from Jhe Jiang University Medical School in 1980. In addition to her duties as a hospital Deputy Director, she also served as Chief Physician for the OB/GYN Department. Dr. Xie was off work for thirty days and then returned, but in a reduced capacity. Since the accident, she was not able to travel and could not do emergency surgeries, which adversely affected her career, and the availability of health care in the community. Based on a comparable salary of a hospital administrator and a Physician in Charge of the OB/GYN Department, the reasonable value of her salary would have been approximately$400,000 per year, therefore her loss of earnings for her thirty-day absence was $33,333.00.The fact that since the accident, She was unable to travel or do difficult surgeries and emergency surgeries was, and did adversely affect her career. Her travel and surgeries probably accounted for approximately 25% of her time and salary. She was relieved of her position due to her lingering disabilities, since she was forty-eight years old, she had a work expectancy of an additional seventeen years. The reasonable value of such a loss was in the area of $100,000 per year for seventeen years or $1,700,000.

8. Yuan Ming Dong, Director, Jing Bei District Medical Department of Ningbo

Dr. Dong graduated from Funing County Medical School in Jung Su Province in 1962. He was in charge of medical administration & hygiene. Dr. Dong was relieved of his duties by the government, due to injuries sustained in this accident. He was permanently disabled and unable to work.

Dr. Dong was forty-eight at the time of his injuries. He had a work expectancy of seventeen years. Based on the salary of a Medical Director in the Los Angeles area of $187,800, and a 50% increase due to his supplemental income, the reasonable value of Dr. Dong's loss of earnings and loss of earning capacity was $187,800 X 17 years X 50% = $4,788,900.

Shao Yuan Jin, President, Yin County Medical Bureau

President Jin was the CEO of the Medical Bureau of Yin County which controls all of the hospitals, doctors and staff in the county, including personnel placement and hospital admissions. It also controlled disease control (public epidemic prevention), public hygiene, hazardous waste management, as well as the organization & maintenance of medical equipment. President Jin returned to work part time in January, 2001, however, all of his work was ultimately done by subordinates. Because of his inability to function, he was forced to retire as of January, 2002. He is permanently disabled and unable to work.

The reasonable value of President Jin's salary would in the area of $200,000 per year. His past loss of earnings would be six months off or $100,000, and twelvemonths part time or $100,000. He had a work expectancy of twelve years, or $2,200,000, and an additional 50% for the reasonable value of his supplemental income for a total of earnings and loss of earning capacity in the amount of $3,500,000.

9. Jian Ping Hu, President, Medical Bureau of Feng Hua City, near Ningbo

President Hu was the Medical Director of Feng Hua City's (population 490,000) public health administration. There were thirty medical and health institutions in the city, including three city level hospitals, one epidemic prevention station, one city public health school for advanced studies, one drug administration organization, one city level obstetrics and gynecology hospital, one dental hospital, four central hospitals, twenty-six township medical institutions, with a total of 1,650 employees under his control. He was the highest ranking leader in the health circles. President Hu returned to work full time thirty days after the accident. His continuation in this capacity is problematic. The reasonable value of Mr. Hu's loss of earnings for forty-five days is $25,000.

The Chinese Communist government did not want the victims to file any kind of claim to recover any damages resulting from the failure of the subject Firestone Steeltex tire. Consequently, any action had to be maintained in the United States and had to be highly confidential and secret and absent any publicity. The driver of the van was to be prosecuted for manslaughter because the California Highway Patrol said the accident was his fault in failing to control his vehicle. He sought legal representation with a criminal defense attorney in Alhambra, California, Fred Witherspoon, who was a colleague of Lisoni & Lisoni and who employed Jiang Ping Zhang, also known as Jiang Ping, as a Chinese interpreter, and legal assistant.

Fred Witherspoon, Esq. called Lisoni & Lisoni, Consumer Advocate attorneys concentrating in the law of product liability, to see if there was a potential product liability action. Joe and Gail advised Fred Witherspoon of the fact that the ten victims who lived in China could bring a claim for compensation in the United States without traveling here from China. Jiang Ping was used as the interpreter between the clients and Lisoni & Lisoni. We would not have been able to prosecute this case without the invaluable assistance of Legal Assistant, Jiang Ping.

The injured doctors retained Lisoni & Lisoni in 2001, and we realized immediately that we had to secure possession of the damaged vehicle and the defective tire. Without the tire, we had no case. We hired private investigator, Ericka McCullen, to review the accident report from the California Highway Patrol in Barstow, California and then set out to locate the vehicle and the defective tire. The police accident report did not indicate where the wreckage of the vehicle was stored. Consequently, Ms. McCullen had to go to the accident scene and locate every auto wrecking yard in the area of the accident where the vehicle wreckage might be located. She spent hours in a hundred-plus degree heat in the Mohave Desert along Interstate 15, going to each wrecking yard in the area of the accident looking for a wrecked fifteen-passenger Ford Club Wagon with a failed Firestone Steeltex tire. It was a long, hard, tedious job, but the whole case rested on her finding and securing the vehicle and the defective Steeltex tire.

After several days of searching the desert area, Ericka found a small wrecking yard several miles east of I-15. When she approached the owner—who was holding a shotgun, she was cautioned to explain what she was doing. At first he was uncooperative, but Ericka managed to gain his confidence and he allowed her to roam around the wrecking yard. After about thirty minutes of looking at junked cars – bingo! She found both the vehicle and the defective tire one day before the yard was going to destroy it. She arranged to buy the vehicle and have it transported to Golden Hands Auto Body Shop in Pasadena, California. Ericka McCullen rode with the driver of the transportation truck all the way from Barstow to Golden Hands Auto Body in Pasadena, a distance of 110 miles, to ensure its safety.

We filed suit against Bridgestone/Firestone, Inc., and Bridgestone Corporation of Japan, alleging that the subject Firestone Steeltex tire was defective and caused this tragic accident. No charges were ever filed against the driver. He retained Lisoni & Lisoni to represent him for his damages associated with his injuries against Bridgestone/Firestone, Inc. and Bridgestone Corporation.

We retained a tire expert, Bill Hagerty, who had inspected several hundred vehicles for tire failure and was an excellent expert in the field of tire forensics. He began his career as a forensic tire consultant in 1995. Prior to 1995, from 1987 to 1993, he operated K & S Tire and Wheel in San Diego County, California. From 1977 to the time we retained him as our independent tire expert, he was a member of the Sports Car Club of America as an owner and driver.

At the time of his retention, he had prepared more than a dozen different race cars at hundreds of race tracks throughout the U.S. He won over 140 races and set 43 track records at high speed race courses such as Willow Springs, Button Willow, Riverside, Laguna Seca, Sears Point, Med Ohio and Road Atlanta. He set a lap record for his class at the Daytona Motor Speedway.

From 1963 to 1985, he was in the United States Navy, retiring as a Commander, among many other positions in the Navy. He served as the U.S. Naval Supply Officer, U.S. Naval Advisory Group, Saigon, Vietnam, the Director of Quality Assurance Industrial Supply Center and was an instructor at the U.S. Naval Academy. While in the Navy, he received and gave training in probability and failure analysis on all types of hardware.

While operating K & S Tire & Wheel, he sold, repaired and adjusted thousands of all makes of tires on all makes of vehicles and light trucks. He received over 200 failed tires to return to the manufacturer for possible warranty replacement. We could not have had a more competent, articulate, and experienced expert. We needed a consummate professional with his world class credentials to opine that the Bridgestone Firestone "C-95" Cost Reduction Program was responsible for the manufacturing defects present in all Firestone Steeltex tires, including the one that failed in the Ford Club Wagon that rolled over due to a tread separation and caused two deaths and eight catastrophic injuries to the eight Chinese doctors and two Chinese hospital administrators.

After being retained, he examined the tire and found it was definitely defective due to weak skim stock and under-curing resulting from the implementation of the cost cutting program, "C-95." He documented the defect and how it lead to the failure mechanism that caused the tire tread to separate from the side walls of the tire and the steel belts that the tread was supposed to adhere to in the normal course of the operation of the tire. Bill Hagerty concluded that the manufacturing process that caused the rubber tread to adhere to the steel belts was defective and the cause of the tire failure. After completing his inspection, he turned to us and said "You've got a great case. This tire is most definitely defective." He prepared a comprehensive report of *how and why* the Firestone Steeltex tire suffered the sudden and unexpected tread separation.

We mailed Bill Hagerty's report to Doug Larson, Esq., Firestone's defense counsel. He commented, after reading the report and examining the photos, that it was the most complete and comprehensive expert report he had ever read and considered in a tire failure case. After reading the report, he suggested that we schedule a settlement conference to try and conclude the entire case.

We knew that Bridgestone/Firestone would treat this case in a special way, based upon Doug Larson's statement to the court at a general status conference, that our case would be handled differently than all the others. Doug Larson, Esq., made an offer of $1,000,000 to settle the entire case, which lead to our plan to go to China to depose our own clients, in secret, to establish the factual basis of the nature and extent of injuries and the mechanics of our clients "red envelope" income to be able to evaluate the clients' loss of income claims, past and future. We took the aggressive posture and told Bridgestone/Firestone, Inc. that we would go to China and depose our clients to preserve their testimony. We did this because we knew the clients would not be able to come to the United States. Jiang Ping had to inform the clients of the deposition, their purpose, the dates, the location, and had to convince them that their confidentiality from the Chinese Communist Party regarding their claims against Firestone would be safe. The success of the depositions was crucial to motivate Firestone's defense attorney, Doug Larson, Esq., to re-evaluate the settlement value of the case.

We had to locate a Certified Shorthand Reporter who would be willing to travel to Communist China; we had to find a hotel in Ningbo, China with a business center and a conference room; we had to get our passports in order, we had to obtain Visas from the Chinese consulate, and make travel arrangements to China for the entire team.

We had to compile and assemble information to be the subject of the deposition of each of the client's in China. We were somewhat apprehensive about traveling to the east coast of Communist China to prosecute the case against Firestone for the defective tire, given the fact that the U.S. and Communist China did not want a claim for compensation to be prosecuted in any manner, shape or form. Jiang Ping became the liaison between the clients in China and us, as their attorneys in Pasadena, California.

Gail and Jiang Ping worked very hard to gather the necessary photos, medical reports, written documentation, medical bills, and biographies—all demonstrating the nature and extent of the damages suffered by each victim. Gail spent hours outlining questions to be asked of the victims at their depositions. When complete, Joe was positioned to take very detailed and organized depositions of the injured plaintiffs. The success of the depositions was crucial to motivate Firestone's defense attorney, Doug Larson, Esq., to re-evaluate the settlement value of the case.

During the investigation and litigation, Lisoni & Lisoni learned of the secret "C-95" cost-reduction program and found that these Steeltex tires were failing all over the country, and foreign countries, as a result of the "C-95" Cost Reduction Program and so advised Doug Larson, Esq.

We sent a doctor, Edith Chung, M.D., to China to document their injuries, both physical and emotional. She video-taped their sessions and prepared a detailed report of their injuries. We also had Robert Gertmanian, PhD prepare detailed reports of their estimated loss of earnings resulting from their injuries in the accident. Bridgestone/Firestone was unimpressed with the magnitude of the tragic loss suffered by the medical infrastructure of Ningbo, China, a city located in the southeast province of China, with a population of five-million people.

We had to borrow money to finance our trip, and it did not come through until two days before we left. Joe met with case financial representatives at the Parkway Grill Restaurant in Pasadena to present a case for them to loan us One hundred thousand dollars ($100,000) for the trip to China and to further prosecute the class action. After the presentation to Harvey Bibicoff, Dan Ahern, and the CEO of Case Financial, they agreed to the loan.

The One Tire that Destroyed 10 Lives

Two days before we were scheduled to leave for China, we still didn't have the check. Joe called Dan Ahern and he pressured the CEO of Case Financial to issue Lisoni & Lisoni a check for $100,000. He delivered the check to us the day before leaving for China. We hired a Certified Court Reporter, Linda Torre, and an interpreter, Jiang Ping, and our group traveled to Ningbo, China, across the Sea of Japan, surreptitiously as tourists.

Bridgestone/Firestone, Inc. sent an attorney, Mark Pearson, Esq. from the law firm of Iverson, Yocum, Papiano & Hatch, who spoke Chinese, unbeknownst to us, to defend the depositions. Mark Pearson, Esq. learned to speak Chinese when he was a Mormon missionary in Taiwan. He was hired for the specific purpose of defending the depositions in China.

We felt a great deal of anxiety as we waited at Los Angeles International Airport (LAX) for our flight, realizing the magnitude of what we were doing and having security issues regarding getting the Certified Shorthand Reporter equipment through airport security. The flight was extremely long, making a stop-over in Tokyo, Japan, and then on to Shanghai, China. We landed in Shanghai and waited for our luggage and our ride from one of our clients to Ningbo, China, where the depositions would be taken. The drive from Shanghai airport to the Nan Yuan Hotel in the City of Ningbo on the east coast of China took four hours. Ping had to speak to the driver the entire trip to make sure the driver did not fall asleep as it was the middle of the night. We arrived at the Nan Yuan Hotel at 6:00 a.m. Chinese time.

Jiang Ping checked the team into the hotel and received room assignments. Jiang Ping and Linda Torre took regular rooms, and Joe and Gail took a suite that would serve as a command center for preparing each client for his or her deposition. The translator took a room across the street from the Nan Yuan Hotel as did Firestone's defense attorney, Mark Pearson, Esq. The certified court reporter, Linda Torre, the niece of former Yankee and Dodger Manager, Hall of Famer, Joe Torre, did a very good job, as it was difficult reporting a deposition involving translations.

After the first few depositions, it was obvious that defense attorney, Mark Pearson, was unconcerned about giving Linda Torre breaks from her tedious job as the court reporter. Joe admonished Mark in the presence of Linda Torre about the need to take breaks stating, "She's not a machine, she is a human being, treat her like one!" After Joe's defense of her need for a break and respect for her professional obligations, she was very appreciative from that day forward, maintaining a strong bond with us. We ate our meals together and every night we had Western food in the hotel restaurant because we were afraid the Chinese food might not agree with us. We were a real team and worked well together. We had to hire a Chinese certified interpreter for the depositions, and she was not very nice. Jiang Ping had to keep her "honest" in her translations, because she was not translating accurately. We suspected that she might be a Communist agent reporting the deposition results to the Communist party. After a period of time Joe and Gail concluded that she was not an agent but just a very unfriendly person.

We spent twenty-one days in Ningbo, China, and took twenty (20) depositions of the Chinese plaintiffs, their spouses and heirs. We stayed at the four-star Nan Yuan Hotel, in Ningbo, China, and to avoid detection, we only left the hotel twice in twenty-one days. We ate all of our meals in the hotel; the plaintiffs met with us for preparation at the hotel; the depositions were taken in the private conference/business center in the hotel and everything remained highly confidential.

One of our doctor clients gave us sleeping pills, which helped tremendously. Gail outlined the questions for each client in great detail, and she used it to prepare the clients and Joe used it for the questioning at the depositions. Each deposition lasted about five hours. Our morning ritual before starting the deposition was to have breakfast in the lobby restaurant, Western food, shower and dress in the room after breakfast, take an elevator ride to the business center to take the deposition. We met our client at 9:45 a.m. for a final preparation before the deposition started at 10:00 a.m. Joe's questioning from Gail's outline lasted about three hours. After Joe finished his questions, the defense attorney would question the witness in a fashion that would last about two hours.

During the period that Mark Pearson was questioning the witness, Joe was there to protect the rights of the client. Gail and Ping would leave the deposition and be preparing the next day's witness for his or her deposition while Mark Pearson was questioning the witness. Gail and Ping's witness preparation was the key element responsible for the success of the deposition of each client. When Joe questioned the witnesses in the context of the formal deposition they knew what the question would be before Joe asked it, thanks to the preparation time Gail and Ping spent with them the day before, which resulted in well organized, articulate, and comprehensive responses to questions.

Documenting the plaintiffs' lost earnings was very difficult because of their custom of the "red envelope." If you want good medical treatment in China, you must put extra money into a red envelope and give it to the doctor to assure good and prompt attention. Unfortunately, there is no record of any payment, and therefore, no documentation.

During our stay, Gail had an ear problem which required medical attention. We were driven to the hospital in a car provided by one of our clients and Joe took a "red envelope" from the hotel room and put $100 American dollars into the envelope. Needless to say, Gail was treated immediately, and we were provided an escorted tour of the entire hospital. After the tour, we were driven back to the Nan Yuan Hotel to continue our deposition work. Gail's waist-length long, blond hair caused a lot of positive attention at the hotel from the salon staff and employees in the hotel. It was quite obvious by the "double-take" looks she received, that Chinese people in Ningbo, China, were not accustomed to seeing a woman with waist-length blond hair and green eyes.

During the deposition of the Surgeon and Army General, who had been with the Chinese Army for twenty-five years, the defense attorney, Mark Pearson, Esq. was suggesting that the group had actually gone to Las Vegas to gamble and have a good time. These questions insulted the General Doctor and made him extremely agitated, so Joe took a break from the deposition and took the defense attorney to the men's room and told him that if he continued with this line of questioning, the Surgeon and Chinese Army General could make a single phone call, and the defense attorney would not go home, and that the United States and President George W.

Bush would not come to his aid because he was not "strategically important" to the United States.

The defense attorney immediately apologized to the General Doctor, in Chinese, for the disrespect and ended the deposition! The next morning the defense attorney, Mark Pearson, looked ill and Joe asked if he was okay. He responded that he had been up all night waiting for the "knock on the door." The Surgeon General was so happy that Joe ended the deposition abruptly that he gave him a Red Cross tie clip. He explained that it had been given to him by the Communist party and it would provide them certain amenities that ordinary people would not have while in Communist China.

Joe, Gail and Mark Pearson, Esq. all celebrated their birthdays during their twenty-one day stay in China. On Gail Lisoni's birthday, March 11th, 2002, Joe, Gail & Jiang Ping took a taxi ride around the city (one of only two times they left the hotel).During the ride, Jiang Ping was speaking to the taxi cab driver in Chinese, telling him that she was with two American lawyers and it was the birthday of one of them and she wanted to get a T-shirt from Ningbo as a memento. Unbeknownst to us, the taxi cab driver called into a talk radio station, explained about us and asked the radio audience if there was a store which sold Logo T-shirts. Then Jiang Ping heard on the radio talk show, in Chinese, the story of our trying to find a T-shirt from Ningbo. Someone called in and gave an address of a sports shop and we went to the shop, only to find that it was closed for re-modeling.

On the only other day Gail, Joe, Jiang Ping and Linda left the hotel, the day before we left, one of our clients drove us around the city of Ningbo, and the countryside, pointing out many places of interest. We drove by a Bridgestone Tire store and took pictures of ourselves in front of the store. Then we drove near the shore of a lake near Ningbo, and decided to walk along the water. We didn't realize that we were very close to a military installation. We heard something over a loud speaker, saying that we should leave immediately. As we were walking back to the van, Gail decided to *surreptitiously* take a picture. Joe told her not to do it, but she did it anyway. When Gail returned home and developed the pictures, she learned there was a "big cannon" pointed directly at us.

The One Tire that Destroyed 10 Lives

Spending time in Ningbo gave us a great insight into the huge work force China has at its command. All bicycles were black and the bike trails on the streets surrounding the hotel looked like ant trails from the upper level of our hotel room. Our client took us on a driving tour of Ningbo and his business-complex, business towers and high rise hotel, and then we had lunch in the hotel restaurant and we ate traditional Chinese food.

Gail made daily phone calls back to Pasadena to report our status and to receive a status report from our paralegal, Kathy Terrazone. We also learned that most American fast-food chains had a physical presence in Ningbo at three large shopping centers spread throughout the city.

On the last day of depositions, one of the plaintiffs was contacted by the Chinese Communist Government and they were questioned about "the American attorneys." Fortunately, he made up a believable story, that the "American attorneys" were investigating manslaughter charges against the United States driver of the van, and that seemed to satisfy them, allowing "the American attorneys" to finish their business and leave the country.

We took a driving tour of the countryside surrounding Ningbo the day before we left for Shanghai to board a flight back to the United States. We arrived in Shanghai and stayed at a hotel across the street from the Shanghai Stock Exchange. We took a walking tour and went shopping until Jiang Ping was attacked and a thief attempted to steal her purse. She warded off the attack, kept her purse and was not hurt.

We flew first class on China Airlines from Shanghai to Los Angeles International Airport. We looked at each other upon take-off and said, "Wheels up!" "What an experience!" We were exhausted and slept most of the trip home. After a sixteen-hour flight, we had a beautiful view of the Pacific Ocean and California beaches as our plane was on approach to Los Angeles International Airport. It was the first time we saw a bright sunny landscape since we arrived in Ningbo, on the east coast of China. No place like home in the U.S.A.!

We informed Bridgestone/Firestone of all of the incriminating evidence that we had amassed during the litigation and that we discovered that these tires were failing all over the United States and foreign countries. In an attempt to resolve the issues involved regarding the defective Firestone Steeltex R4S, R4SII and A/T tires, we advised the defense attorneys that if we could not obtain a voluntary recall of the defective Firestone Steeltex tires still in service, we would file a nationwide class action against Bridgestone/Firestone, Inc. and Bridgestone Corporation of Japan for the recall all of the eleven-million Steeltex tires still in service. These tires came as original equipment on seventy-one models of vehicles, including but not limited to, all Ford and General Motors pick-up trucks, SUV's, motor homes and ambulances in all fifty states.

The class action would provide the class members with damages for their failed tires and would provide some retribution to the Japanese government for the sins of their ancestors. Bridgestone/Firestone, Inc. and Bridgestone Corporation of Japan refused to discuss the settlement and refused to believe that Lisoni & Lisoni would file such a massive nationwide class action against Bridgestone/Firestone, Inc. and Bridgestone Corporation of Japan.

A Mediation Settlement Conference was held in early April, 2002. Arlen Gregorio, from San Francisco, was the Mediator, and Frances Pearl, Esq. of Holland & Knight in Chicago, Ill, and Arnold Douglas Larson, Esq. and Mark Pearson, Esq. of Iverson, Yocam, Papaiano & Hatch in Los Angeles, California, represented Bridgestone/Firestone.

At the Mediation, we advised Doug Larson, Esq. and Frances Prell, Esq. that we would file a class action lawsuit against Firestone and its parent company, Bridgestone Corporation, to recall all Firestone Steeltex tires if Firestone did not voluntarily conduct a nationwide recall of all Firestone Steeltex tires. The doctors' case settled that day, however, as always, Bridgestone Firestone required the ten plaintiffs to agree to a confidential settlement all in furtherance of the Bridgestone/Firestone and the National Highway Traffic & Safety Administration (NHTSA) Conspiracy of Death & Destruction.

Doug Larson refused to recommend a voluntary recall of the subject tires and he indicated to us that he didn't believe that we would file a class action. Lisoni & Lisoni's goal was to get the defective Steeltex tires off of the roads and highways of the U.S.

through a nine-step nationwide public information campaign to force a tire recall. We decided to go after Bridgestone/Firestone, Inc. and Bridgestone Corporation of Japan as the retailer selling defective tires in the U.S. and foreign countries.

In California, there is a doctrine called "post-sale duty to warn, recall and retrofit defective products." A July, 2003 article in The Advocate on "Post-Sale Duties to Warn, Recall and Retrofit Defective Products" by John D. Rowell, suggests that sellers and distributors may have a duty to warn customers of defects and could be liable for harm to persons or property caused by the seller's failure to provide a warning after the time of sale or distribution. The mediation concluded and each party went their own way.

Lisoni & Lisoni settled the case for the Chinese doctors in May, 2002, and filed the class action lawsuit in August, 2002. Before filing the lawsuit, Lisoni & Lisoni obtained mailing lists of owners of Ford & Chevy vehicles which came with Firestone Steeltex tires as original factory equipment and sent out thousands of letters to consumers about the Firestone Steeltex on July 2, 2002. It stated:

"Dear Consumer:

Our firm is handling a civil action involving a Firestone Steeltex R4S tire on a motor vehicle, which failed causing an accident. The National Highway Traffic & Safety Administration began a Defect Investigation into Steeltex R4S tires September 29, 2000, which is a preparatory step to a formal recall of the tire. This was done less than two months after the recall of 6.5 million Firestone ATX, ATXII and Wilderness AT tires. On April 15, 2002, National Highway Traffic Safety Administration closed its investigation into the Firestone Steeltex R4S and R4SII and A/T light truck tires, finding no defect trend. The agency said it found the evidence does not support a defect finding against the tires, but <u>also that it would re-open the investigation if new evidence becomes available</u>. We have information that these tires are failing all over the United States. It should be noted that our subject accident was not included in the more than 350 reported failures reported to NHTSA, and we believe that many more complaints about this subject tire have also not been included in the reported failures. NHTSA has left the door open for a formal recall campaign if new evidence is brought to its attention. We believe that there are more than enough complaints against this subject tire to demand that Bridgestone/Firestone formally recall these tires as they did with the Firestone ATX, ATXII and Wilderness AT tires, and we intend to formally demand that Bridgestone/Firestone, Inc. recall these subject tires, for the safety of the driving public. If you have had a tire problem with any of your Firestone Steeltex tires, please contact us. If you want any additional information regarding the status of the investigation, please contact us. Thank you for your courtesy and cooperation in this matter."

Lisoni & Lisoni also purchased lists of all tire dealers in the United States, including but not limited to, Firestone Dealerships, Sears, Pep Boys, and Big O Tires.

On September 12, 2002, Lisoni & Lisoni sent the following sample letter:

"Dear Pep Boys:

The National Highway Traffic & Safety Administration (NHTSA) began a Defect Investigation into Steeltex R4S tires on September 29, 2000, as a preparatory step to a formal recall of the Steeltex R4S, R4SII, and A/T light truck tires. This was done less than two months after the recall of 6.5 million Firestone ATX, ATXII and Wilderness AT tires. On April 9, 2002, the National Highway Traffic & Safety Administration closed its investigation into the Firestone Steeltex R4S, R4SII and A/T light truck tires, finding no defect trend. The agency said it found the evidence does not support a defect finding against the tires, but <u>also that it would re-open the investigation if new evidence becomes available</u>. We have information that these tires are failing all over the United States and that most failures have not been reported to NHTSA, and further, we believe that many more failures of these subject tires will fail in the future. NHTSA has left the door open for a formal recall campaign if new evidence is brought to its attention. We believe that there are more than enough complaints against this subject tire to demand that Bridgestone/Firestone formally recall these tires as they did with the Firestone ATX, ATXII and Wilderness AT tires, and we intend to formally demand that Bridgestone/ Firestone, Inc. recall these subject tires, for the safety of the driving public. If a customer brings a vehicle into your dealership equipped with a Firestone Steeltex R4S, R4SII, or A/T tire, you may be held liable for any property damage or personal injury which results from their failure, if you don't warn the customer of the known or suspected problems with the subject tire. We have requested the Department of Transportation to re-open its investigation of the subject R4S, R4SII, and A/T light truck tires."

The successful conclusion of the underlying "China case" served as the Gateway to the development and execution of the Nine-Point Plan to Remove the Defective Firestone Steeltex tires from the roads and highways of the United States.

The Chinese victims of the one defective Firestone Steeltex tire which ruined their lives, taken in Chicago, Illinois, before the accident

The Nan Yuan Hotel, Ningbo, China

Deposition participants

Gail, Joe, Ping & Linda having dinner after first deposition
at the Nan Yuan Hotel restuarant

Gail & Joe at a Bridgestone dealership in Ningbo, China

The legal team at the lake directly across from the Chinese military installation

The "cannon" is pointed directly at the legal team after it was warned over a loudspeaker to leave the vicinity of the lake adjacent to the military installation immediately!

The beautiful sky over the California coastline as viewed by Gail & Joe from their seats on the airplane on approach to Los Angeles International Airport

Chapter VII

THE FIRESTONE STEELTEX NATIONAL CLASS ACTION TO REMOVE THE DEFECTIVE STEELTEX TIRES FROM THE ROADS & HIGHWAYS OF THE U.S.

"Bad acts give birth to drastic remedies"

Section 382 of the California Code of Civil Procedure authorizes national class action suits in California when "the concern is one of common or general interest, of many persons, or when the parties are numerous, and it is impracticable to bring them all before the court." The plaintiffs have the burden of establishing all prerequisites of class certification, and of convincing the court that certification will confer substantial benefits. Plaintiffs' Class definition was modified and defined as follows: "Those persons residing in the United States who currently own or owned a vehicle which came factory equipped with Firestone Steeltex R4S, R4SII, or A/T tires, which were manufactured in Decatur, Illinois, Jolliette, Quebec, Canada, Mexico, Lavergne, Tennessee, and Aiken, South Carolina, between 1995 and the present."

Subclasses were defined as follows:

1. Those persons residing in the United States who currently own or owned a vehicle which came factory equipped with Firestone Steeltex R4S, R4SII or A/T tires, and who sustained property damage to their vehicle as a result of the failure of the Firestone Steeltex R4S, R4SII or A/T tire(s);
2. All class members who are "consumers" as that term is defined in California Civil Code Section 1760(d), and who have not suffered monetary damage;.
3. Those individuals who received a "'replacement tire(s)" after their original Steeltex tire(s) failed, and who suffered a failure of the "replacement tire".

To obtain certification of a class action, a party must establish the existence of both an ascertainable class and a well-defined community of interest among the class members. "The community of interest requirement involves three factors:

1) predominant common questions of law or fact;
2) class representatives with claims or defenses typical of the class; and
3) class representatives who can adequately represent the class." (*Linder v. Thrifty OilCo.* (2000) 23 Cal. 4th 429, 435)

The ultimate question concerning the propriety of maintaining a class action, given a sufficiently numerous and ascertainable class, is whether the issues that may be jointly tried—compared with those requiring separate adjudication—are so numerous or substantial that maintenance of the action as a class action would be advantageous to the judicial process and the litigants." (*Collins v. Rocha* (1972) 7 Cal 3rd 232, 238. The requirement that common issues predominate mandates that "proof of most of the important issues as to the named plaintiffs will supply the proof as to all." Common issues are predominant when they would be "the principal issues in any individual action, both in terms of time to be expended in their proof and of their importance." *Vasquez v. Superior Court of San Joaquin County* (1971) 4 Cal 3rd 800, 810.

In our class action, plaintiffs sought damages for the replacement of their Firestone Steeltex tires as a result of their defective condition, and for any property damage resulting from the failure of their Firestone Steeltex tire(s). The common issues to be decided were:

1. Was the member of the class an owner of a vehicle which came equipped with Firestone Steeltex tires as original equipment?
2. Did the class member suffer a failure of their Firestone Steeltex tire?
3. Was the failure caused by the defective de-engineering of the Firestone Steeltex tire?
4. Did the class member sustain property damage?
5. Did the class member replace all of the Firestone Steeltex tire(s) on their vehicle after the failure due to safety concerns?

In Product Liability law, a defective product is "an imperfection in a product that has a manufacturing or design defect, or is faulty because of inadequate instructions or warnings. A product is in a defective condition if it is unreasonably dangerous to the user or to consumers who purchase the product and causes physical harm." In the law of product liability, a manufacturing defect in a product that was not intended is the kind of defect which occurs when a product departs from its intended design and is more dangerous than consumers expect the product to be.

On August 12, 2002, we, Joseph and Gail Lisoni, of Lisoni & Lisoni, filed the national class action in California Superior State Court, entitled Roger Littell, Lou Ann Pleasant vs. Bridgestone/Firestone, Inc., and Bridgestone Corporation, in Riverside County Superior Court, Case No.INC 030708, before Judge Christopher J. Sheldon in Indio, California. The national class action alleged fraudulent concealment, unfair business practices, and product liability. It claimed damages on behalf of all members of the class, and demanded a recall of eleven million Firestone Steeltex R4S,

R4SII and A/T tires, which came as original factory equipment on seventy-one different model vehicles including many Ford and GMC pick-ups, SUVs, ambulances, rescue vehicles and motor homes.

Lisoni & Lisoni contended that these defective tires were the result of the Cost Cutting Program "C-95", which affected all of the Firestone tire brands, including the history making Wilderness tires, recalled in 2000. There were still approximately eleven million Firestone Steeltex tires still on the road, ready to suddenly, and without warning, suffer a sudden and catastrophic tread separation. Routine maintenance was irrelevant, because it was a latent defect, which the consumer could not notice until after the tire had failed.

Bridgestone Corporation stock dropped 5.7% as a result of the announcement. Bridgestone Corporation was required by its outside auditors to advise its investors of the contingent liabilities presented by the class action in its Annual Report. The contingent liabilities were explained in a one-third-page long report in their Annual Report, which cost Bridgestone Corporation millions of dollars, and which gave credibility to our class action.

On August 14, 2002, Bloomberg News reported:

"Bridgestone Corporation shares fell 5.7 percent after a California man yesterday sued the U.S. unit of Asia's biggest tire-maker, claiming its Steeltex tires used on Ford Motor Co. and General Motors Corp. vehicles were defective. Shares of Tokyo-based Bridgestone fell 94 yen to 1,555 yen in trading today. It was the fourth most actively traded stock by value on Japan's equity markets, with shares worth 10.96 billion yen ($93.6 million) changing hands."

Business Wire reported: August 19, 2002: In a Reuters article published August 13, 2002, Clarence Ditlow, spokesman for the highly respected national nonprofit consumer protection agency the Center for Auto Safety in Washington, DC, as quoted as saying, "The Steeltex is the utilitarian version of the Wilderness tire. They are just as bad." Lisoni stated, "This week we have sent a letter to every member of the

United States Congress demanding a congressional investigation into what is a national health and safety tragedy in the making. There are currently thirty million of these tires on the road, since more are being manufactured each day. We have also written to each Firestone tire dealership in the United States asking them to voluntarily advise their customers of the dangers of the Steeltex tires."

Further, on August 26, 2002, Business Wire reported:

August 26, 2002: "Lisoni emphasized that 'As Steeltex tire owners become aware of the lawsuit through media reports and other means, many are contacting the law firm to report defects and negative experiences with their Steeltex R4S, R4SII and A/T light truck tires. The law firm has set up a special website www.firstonesteeltexclssaction.com where people can file complaints with the law firm or directly to the Department of Transportation'...Commenting on the response from the public to the filing of this lawsuit, Lisoni remarked, 'From the reports we have received, it certainly appears that there are a growing number of Bridgestone/Firestone customers who own Steeltex tires who are extremely dissatisfied and need an outlet to vent their anger. Many have told stories of near-death experiences from total tread separations and others are frustrated that the manufacturer doesn't seem to care and many dealers refuse to help. It is imperative that Bridgestone/Firestone recall the Steeltex tire series. Another area of utmost concern relating to Steeltex tire defects,' Lisoni pointed out, 'are nationwide reports of tire failures on law enforcement and emergency vehicles, including sheriffs' vehicles, ambulances and fire trucks, as reported by CBS News in March of last year.' According to CBS News, there were 18 cases of ambulance tire failures reported by Emergency Medical Service agencies in the state of Kansas, and ambulance services in Sun City, Arizona, and Augusta, Georgia, have replaced all Firestone tires on emergency vehicles."

On September 2, 2002, Business Wire reported:

"The purpose of this lawsuit is not about money, Lisoni stressed, adding, 'First and foremost, it is to motivate Bridgestone/Firestone to take responsibility for their defective product and do what is best for the safety of its customers – immediately recall the entire Steeltex tire series."

On September 9, 2002, Blue Oval News, the Independent Voice of the Ford Community since 1998, published an Exclusive Report, stating:

"Plaintiffs' lawyers representing owners of Firestone Steeltex R4S, R4SII and A/T tires are mapping out a new legal strategy – go after the retailers selling the product... Plaintiffs' lawyers are waging a new kind of war against Firestone though memos sent to Firestone Retailers stating 'If a customer brings in a vehicle into your dealership equipped with Firestone Steeltex R4S, R4SII or A/T tires, or you sell such a tire to a customer, you may be held liable for any property damage or personal injury which results from their failure if you don't warn the customer of the known or suspected problems with the subject tires...'"

CBS Evening News with Dan Rather, along with investigative reporter, Sharyl Attkisson, aired several reports regarding these defective Steeltex tires, based upon evidence provided by Lisoni & Lisoni. Dan Rather, at the time, was the News Anchor and Sharyl Attkisson was the investigative reporter. Rather was one of the "Big Three" news anchors in the U.S. when he took on the Firestone Steeltex tire defect investigation along with the ABC News Anchor, Peter Jennings, and Tom Brokaw, the NBC News Anchor. He assumed the position as the Anchor of CBS Evening News on March 9, 1981 upon the retirement of Walter Cronkite – the most trusted man in America at the time.

Sharyl Attkisson, at the time of the Firestone National Steeltex Tire Recall Campaign was launched, was the CBS News investigative correspondent in the network's Washington, DC news bureau. Attkisson was an anchor for CNN from 1990 to 1993 when she moved to CBS and began her Emmy-Award winning career as an investigative reporter in our Nation's Capital.

Gail and Joe made it clear to CBS Evening News in New York City and Washington, DC that we did not want to be part of the story because then the focus would be on us, as attorneys, and not the defective tires. We told CBS Evening News that we would give them all of our evidence to further our public information campaign through the news media to get these dangerous Firestone Steeltex tires off of the roads and highways of the U.S. and several foreign countries. We told CBS that it's "Evening News" would win an Emmy Award for its reporting. In fact, Sharyl Attkisson was nominated for an Emmy Award for her coverage of the campaign to recall the defective Firestone Steeltex tires (the "Firestone Fiasco"). She did not win the Emmy for the Firestone stories but won five other Emmys during her career which continues to this day.

The Bridgestone Corporation 2004 Annual Report stated:

"In November, 2002, an attorney who had filed a purported class action suit alleging that all the BSA Steeltex tires (eleven million of which are estimated to be in service as of December 31, 2004) were defective and petitioned the NHTSA to re-open an investigation of such tires which that agency had closed in April 2002. The NHTSA denied that petition in June, 2003, and in March 2004, the court denied plaintiffs motion for class certification. Plaintiffs then filed a renewed motion for class certification and another petition for NHTSA to investigate (i) all Steeltex tires generally and (ii) those Steeltex tires used on ambulances. The NHTSA denied this petition in September 2004 and closed its investigation and the court denied plaintiffs renewed motion for class certification in February, 2005. BSA management has thoroughly investigated this issue, and continues to monitor the performance of the tires in question. However, except with regard to the February 2004 voluntary safety campaign addressed below, BSA (i) does not believe that a recall or similar action concerning its Steeltex tires is necessary or appropriate; (ii) strongly believes that the related litigation is without merit, and (iii) plans to vigorously defend its position. Accordingly, BSA had made no provision for any related-contingent liability. In February, 2004, BSA announced a U.S. voluntary safety campaign to replace, free of any charge to consumers approximately 230,000 (initially estimated at 297,000 tires). The tires are Firestone brand Steeltex Radial A/T tires in size LT265/75R16, and in Load Range D, which are on 2000-2002 and some early model year 2003 Ford Excursion vehicles. All the affected tires were made between March 1999 and December 2002 at BSA's plant in Joliette, Quebec, Canada, and none are presently being manufactured by BSA. BSA also agreed to replace approximately 20,000 exported tires meeting the same criteria. BSA estimates that the total direct costs of the voluntary safety campaign will approximate $30 million. The voluntary safety campaign is substantially complete as December 31, 2004."

Lisoni & Lisoni created a website, www.firestonesteeltexclassaction.com which produced over 3,500 documented claims of Steeltex tire failures and over 20,000 information requests from concerned owners of vehicles equipped with the defective tires. In addition to over 3,500 reported claims resulting from the defect notices mailed to owners of vehicles equipped with defective Steeltex tires as stock factory equipment, the Firestone class action website received over 20,000 contacts ("hits") from owners of the seventy-one models of vehicles equipped with defective Steeltex tires. To review the website contents as it was presented during the Firestone Steeltex National Recall Campaign, go to Google and enter the caption "WAY BACK The www.firestonesteeltexclassaction.com." For articles not included in the website see on Google "WAY BACK the firestonesteeltexclassaction.com."

CBS News Correspondent, Sharyl Attkisson reported on CBS Evening News that

"The government will decide whether to re-open the investigation based on a petition from a lawyer who says there's new evidence of catastrophic failures in thousands of complaints, hundreds of serious injuries and eleven deaths."

CBS Evening News with Dan Rather reported:

February 9, 2004: "Referencing a news report which aired on the 'CBS Evening News' on Friday evening, Attorney Joseph Lisoni reiterated today that Bridgestone/Firestone, Inc.'s Steeltex tire series is defective in both design and manufacturing and that the tire manufacturer is involved in a 'cover-up' of these defects while also illegally destroying defective tires in violation of a court order...In its special report which aired Friday, the 'CBS Evening News' reported that 'questions are being raised' about the Steeltex tires and that it appears that Firestone is 'trying to cover up the problem.' The news report alluded to hundreds of letters that the tire manufacturer had sent out to customers saying that the allegedly defective tires they sent in 'would be returned or destroyed' even though the latter would be a violation of an existing court order. The news report cited an instance in which Firestone had claimed there were no defects in a set of tires sent in by a customer. CBS had Alan Hogan, an outside expert, analyze the tires. He reported that the damaged tires were defective and there were even cracks in the ones that hadn't malfunctioned yet, concluding they were a 'recipe for disaster.' Lisoni noted that it is significant that CBS sought Hogan's analysis as he is a former employee of Bridgestone/Firestone who was intimately involved with the manufacture of Firestone's ATX, ATXII and Wilderness A/T tires. Hogan had previously testified before a federal grand jury which was investigating 270 deaths attributed to tread separations suffered by the recalled Wilderness tires. Commenting on the report, Lisoni remarked, 'This only validates what we have found to be true through our investigations since we filed the class action lawsuit eighteen months ago. It is unconscionable that Bridgestone/Firestone not only refuses to acknowledge that these tires are defective and recalls them, but it is clearly knee-deep in a program to deny that any problems exist and to cover up evidence of such defects by destroying tires... It is important that Bridgestone/Firestone understand that this lawsuit will not go away, not as long as there are over thirty-million Steeltex tires on the road whose defects have already been proven to be a threat to the health and safety of the American public,' Lisoni stressed. He added that more reports of tire failures from all over the country are coming into the lawsuit's website, www.firstonesteeltexclassaction.com on a daily basis."

Upon reading this story, Joe realized he had erred on the number of Firestone Steeltex tires that were still on the road and sent notice of this error to over 400 newspapers (every newspaper with a circulation of 15,000 or more subscribers) in the U.S. and to the ABC, NBC, CBS, CNN and Fox News television stations. The general response he received from the media was "After eleven million, what difference does this error make as to the serious nature of the problem with the Firestone Steeltex tire?" Nonetheless, the error had to be corrected to maintain the credibility of Lisoni & Lisoni.

HOME / TOP NEWS

New Firestone recall sought

By MARCELLA S. KREITER, United Press International | Nov. 15, 2002 at 12:13 PM

Follow @upi

Comments

A California law firm Friday asked the federal government to reopen its investigation of Firestone Steeltex tires, saying their failure rate is even greater than that of the 10 million Wilderness AT, ATX and ATX II tires already recalled.

Attorney Joseph Lisoni said the failures of Steeltex tires have led to at least 12 deaths and hundreds of injuries. He has filed a class-action lawsuit in California seeking a full recall and Friday presented Transportation Secretary Normal Mineta with a petition demanding immediate action.

"The mission of this lawsuit is to get the Steeltex line of tires recalled," Lisoni said. "... Our primary mission is to get this tire off the streets. It's killing people. It's injuring people."

Bridgestone-Firestone spokeswoman Christine Karbowiak said the company stands behind the tires and maintained it has a lower failure rate than tires from other manufacturers.

Lisoni investigator William Hagerty said the tires are made at the same plants that produced the Wilderness AT, ATX and ATX II, which were linked to 217 deaths and more than 800 injuries, mostly involving Ford Explorers. Ford expanded the government recall to include another 13 million tires on its vehicles, leading to a rupture in relations between the two manufacturers that had been doing business for more than a century.

The National Highway Traffic Safety Administration suspended its investigation of Steeltex tires after investigating 872 Steeltex failures but said it would reopen the inquiry if evidence warranted such action. Lisoni said, however, federal officials have refused to accept the evidence his investigation turned up.

Lisoni, who represented a number of doctors and hospital administrators killed and injured in an accident involving Steeltex tires, said he opened a wider investigation after the suit was settled because Bridgestone-Firestone "categorically refused" to recall the 30 million Steeltex tires on the road despite alleged evidence of manufacturing defects.

Lisoni said NHTSA already has evidence of nearly 3,000 Steeltex tire failures and his limited, 3-month investigation turned up 7,000 more. He said he has confirmed 12 deaths related to the Steeltex tires and is in the process of confirming 11 others.

Lisoni said most of the problems are showing up on motorhomes and a number of Ford trucks. Ford spokesmen were unavailable for comment Friday.

"There is compelling evidence to reopen this investigation," Lisoni told a National Press Club news conference in Washington, adding he is confident a full federal investigation would increase the number of confirmed instances substantially.

In his petition to Mineta, Linsoni accused Bridgestone-Firestone of showing a "willful disregard" for the safety of motorists.

He cited an anonymous letter from a Firestone executive referring to court documents involving the earlier recall in which admitted the company sought to reduce costs by taking out failsafe mechanisms and offered cash bonuses to dealers for failing to report tread separation failures to both the company and federal government.

"We frankly believe the anonymous letter from the Firestone executive (gets to) the root of the problem," Lisoni said.

Hagerty, who owned a tire store and became an expert on tread separation, said he has determined efforts by the tiremaker to cut costs may have led to shortcuts in the manufacturing process that make the tire dangerous.

He said the company sought 153 cost reductions, including alterations to the natural rubber content, curing temperatures and number of body plys. Hagerty also blamed the failures in part on carbon black produced by Continental Carbon, which is involved in a labor dispute with the Paper, Allied, Industrial Chemical and Energy Workers union.

Hagerty noted Firestone already has recalled 40,000 Steeltex tires in Brazil and Saudi Arabia has banned the importation of Firestone tires and any vehicles that come equipped with them. Additionally, Lisoni said a number of states have ordered Steeltex tires removed from all emergency vehicles.

Related UPI Stories
- New Firestone recall sought
- Firestone paying Ford Motor $240 million
- Firestone recalls another 3.5 million tire
- Ford tire recall ending

Independent Voice of the
Ford Community since 1998.

Exclusive Report
Lawyers Target Firestone Retailers

09 September 02
Robert Lane

Plaintiff lawyers representing owners of Firestone Steeltex R4S, R4SII and AT tires are mapping out a new legal strategy - go after the retailers selling the product.

Attorneys Joseph and Gail Lisoni filed a lawsuit against Bridgestone-Firestone on 13 August 2002 demanding that they recall over 27.5 million Steeltex tires due to claims of tread separation. Clarence Ditlow told Reuters "The problem with tracking these problems in the Steeltex ... is that it is was not associated with a particular make and model (of automobile)." and that "The Steeltex was the utilitarian version of the Wilderness. They are just as bad." Steeltex tires are widely used on Ford SuperDuty F-Series trucks as original equipment.

Safety groups and attorneys claim that the steeltex tires contain a lamination defect whereupon the tread separates from the carcass of the tire.

Bridgestone has countered that the NHTSA tested the steeltex tires from September 2000 through April 2000 and found no defects. On 15 April 2002, the NHTSA closed its investigation finding no defect trend. NHTSA also reported that "Claims of tread separation are not necessarily evidence of a tire defect. Tread separations can also result from external factors, such as tire injury or poor maintenance." NHTSA also added that it would reopen the investigation if new evidence becomes available.

Plaintiff's lawyers are waging a new kind of war against Firestone though. Memos sent to Firestone retailers states "*If a customer brings a vehicle into your dealership equipped with Firestone Steeltex R4S, R4SII or AT tire, or you sell such a tire to a customer, you may be held liable for any property damage or personal injury which results from their failure if you don't warn the customer of the known or suspected problems with the subject tires.*" Read the entire memo here.

A retailer selling Firestone tires told BlueOvalNews that after becoming aware of the memo, he would shy away from selling Firestone Steeltex tires and discourage customers from buying them for fear of a lawsuit.

If you have had a Firestone Steeltex tire fail, please contact lisoni@earthlink.net or go to Firestonesteeltexclassaction.com.

BlueOvalNews.com

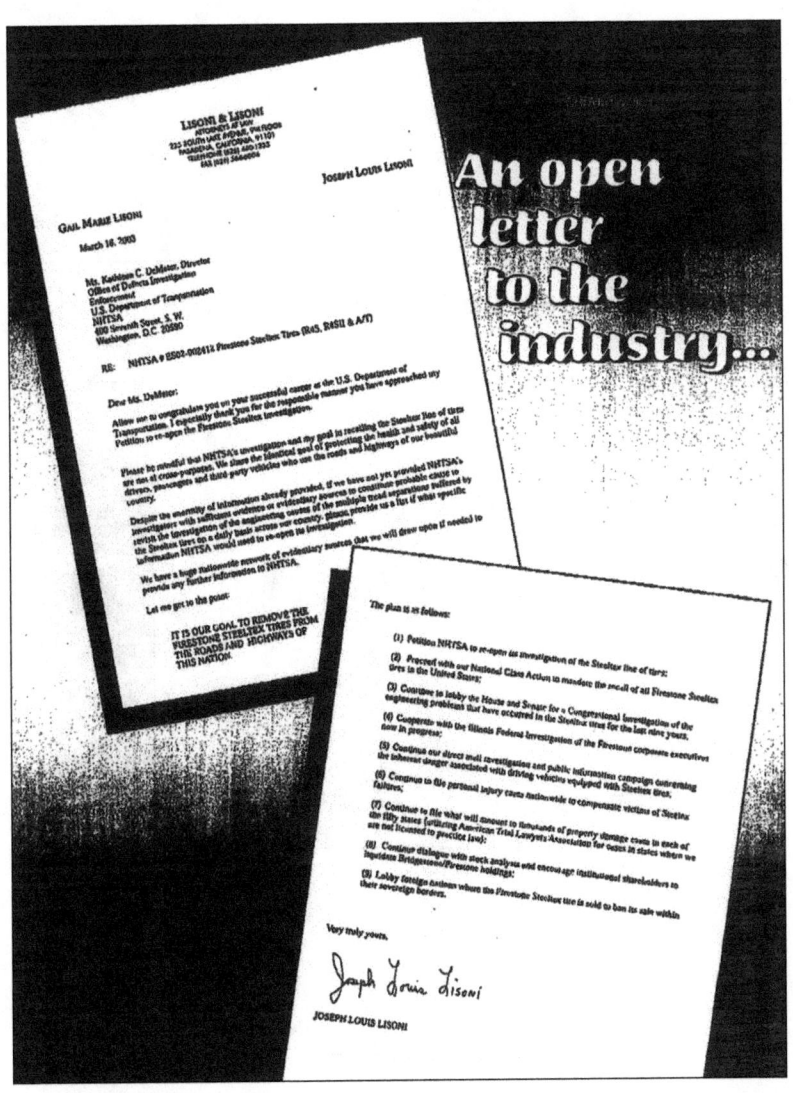

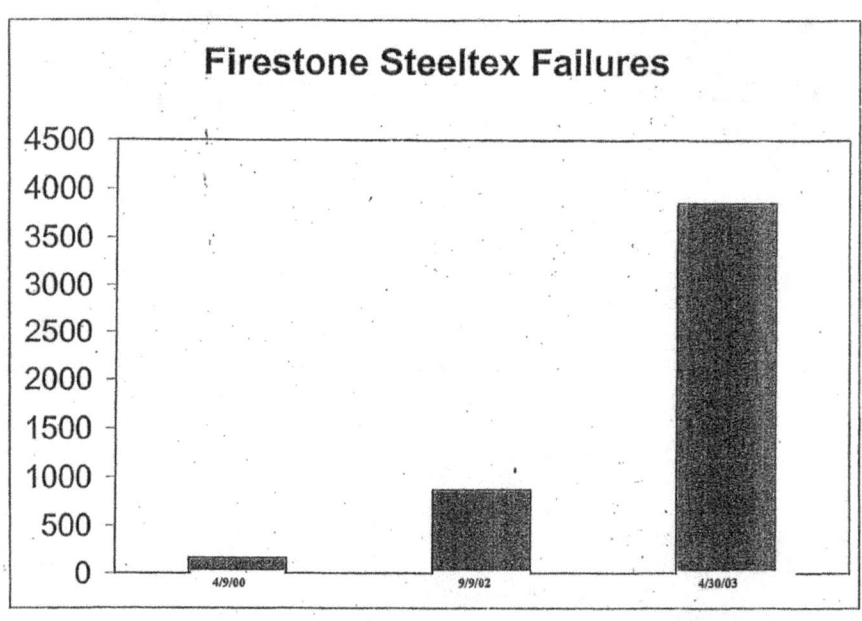

Firestone Steeltex R4S, R4SII, and A/T CLASS ACTION LAWSUIT INFORMATION

| Home Page Welcome! | Breaking News and Documents | NHTSA Vehicle Owner Questionnaire | Class Action Contact Form | Seeking Other Legal Support? Contact Us |

LIVE VIDEO WEBCASTS - News Conferences
Monday, May 5, 2003 at 9:30 AM EST
Friday, November 15, 2002 at 9:30 AM EST

Mission Statement

The law firm of Lisoni & Lisoni filed one of the largest class action lawsuits in history. Filed in Riverside County, California, its goal is to bring about a nationwide recall of dangerous and defective Firestone Steeltex R4S, R4SII, and A/T tires. Tread separation and other failures indiscriminately can occur on these tires with catastrophic consequences to the motoring public.

Since this nationwide class action lawsuit was filed, we have received hundreds of additional complaints regarding these tires. In addition, ongoing investigation efforts have uncovered literally thousands of Steeltex tread separation complaints that were not previously taken into account by the National Highway Traffic Safety Administration (NHTSA) during their 18 month investigation into the Steeltex tire line.

Today, there are millions of these tires on roads around the world and they are failing at an alarming rate. In addition to the common usage of these tires on trucks, SUV's and vans, these tires are used on vehicles ranging from school buses to ambulances and fire and public safety vehicles. The following is a representative but not all-inclusive list of the vehicles on which the Steeltex tire brand can be found:

Trucks, SUV's & Vans

Ford
Ford E 100
Ford E 250 Ford E 350
Ford E 450 Ford F 150
Ford F 250
Ford F 350
Ford F 450
Ford Econoline Van
Ford Excursion

Chevrolet
Chevy Silverado
Chevy Express
Chevy Full Size Pickups
Chevy Full Size SUV's
Chevy Full Size Passenger & Cargo Vans

GMC
GMC Suburban
GMC Sierra
GMC Savannah
GMC Full Size Pick Ups
GMC Full Size SUV's
GMC Full Size Passenger & Cargo Vans

Class C Motorhomes

Airstream
Aliner
American Motors
Amtran
Arizonian
Country Campers
Chinook
Country Coach Damon
Dutch
Dutchman
Big Four
Carleton
Carriage
Chevy Motorhomes
Georgie Boy
Getty
Gulf Stream
Holiday Rambler
Home & Park
Itasca
Jayco
King of the Road

Lazy Daze
Mallard
National RV Newmar
Nuwa
Fisher Price
Fleetwood
Ford Motorhome
Four Winds
Osh Kosh
Olympic
Pace American
Pace Arrow
Roadtrek
Rockwell
Shasta
Starcraft
Stoughton
Thor
Tiffin
Trailmaster
Winnebago
Workhorse

If you wish to participate in this class action lawsuit, please contact us by using our simple **Class Action Contact Form**. To review developments on this case, and stay abreast of breaking news, visit our **news and documents** section. Return to this site often for updates, press releases and media coverage.

Thank You.

Lisoni & Lisoni

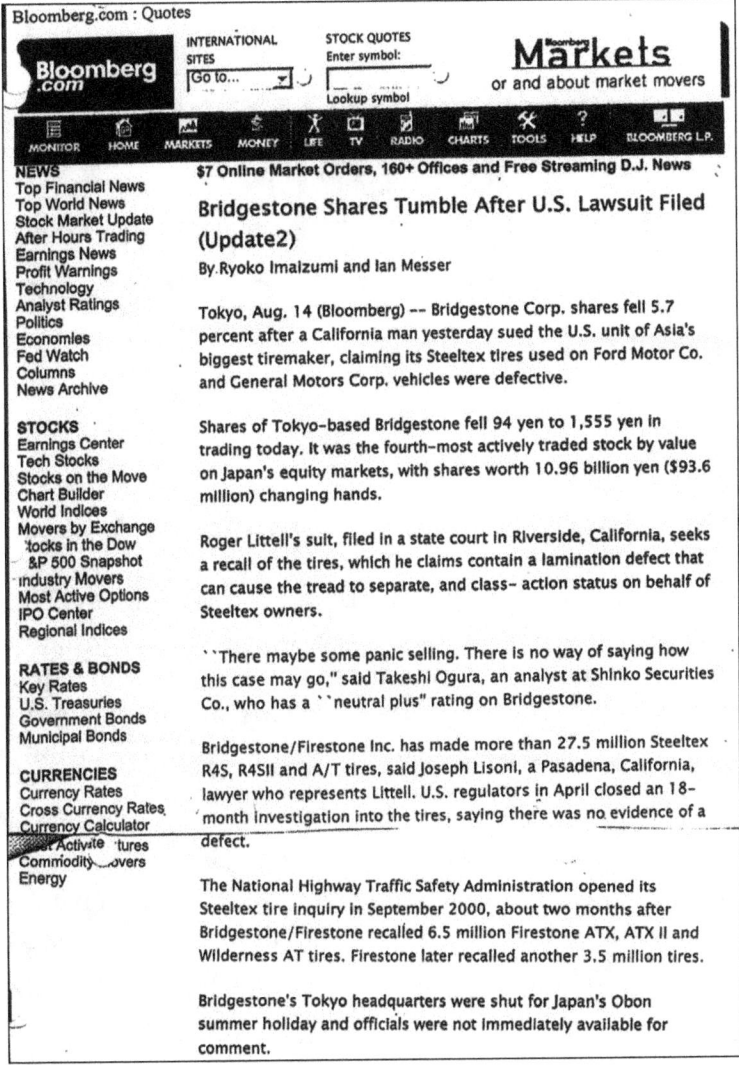

Bridgestone Shares Tumble After U.S. Lawsuit Filed (Update2)

By Ryoko Imaizumi and Ian Messer

Tokyo, Aug. 14 (Bloomberg) -- Bridgestone Corp. shares fell 5.7 percent after a California man yesterday sued the U.S. unit of Asia's biggest tiremaker, claiming its Steeltex tires used on Ford Motor Co. and General Motors Corp. vehicles were defective.

Shares of Tokyo-based Bridgestone fell 94 yen to 1,555 yen in trading today. It was the fourth-most actively traded stock by value on Japan's equity markets, with shares worth 10.96 billion yen ($93.6 million) changing hands.

Roger Littell's suit, filed in a state court in Riverside, California, seeks a recall of the tires, which he claims contain a lamination defect that can cause the tread to separate, and class-action status on behalf of Steeltex owners.

``There maybe some panic selling. There is no way of saying how this case may go,'' said Takeshi Ogura, an analyst at Shinko Securities Co., who has a ``neutral plus'' rating on Bridgestone.

Bridgestone/Firestone Inc. has made more than 27.5 million Steeltex R4S, R4SII and A/T tires, said Joseph Lisoni, a Pasadena, California, lawyer who represents Littell. U.S. regulators in April closed an 18-month investigation into the tires, saying there was no evidence of a defect.

The National Highway Traffic Safety Administration opened its Steeltex tire inquiry in September 2000, about two months after Bridgestone/Firestone recalled 6.5 million Firestone ATX, ATX II and Wilderness AT tires. Firestone later recalled another 3.5 million tires.

Bridgestone's Tokyo headquarters were shut for Japan's Obon summer holiday and officials were not immediately available for comment.

Chapter VIII

PETITION NHTSA TO RE-OPEN ITS INVESTIGATION OF THE STEELTEX LINE OF TIRES

"If at first you don't succeed, try, try again."

While the official goal of the National Highway Traffic & Safety Administration (NHTSA) is to police the automobile and tire manufactures, however, it actually supports and defends the automobile and tire manufacturers. NHTSA closed its investigation on April 15, 2002, stating that there were only 872 Steeltex tire complaints and no defect trend.

On November 15, 2002, Lisoni & Lisoni filed a Petition to Re-open the Investigation and provided NHTSA with 1,000 individual claims and 2,972 complaints that were listed on the NHTSA website at the time it closed its investigation, seriously challenging its claims of only 872 complaints. The denial alleges that there were only two deaths (which were counted twice). This is absolutely incorrect because our firm represented the heirs of two doctors killed in a Firestone Steeltex tread separation accident on July 30, 2000 on Interstate 15 near Barstow, California.

The Lisoni & Lisoni discovery of NHTSA's misconduct in not accurately posting Steeltex tire failures was reported by them in a Press Conference held in Washington, DC at the National Press Club's Holeman Lounge. It was televised to viewers nationwide on November 15, 2002. The Mission Statement of the National Press Club is "To promote social enjoyment among the members, to cultivate literary taste, to encourage friendly intercourse among newspaper men and women and those with whom they were thrown in contact in the pursuit of their vocation, to aid members in distress and to foster the ethical standards of the profession." The organization administers the annual Freedom of the Press Award, which honors two recipients, one foreign and one domestic, who have demonstrated the "principles of press freedom and open government."

Speaking at the National Press Club to mark his retirement, CBS Commentator, Eric Severeid, called the club the "sanctum sanctorum of American journalists...for everybody in this country having anything to do with the news business; only hallowed place I know of that's absolutely bursting with irreverence."

Bridgestone/Firestone tried to convince the National Press Club not to host the press conference, but they were unsuccessful. The Press Conference was available on television upon request by subscribers for weeks following the live presentation. The Press Conference informed millions of viewers nationwide about the defects in the Steeltex tires caused by the "C-95" cost reduction program. CBS Evening News covered the Press Conference and featured a report of its message that night on CBS Evening News with Dan Rather and Sharyl Attkisson was the investigative reporter who presented the story.

Lisoni & Lisoni arranged to have NHTSA picketed by the Plastic, Allied-Industrial, Chemical and Energy (P.A.C.E.) Union while the press conference was in session, demanding the recall of all of the eleven million remaining of thirty million Firestone Steeltex tires manufactured by Bridgestone/Firestone, pursuant to procedures set forth in the "C-95" cost reduction program.

On March 18, 2003, Lisoni & Lisoni sent a letter to Kathleen Demeter, Enforcement Officer of the Office of Defects Investigations for the National Highway Traffic & Safety Administration (NHTSA), documenting the detailed Nine-Step Plan to remove the defective Firestone "Steeltex" tires from the roads and highways of the United States.

The letter stated:

"RE: NHTSA # ES02-002412 Firestone Steeltex Tires (R4S, R4SII & A/T)

Dear Ms. DeMeter:

Allow me to congratulate you on your successful career at the U.S. Department of Transportation. I especially thank you for the responsible manner you have approached my Petition to re-open the Firestone Steeltex investigation. Please be mindful that NHTSA's investigation and my goal in recalling the Steeltex line of tires are not at cross-purposes. We share the identical goal of protecting the health and safety of all drivers, passengers and third-party vehicles who use the roads and highways of our beautiful country. Despite the enormity of information already provided, if we have not yet provided NHTSA's investigators with sufficient evidence or evidentiary sources to constitute probable cause to revisit the investigation of the engineering causes of the multiple tread separations suffered by the Steeltex tires on a daily basis across our country, <u>please</u> provide us a list of what specific information NHTSA would need to re-open its investigation. We have a huge nationwide network of evidentiary sources that we will draw upon if needed to provide any further information to NHTSA.

Let me get to the point:
IT IS OUR GOAL TO REMOVE THE FIRESTONE STEELTEX TIRES FROM THE ROADS AND HIGHWAYS OF THIS NATION.

The plan is as follows:

(1) Petition NHTSA to re-open its investigation of the Steeltex line of tires.

(2) Proceed with our National Class Action to mandate the recall of all Firestone Steeltex tires in the United States.
(3) Continue to lobby the House and Senate for a Congressional Investigation of the engineering problems that have occurred in the Steeltex tires for the last nine years.
(4) Cooperate with the Illinois Federal Investigation of the Firestone Corporate executives now in progress.
(5) Continue our direct mail investigation and public information campaign concerning the inherent danger associated with driving vehicles equipped with Steeltex tires.
(6) Continue to file personal injury cases nationwide to compensate victims of Steeltex failures.
(7) Continue to file what will amount to thousands of property damage cases in each of the fifty states (utilizing American Trial Lawyers Association for cases in states, where we are not licensed to practice law).
(8) Continue dialogue with stock analysts and encourage institutional shareholders to liquidate Bridgestone/Firestone holdings.
(9) Lobby foreign nations where the Firestone Steeltex tire is sold to ban its sale within their sovereign borders.

In conclusion, it is a scientific certainty that as long as the Firestone Steeltex tire is driven on the road, it will continue to cause deaths, injuries, and property damage."

Through Joe's tenacity and skills, he was able to convince the editors of Rubber & Plastic News, the leading tire industry publication, of the importance of this letter being published in their monthly magazine. He convinced them that it was a "Public Safety Campaign". The cost was $15,000 and it was published as a full-page ad in the Rubber & Plastic News magazine, and it described in detail our nine-point plan for a public information campaign to remove the defective Steeltex tires from the roads and highways of the United States and foreign countries.

On April 7, 2003, this letter was published world-wide in Rubber & Plastic News as "An Open Letter to the Industry," which stated, "It is our goal to remove the Firestone Steeltex tires from the roads and highways of this nation." Some people missed the message.

On May 19, 2003, in the Rubber & Plastic News, Letter to the Editor, Tim Morris wrote: "Editor: Reading the April 21 issue of Rubber & Plastic news I was shocked to see you published an ad for trial lawyer Joseph Lisoni (who is leading a class action suit against Bridgestone/Firestone). I believe that your responsibility to be independent and unbiased. You should stop at reporting the news and not to advertising that tries to become news. RPN is for our industry and should not be used as a platform to slam one of our industry's leaders, just because someone can afford to run a full-page ad. We do not want or need to see these types of ads. Your loyalty has to align at some point with our industry and attempt to build us up instead of tearing us down. I would not attempt to argue the merits of Lisoni's claim as a news story, but you should not take money to advertise his stance. Competitive ads are one thing, but an ad that attempts to start litigation against another in our industry is it what I believe your mission should be. I have always respected your reporting of the news in our industry, but I feel running this ad was one of your low points."

Rubber & Plastic News reported:

May 5, 2003: "The attorney leading a class action suit against Bridgestone/Firestone produced a memo at a press conference May 5. His claims show the firm deliberately made shoddy Steeltex tires, a document BFS said isn't new and proves nothing... The document outlined 'Project 95,' a Bridgestone plan to reduce operating costs between 1994 and 1997. The recommended actions included the purchase of off-spec synthetic polymers and pigments, as well as making manufacturing decisions that would result in increased belt-edge separations, according to the document.

A BFS spokesman, however, gave no merit to the memo. 'They're always trotting out that document in every court case that involves us,' he said. Mr. Lisoni claimed that the National Highway Traffic & Safety Administration –which, in 2002, investigated the tire and found no defect trend with it – has more than 4,000 accidents on file directly attributable to Steeltex failures, and he has proof of 7,000 others."

On May 7, 2003, we met with administrators, engineers, and legal counsel of the National Highway Traffic & Safety Administration (NHTSA) together with William J. Orr, the Firestone whistle-blower, and demonstrated the defects in the Steeltex tire resulting from the implementation of "C-95," which weakened the tire's engineering strength and integrity.

Public advocates, Joan Claybrooke of *Public Citizen* and Clarence Ditlow of *Center for Auto Safety*, accompanied Lisoni & Lisoni to NHTSA on May 10, 2003. Joan Claybrooke was the former Director of the National Highway Traffic & Safety Administration. Joan Claybrooke, in her closing remarks referred to Bridgestone/Firestone's conduct as "criminal".

When Clarence Ditlow, III, came on board with the Firestone Steeltex National Tire Recall Campaign, he was widely regarded as "America's foremost advocate for automobile safety" that had lead numerous campaigns to force the recall of millions of dangerously-flawed motor vehicles. As head of the *Center for Auto Safety* in Washington, DC, he was instrumental in forcing manufacturers to recall the Ford Pinto with the infamous exploding gas tanks, Toyotas that suddenly accelerated out of control and General Motors pick-up trucks with side-saddle gas tanks that blew up in collisions, killing more than 1,000 people. Ralph Nader has described Ditlow as "The nightmare of the misbehaving auto industry and the dream of safety-conscious motorists." Mr. Ditlow received a Juris Doctorate from Georgetown University in 1970 and a Master's Degree in Law at Harvard University in 1971.

At the time Joan Claybrooke appeared at NHTSA with Lisoni & Lisoni and the Firestone Steeltex National Tire Recall team, she was President of *Public Citizen*, a powerful consumer advocate lobby in

Washington, DC. *Public Citizen* was founded by Ralph Nader. In 1966, she teamed up with Nader to successfully lobby the passage of the nation's first auto safety laws—the National Traffic and Motor Vehicle Act and the Highway Safety Act. These acts empowered the government to establish safety standards for new vehicles and issue recalls for defective vehicles and parts. She was head of the National Highway Traffic & Safety Administration in the Carter Administration from1977-1981. Joan Claybrooke earned her Juris Doctorate degree from Georgetown University Law Center in 1973.

In 2000, she held a press conference at *Public Citizen* about the Ford-Firestone Wilderness tire problems. That morning, the telephone lines at *Public Citizen* would not work. Later that day, the telephone company reported that *Public Citizen's* telephone lines had been cut, prompting it to install a lock box to prevent such disruption of its high-profile consumer advocacy work.

The National Class Action, a daily electronic newspaper delivered via email that is devoted solely to the key details of virtually every major class action suit filed in the U.S., reported: "In a rare and valuable display of support, Ms. Joan Claybrooke, the former Administrator of the NHTSA and current President of Public Citizen (a Washington DC based national, non-profit, public-safety organization founded by Ralph Nader), appeared at the meeting with the Lisoni law firm urging the NHTSA to re-open the Firestone Steeltex safety-defect investigation. Equally significant was the appearance of Clarence Ditlow, Executive Director of *Center for Auto Safety*. To further document the national public concern with the safety of the Firestone Steeltex tire series, both *Public Citizen* and *Center for Auto Safety* indicated they would submit formal letters recommending that NHTSA re-open the Firestone Steeltex safety-defect investigation. In addition *Safety-forum.com* has joined Lisoni & Lisoni in criticizing the safety of the Firestone Steeltex tire series and called on NHTSA to re-open their defect investigation."

CBS Evening News filmed the Lisoni & Lisoni contingent entering the offices of NHTSA on the day of the meeting with NHTSA to document the existence of "C-95" and the deadly tire failures it produced. Bill Orr made the presentation to NHTSA of the sixth tire from the vehicle of Roger Littell, the lead-named plaintiff in the class action. He had dissected the tire and documented the failures and their relationship to C-95. He demonstrated the mechanics of the defect through photos, the pre-failure tire belonging to Roger Littell, and the probable catastrophic results, as follows:

"The ten most important items in the document referred to as "C-95" or "Project 95," which formed the basis of the Bridgestone/Firestone conspiracy of death and destruction and furthered by the National Highway Traffic & Safety Administration (NHTSA) in order of significance are:

1. Using less-expensive input materials.
One example of the cheap materials used in the production of the Steeltex tires is poor quality carbon black, which is a major bonding material, and substandard or contaminated carbon black which can lead to defects, including but not limited to, cracking which can lead to tread separations and a variety of other failures.

2. Increasing line speed and shortening cycle time.
Line speed and cycle time are a consideration in the entire manufacturing process. It ranges from when the materials are received and processed from the mixer, the Banbury, until the finished product is put into the warehouse. Each department in the tire factory has cycles or line speeds for the processing of IPI (In Process Inventory). Each of these cycles has a specific time allotment.
    a. The Banbury. The longer or shorter the time the Banbury mixes the rubber, the more or less is the uniformity of the mixing, which results in the improper mixing of ingredients, which is very important for rubber-to-rubber and rubber-to-steel adhesion.
    b. The Calendar, the Tuber/Extruder and the Stock Preparation departments have set line/conveyor belt speeds, depending on how difficult the material being processed is to handle. This is where components are shaped and pre-assembled. If the line speed of these

three departments is too fast, the components can be stretched. These stretched components will lose some of their dimensions, or gauge, and will become a weak spot in the finished product. This weak or light spot can often be identified by a wheel balance weight seemingly large for the size of the tire. If the line speeds of these departments are too fast then the alignment of the pre-assembled components will be irregular and out-of-specification.

c. The Tire Room, where all the components are assembled into a green (uncured) tire, functions on time cycles. Cycles that are too fast in the Tire Room will result in: 1. Improper splicing of components; 2. Mis-alignment of components; 3. Air trapped between components, and 4. Poor compression of components. Also, the machine operator will not be allowed enough time to properly inspect the tire, materials or components. Reduction of cycle time here results in a wide variety of failure modes. Trapped air. Reduction of cycle time in the tire assembly room contributes to this condition.

d. The Curing department, where tires are vulcanized, operates on exact time temperature specification. Each tire has a time and temperature requirement, depending on the tire size, function, and the amount of curing agents added to the original rubber recipes. The tolerance for variation in time and temperature here is small. If time or temperature is outside tolerance the tire will fail early in its utility. Shiny brass on steel, in a tire, is evidence of an under cure, or use of improper materials. Shiny brass will be found, in failed tires, where under cure occurred and when weak curing agents were used. The number of Steeltex tires inspected in Marengo, Indiana with evidence of shiny brass was disturbing. Forty of the one-hundred and fourteen tires inspected at Marengo Indiana exhibited shiny brass (40%).

3. Buy at discount certain pigments which have been downgraded by their manufacturers for failing to meet some portion of the purchase spec.

Uncured, tire components can be analyzed for the type and quality of chemical ingredients. Once the rubber is cured it becomes a different material and few of the ingredients can be analyzed for the percentage or quality of its composites. Blending expensive ingredients with less expensive ingredients created a product of questionable quality. The Wilderness tires did fail and were recalled. The Steeltex is a similar tire, considered the "big brother" of the Wilderness, and is experiencing the same mode of failures as the recalled tires of August 2000.

4. Purchase at discount and blend out of spec synthetic polymer.

Engineering Cliché: "junk in equals junk out". Out-of-spec, inexpensive, ingredients were often blended with in-spec, expensive ingredients at Firestone factories in an attempt to save fractions of a penny per tire. Because some of these savings had worked, "C-95" was allowed to take the process further. When quality (expensive) ingredients are combined and blended, with out-of-spec (less expensive) ingredients, the consequence is an ineffective tire. The cheap materials are cured into the tires. The only evidence remaining of the cheap materials is the resulting failure of the tires.

5. Reduce NR content in 14 BFSPSR and LTR compounds.

Natural rubber content is reduced by substituting a larger proportion of synthetic rubber into the tire component formula. Natural rubber will resist heat better than synthetic rubber. Adding more, less expensive, synthetic rubber, reduces the heat resistance of the rubber. Excessive ambient and internally generated heat is what causes tires to wear and fail earlier in their utility.

6. Reduce inner liner gauge to minimum acceptable air retention. BFTE advises current performance may require an increase in air retention. Approximately 20% of current production fails permeability standard within three weeks. The purpose of the inner liner is to prevent the air and the air's moisture in the chamber, from migrating into the body ply, sidewalls, bead area, belts and tread of the tire. Many of the failed tire reports issued by Bridgestone/Firestone state that the failed tires were the result of over-deflection. Over-deflection resulted from over loading and/or under inflating a tire, which causes the sidewall to over deflect, and flex, beyond its design. This excessive internal heat generation caused a premature tire failure. Over deflection, caused by overloading or under inflating, leaves evidence of abuse—evidence of over deflection and under inflating is abnormal tread wear on both tread shoulders and excessive bead grooving.

In excess of two thousand Wilderness and Dueller tires inspected in the summer of 2000, by my team experienced no excessive shoulder wear on the tread. The Lisoni & Lisoni inspection team in Marengo, Indiana, on April 12 & 13, 2004, documented no excessive tread wear in the failed Steeltex tires. All used tires exhibit modest bead grooving. Abnormal bead grooving was not observed in any of the inspection of failed Firestone tires. If one in five of Bridgestone/Firestone products fail permeability standards, losing air pressure within three weeks of use, then 20 % of these failures were premeditated into the product design.

Reduced inner-liner gauge increases the frequency of cord shadow. This is a design defect allowing easier air and moisture migration into the tire through the inner liner. In this condition the major structure of the tire, the body ply, can be seen through the inner liner. Reducing the gauge and thickness of the inner liner contributes to a defect called cord shadow. In this condition the primary structure of the tire, the body ply, is raised into view through the inner liner. This condition allows the migration of air and its moisture into the tire causing tire failure.

7. Thinner steel filament

Steel filaments are round strands of steel. These strands are pulled through a die, giving the filament the required diameter and then given brass plating. Bill Orr analyzed filaments as small as .11 millimeters and as large as .36 millimeters. Steelcords are comprised of as few as six and as many as twenty-eight filaments. These brass-plated filaments allow the sulfur, of the skim stock, to adhere to the steel cord, provided quality sulfur is used. The skim stock will bond with the brass, whereas rubber will not bond to steel effectively. This discovery allowed the development of radial tires, in Europe, just prior to World War II.

Reducing the diameter of steel filaments also reduces the tensile strength of the filament, the steel belt and the tire. The smaller the steel filaments of a cord the less is the migration of skim stock into the voids of the cords, during the cure cycle, which results in a weaker bond of rubber to steel. The gist of steel to rubber adhesion is the bond of the sulfur, an additive in the skim stock recipe, to the brass plating of the steel cord filaments and the skim stock.

Creating thinner steel filaments also creates less steel cord surface area for the required steel cord to rubber adhesion. This makes the tire more susceptible to cord and rubber separation.

8. Reduce gauge or eliminate top body ply insert.

The top body ply insert is the cushion and stability for the steel belts, which complements the purpose of the belt wedge. Eliminating or reducing the width or thickness of this insert results in more heat generation. Heat destroys the rubber components of the tire.

9. Reduce LTR wedge gauge to 0.75".

The purpose of a wedge is to cushion the edges of steel belts. This prevents the belts from over flexing and rubbing against each other. This also prevents excessive internal heating and alters the tread crown radius to the required slope. Reducing the wedge allows excessive internal heat generation. Heat is the primary factor in tire durability. Reducing the wedge also changes the tire's footprint. This is the shape of the contact area between the tire and the highway. Changing a footprint can produce irregular tread wear, shorten the life of the tread, reduce wet and dry traction and change the distribution of weight. The size of the belt wedge provided a function. Changing the belt wedge changes the performance of the steel belts, thus influencing the concert of the tire.

10. Extending the life of consumable and eliminating or reducing of supplementary materials. The consumables of tires have a limited usable period in the production environment. Extending the life of consumables allowed the materials and components to be stored longer before their assembly into the tire, which allowed moisture to accumulate in dry materials and moisture to be lost in moist materials. Tire components, ready for assembly, if allowed to set idle too long will bloom, meaning the chemicals will migrate to the surface of the components, creating a gray powder appearance, resulting in a weak bond to the adjacent component properly. This will result in components separating from each other. Reducing the volume of materials refers to omitting material from the recipe of the compound, which produces a tire that is not according to the design specifications."

Incredibly, NHTSA denied the Petition, concluding that it could not identify a "defect trend," but never concluded that the tires were *not* defective. After the press conference and the meeting with NHTSA, CBS Evening News interviewed us at our home office in Pasadena, California regarding the merits of the national class action. Sharyl Attkisson was the correspondent in the Washington, DC, CBS Evening News studio, questioning us regarding our recall campaign and how the "C-95" cost reduction program was responsible for the defects in the Steeltex tire line. It should be noted that Alan Kam, Esq. (former NHTSA Compliance Attorney) set up the meeting with Joan Claybrooke and Clarence Ditlow, which resulted in their being present at the presentation before NHTSA of the "failure mode tire". Their attendance gave a great deal of validity to the Lisoni & Lisoni NHTSA Petition and the other aspects of the Firestone Steeltex Recall Campaign. However, due to the on-going conspiracy between Bridgestone/Firestone, Inc., Bridgestone Corporation of Japan and NHTSA, the presentation and the evidence fell on deaf ears. On May 23, 2003, Rubber & Plastic News reported:

> "The president of a company that processes and investigates road hazard warranty claims on tires said she has documented hundreds of tread separation complaints against Firestone Steeltex tires on recreational vehicles in the past three years. 'We've had complaints from mobile home owners whose Steeltex tires lost their treads, one right after the other in the course of a year, said Diana Becker, president of Capital Administrators, which investigates claims for the tire road-hazard warranty company Tire Guard. Bridgestone Firestone however, said the high number of Steeltex claims on RVs is due to chronic tire under-inflation and overloading in those vehicles, as well as the sheer numerical popularity of the Steeltex as an original equipment tire on them.' 'This is a case where you really have to check the ratio of failed tires, not the numbers,' said a spokesman for BFS, which regularly issues consumer advisories about the dangers of under-inflating and overloading RV tires. When the National Highway Traffic & Safety Administration dropped its investigation of Steeltex tires in April 2002, it noted these very facts, the spokesman said. 'While the Steeltex Load Range E failure frequencies are relatively high when compared with other Steeltex tires, these figures are low when compared with some competitor tires of the same load rating, NHTSA wrote."

Clarence Ditlow, President of *Center for Auto Safety*, issued a statement:

May 8, 2003: "In the June 2001 hearings where Dingell knew there was a cost-cutting program based on public statements about Firestone controlling its costs, Lampe did a good job in avoiding any specific disclosure of Project 95 and nothing shows he turned over the memos describing the project. After all, this Committee and Congressman Dingell were not at all shy about airing Firestone's dirty laundry and documents. If the Committee had these documents, they would [have] had a field day."

On June 16, 2003, NHTSA denied our first petition to re-open the investigation of the Firestone Steeltex tire series. Rubber & Plastic News reported: June 23, 2003:

"Clarence Ditlow, III, Executive Director of the *Center for Auto Safety* and a supporter of Lisoni's Petition, said the failure rate for the Firestone ATX, ATXII and Wilderness A/T recalled in 2000 was actually lower than that of the Steeltex tires. 'This decision does not square with NHTSA's earlier decisions,' Ditlow said. 'I think you're talking about an agency that is more concerned with Bridgestone/Firestone's financial health than with public safety. If you did it by the numbers, there would be a recall.' (Rubber & Plastic News)" Emphasis added.

On May 10, 2004, Lisoni & Lisoni filed a Second Petition with NHTSA to Re-open its Investigation into the Firestone Steeltex tires, comprised of two petitions, one for ambulances and emergency/rescue vehicles, and one for other subject vehicles. Lisoni &Lisoni held a Press Conference at the National Press Club in Washington, DC, to announce the filing of the new petition, but also to provide the secret "C-95" cost-cutting document to the media, which Joe and Gail had received anonymously. Richard Williams, Esq., attorney for Bridgestone Firestone, Inc. was furious. He challenged Lisoni & Lisoni in a letter dated May 7, 2003, stating that the document released at the press conference was a "typed copy of a confidential document." His letter was an admission by him, attorney for Bridgestone/Firestone, Inc., and therefore was an admission by Bridgestone/Firestone, Inc. that the document existed, and that the copy we provided to the media was legitimate and accurate. We did not deny it.

Eighteen million people viewed this Press Conference at the National Press Club. The story was covered by the media nationally and internationally and was aired on CBS Evening News and its affiliate stations nationwide. Dan Rather introduced the story and Sharyl Attkisson narrated the story of this most important release of information by the Lisoni & Lisoni investigation.

In the weeks and months following the "C-95" Press Conference, the motoring public in the United States began to purchase vehicles that came "stock" with Steeltex tires only on condition that the defective tires be replaced with tires from other manufacturers. Bridgestone/Firestone, Inc. was furious. Its brand name integrity was being destroyed by the Lisoni & Lisoni's Public Information Campaign. On June 17, 2003, the Wall Street Journal reported:

"A federal highway safety agency said it won't re-open an investigation into Bridgestone/Firestone's Steeltex tires, despite evidence that tread separation has caused thirteen deaths. At issue are thirty-million Steeltex Radial R4S, R4SII and A/T tires manufactured by Bridgestone/Firestone since 1990...The National Highway Traffic & Safety Administration (NHTSA) investigated the tires previously because of reports of injuries and deaths because of tire blow-outs. It closed an eighteen-month investigation last year after concluding the thirty-nine vehicle crashes linked to tire defects were a very low failure rate, when compared with the total number of tires in use. Those crashes killed eight people and injured forty.

Bridgestone Firestone spokesman, Dan McDonald, said there are no similarities between the Steeltex case and the Wilderness A/T and ATX case. Bridgestone/Firestone recalled 6.5 million Wilderness tires in August, 2000. It also has paid $41.5 million to settle lawsuits over Wilderness tires, which federal agency officials found were prone to separate at high speeds."

The Lisoni & Lisoni National Steeltex Recall Campaign was elevated to the highest level of credibility when, on Sunday, February 24th, 2004, the Nashville Tennessean in its front page head line story, indicted Bridgestone/Firestone, Inc. for manufacturing millions of defective Steeltex tires. The article was authored by its automotive industry reporter, Bush Bernard. Lisoni & Lisoni for two years before his block-buster, game-changing article, had provided him monthly status reports of the steps it was taking pursuant to its Nine-Point Plan to recall the defective Steeltex tires. He was given the number of tread separations, accidents, injuries and deaths. In addition, he was given a copy of the "C-95" Cost Reduction Program, as well as the testimony of Bridgestone/Firestone, Inc. whistle-blower, Bill Orr. Further, he was given the results of the inspection of the warranty claim tires that were ordered by the court to be stored for six months starting in January of 2003. The tires were stored in a limestone cave in Marengo, Indiana and the Firestone Research & Development facility in Akron, Ohio.

For many years prior to the Lisoni & Lisoni Firestone Steeltex National Tire Recall Campaign, Bush Bernard wrote numerous articles praising Bridgestone/Firestone, Inc. and its predecessor corporate entities for its success in the field of tire manufacturing. He was a dedicated apologist for the company during the Wilderness Tire Recall of 6.5 million tires. He endorsed Bridgestone/Firestone, Inc.'s position that the rollovers that had caused so many deaths and injuries to drivers and passengers of the Ford Explorer were not caused by the Wilderness tire, but were caused by an inherent defect in the Ford Explorer, that caused the vehicle to be unstable and subject to rollover accidents.

When Joe first contacted Bush Bernard regarding the National Firestone Steeltex Tire Recall Campaign being waged by Lisoni & Lisoni, he was very hostile and would always argue against its indictment of the safety of the subject tires. After several months of reviewing the status reports faxed to him by Lisoni & Lisoni, he began to be more receptive to the prospect that the Firestone Steeltex Tire Recall Campaign was a legitimate consumer safety public information project. Finally, Lisoni & Lisoni convinced him to interview the "whistle-blower", Bill Orr, regarding the alleged defects in the tires that resulted from the implementation of the "C-95" Cost Reduction Program.

Bush Bernard traveled to Bill Orr's home in Murfreesboro, Tennessee and interviewed him for several hours. Shortly before the date of the interview, he had learned of the "CBS Evening News" interview with Bill Orr and his statements detailing the manufacturing defects present in all Firestone Steeltex tires. The interview was introduced by CBS Evening News Anchor, Dan Rather and presented by correspondent, Sharyl Attkisson. The endorsement by "CBS Evening News with Dan Rather" gave Bill Orr's statement regarding the life-threatening defects present in the entire Steeltex tire line great credibility.

Bill Orr had "hands on" experience with the defective Firestone tires dating back to the first warranty claims presented to the tire manufacturer by angry owners of vehicles that came factory equipped with the dangerously defective tires. While interviewing Bill Orr, he was shown the "Littell tire." This tire was the sixth tire from his RV. Five tires had suffered tread separations and the sixth tire had not yet failed, but was in "failure mode."

Bush Bernard spent several hours with Bill Orr questioning him about his twenty-five-year career at Firestone, his research and investigation of the Wilderness tire failures, the work he did in his lab to uncover the causes of the failures of Steeltex tires on ambulances, his termination from the company, his motives for supporting the Lisoni & Lisoni National Steeltex Tire Recall Campaign, his experience at a meeting at the NHTSA to support the recall campaign, how he had been black-listed in the industry by Bridgestone/Firestone, Inc., how he successfully presented his case for wrongful termination with the Tennessee State Agency in charge of unemployment benefits and the state of his wrongful termination case against Bridgestone/Firestone, Inc.

After ending the interview and "fact checking" Bill Orr's testimony, he came to the shocking conclusion that Bridgestone/Firestone, Inc. had been lying to him about the quality of the millions of tires it had manufactured over a period of many years. He realized he had been used and abused by the tire manufacturer and set out to destroy the credibility of the Firestone tire brand name. He used his position as the automotive industry reporter for the Nashville Tennessean to "inform the motoring public across the U.S. about the corruption that permeated Bridgestone/Firestone, Inc. at every level." He then authored the front page, February 24, 2004 article lambasting the Bridgestone/Firestone, Inc. cover-up of the defects in the Firestone Steeltex tire line. At this point in time, the Lisoni & Lisoni National Tire Recall Campaign had gained national prominence, but was not yet successful in causing NHTSA to recall the Steeltex tire line from the roads and highways of the U.S.

Bush Bernard's February 24, 2004 front-page article in the Sunday Edition of the Tennessean marked the beginning of the end of the Lisoni & Lisoni National Firestone Steeltex Tire Recall Campaign. Two days after Bush Bernard's article appeared in the Nashville Tennessean—and was republished in over 400 newspapers across the U.S.—NHTSA issued a Recall Order for 490,000 Firestone Steeltex tires.

> The February 26th CBS Evening News reported the story as follows: February 26, 2004: "Bridgestone/Firestone announced a recall Thursday of about 490,000 16-inch Steeltex tires linked to sport utility vehicle crashes that killed five people...' We haven't identified a specific problem with the tires,' company spokesman Dan McDonald said. 'The data suggested that there's an issue,' and the decision was made that instead of having a long drawn-out investigation to figure out if there is a problem, let's just step up and replace the tires.' The tire maker said it learned two months ago that there were six crashes involving SUVs with Steeltex tires. It said it reported the information to the National Highway Traffic & Safety Administration, as required, and announced the voluntary recall. The safety administration first noticed a pattern of crashes and blowouts with Steeltex tires, federal officials said."

Bush Bernard authored another front-page article the day after the NHTSA Recall entitled, "Firestone Recalls 490,000 Steeltex tires." It was his personal redemption for having unwittingly apologized for and promoted the huge profits of Bridgestone/Firestone, Inc. for over a dozen years. Lisoni & Lisoni issued a Press Release commenting on the recall:

"The credibility of Lisoni & Lisoni was validated in the national print and electronic media when CBS reported: February 26, 2004: 'Bridgestone/Firestone announced a recall Thursday of about 490,000 16-inch Steeltex tires linked to sport utility vehicle crashes that killed five people... 'We haven't identified a specific problem with the tires,' company spokesman Dan McDonald said. 'The data suggested that there's an issue,' and the decision was made that instead of having a long, drawn-out investigation to figure out if there is a problem, let's just step up and replace the tires.' The tire maker said it learned two months ago that there were six crashes involving SUV's with Steeltex tires. It said it reported the information to the National Highway Traffic & Safety Administration, as required, and announced the voluntary recall. The safety administration first noticed a pattern of crashes and blowouts with Steeltex tires, federal officials said."

As a result of Bush Bernard's front page articles, on the day of the recall, Bridgestone/ Firestone, Inc. tried to perform "damage control" by saying it was a "voluntary customer satisfaction," but a NHTSA spokesperson clearly identified it as a formal government recall. The recall was then, and remains to today, the third largest tire recall in U.S. history. The first (Firestone 500) and second (Bridgestone/Firestone Wilderness) largest tire recalls in history also belong to Bridgestone/Firestone, Inc.

Nonetheless, the two front-page articles authored by Bush Bernard, together with the NHTSA recall of 490,000 defective Firestone Steeltex tires, resulted in the absolute destruction of the Firestone Steeltex tire's brand name.

NHTSA's attempt to mitigate the damage it did to Bridgestone/Firestone, Inc. and the Bridgestone Corporation of Japan caused it to be characterized for the first time as a newly identified facilitator of the Bridgestone/Firestone Conspiracy of Death & Destruction.

Incredibly, on September 24, 2004, NHTSA <u>again</u> denied Plaintiffs Petition to Re-open the investigation. The Third Petition claimed that NHTSA misstated the number of complaints, and manipulated the statistics. Lisoni & Lisoni documented 57 deaths and 162 serious injuries, as of May 1, 2006, and the numbers grew larger with the passing of each day.

Subsequent to the recall, a Federal Court ruled that NHTSA recall investigation reports were not admissible in evidence in product liability cases because they were "untrustworthy." NHTSA was aware of the design change of adding the nylon cap to prevent the tread separations, however, due to the "confidentiality" given to manufacturers, requested by Bridgestone/Firestone, the motoring public was again left in the dark. Bridgestone/Firestone's strategy was to wait anxiously for time to pass so that the defective tires would wear out and be replaced at the consumer's cost, and not Bridgestone/Firestone's. They also knew that there would be tread separations, which would cause injuries and possible deaths, but to Bridgestone/Firestone, it was a "numbers game". It would pay the claims it was required to, and in the long run, it would be much cheaper than to recall the defective tires. However, the Public Information Campaign was nullifying this strategy. The February 26, 2004 recall of 490,000 Firestone Steeltex tires cost Bridgestone/Firestone, Inc. two-billion dollars.

From the filing of the class action lawsuit in August, 2002, Lisoni & Lisoni, through its Public Information Campaign, amassed over 3,500 class members. These individuals usually visited our website, which had a claim form which they could print out and mail to us, along with any documentation of damages.

Gail was in charge of, including but not limited to, maintaining the class action directory, sending status reports to class members, preparing 177 declarations signed by class members, and preparing individuals for their depositions.

During the litigation, the Superior Court in its Case Management Order, ordered Bridgestone/Firestone to store warranty claim tires.

On August 10, 2003, Lisoni & Lisoni sent the following Status Report of Firestone Steeltex Class Action:

"Dear Class Member:

We have defeated Bridgestone/Firestone, Inc's attempts to dismiss this lawsuit. We are now in the first phase of discovery. We have filed our Motion to Certify the Class, and the hearing will be sometime in February, 2004. During this period, the attorneys will be conducting discovery on the issue of class certification. The court will grant class certification if all of the claims involve the same facts (defect), and that the class is an easily identifiable class. There is a possibility that the defense attorneys will want your testimony under oath. If that is the case, we will contact you directly and work out the details. Pursuant to Court Order, Bridgestone/Firestone, Inc., has established facilities to accept the alleged defective tires from the class members, in Akron, Ohio and Nashville, Tennessee. Bridgestone/Firestone, Inc. will pay all costs of shipping. You will be responsible for packaging the tire. We have enclosed a copy of: 1) Steeltex Tire Shipping Instructions to Declarants and 2) Label for Shipping Package. At your earliest convenience, please ship your defective tires to Bridgestone/Firestone, Inc. Please advise us in writing that you have returned the tire(s) so that we can track the tire. Thank you for your continued cooperation and support. Your participation is extremely meaningful and important in our class action lawsuit efforts. Please feel free to call at (626) 440-1333."

Chapter IX

DOCUMENTATION OF THE LITIGATION OF THE NATIONWIDE CLASS ACTION

"The Nature of the Medium is the Nature of the Message"

Lisoni & Lisoni served the class action lawsuit on Bridgestone/Firestone, Inc., and Bridgestone Corporation, and "the game was on." Holland & Knight, a law firm of over 1,100 lawyers in twenty-one offices in the U.S. represented Bridgestone/Firestone, Inc. Squire, Sanders & Dempsey, LLP, a law firm of over 1,300 lawyers in forty offices around the world represented Bridgestone Corporation.

The defense attorneys scheduled thirty depositions in three weeks, all over the country, thinking that we could not possibly handle them, because we were only two lawyers and they had lawyers in offices all over the country. However, we called around the country and, through the American Trial Lawyers Association, we were able to get attorneys in the different states to sit with our clients and let them tell their story. At the depositions, there was one tragic story after another about the sudden and unexpected tread separation and the aftermath in their lives caused by the defective Steeltex tires.

The defense attorneys took the deposition of Roger Littell in Los Angeles and Lou Ann Pleasant in Modesto, California. Roger

Littell had lost five of his six Steeltex tires on his motor home, and Lou Ann Pleasant had lost one tire on her Ford F-250 pick-up truck. Roger Littell and Lou Ann Pleasant were excellent plaintiffs for the class action. Roger Littell was a former employee of Firestone. He worked in quality control and participated in numerous road tests of Firestone tires. Lou Ann Pleasant used her Ford F-250 truck, equipped with Firestone Steeltex tires, to conduct a business which produced dog shows around the state of California and other venues. Roger Litttell's participation was critical because he had lost five of his six tires on his mobile home within a few months. The sixth tire had not yet failed. We sent the tire to Bill Orr and asked him to dissect the tire as he would have done in his lab at the Firestone plant, and show how the defects were being manifested and the likely catastrophic results caused by the implementation of the cost reduction program, "C-95".

After we served Bridgestone Corporation with the class action lawsuit, its defense attorneys filed a Motion to Quash the Service of Summons, alleging that Bridgestone Corporation was a Japanese corporation and did not do any business in the United States. Judge Christopher Sheldon ruled in our favor, holding Bridgestone Corporation in the lawsuit. We made a deal with the attorney for Bridgestone Corporation that we would dismiss Bridgestone Corporation in exchange for an agreement by Bridgestone Corporation to toll the statute of limitations, preserving the class members' right to file a new class action against Bridgestone Corporation at a later point in time. Bridgestone/Firestone then attempted to force Joe Lisoni into submitting to a deposition. We had to fight it with everything we had because the defense attorneys would be allowed to ask just about anything, and Joe would have to answer under penalty of perjury. We filed a motion in court for a "Protective Order" and, after a lengthy argument, the court ruled in our favor and Joe did not have to submit to the deposition.

Chapter X

DIRECT MAIL INVESTIGATION AND PUBLIC INFORMATION CAMPAIGN

"Knowledge is Power"

Lisoni & Lisoni purchased mailing lists of owners of the seventy-one models of vehicles which came equipped with Firestone Steeltex tires from Hugo Dunhill Mailing Lists of New York. They sent thousands of letters—over 300,000—to registered owners of vehicles which had come factory equipped with Firestone Steeltex tires, warning them of the potential for sudden and unexpected catastrophic tread separation of their Steeltex tires. Notices were sent to 3,500 independent tire stores, and the P.A.C.E. Union mailed a notice to every Ford and Chevy dealership in the United States, over 40,000, relating to their *"post-sale duty to warn consumers"* of the known dangers associated with Firestone Steeltex tires. It stated:

> "A new class action lawsuit has been launched against Bridgestone/Firestone. This time for scores of injuries and deaths linked to its Steeltex tires. A CBS Evening News report in November reported Steeltex tire failures in twenty-six states."

Direct Mail Investigation and Public Information Campaign

A July 2003 article in the Advocate on *"Post-sale Duties to Warn, Recall and Retrofit Defective Products"* by Attorney John D. Rowell suggests that sellers and distributors may have a duty to warn customers of defects and could be liable 'for harm to persons or property caused by the seller's failure to provide a warning after the time of sale or distribution'. Are you informing customers of potential problems with your Steeltex tires? Is Bridgestone/Firestone in denial over problems with the Steeltex tire, similar to how the company reacted to the Wilderness debacle? Get all the information to protect your customers and yourself. Put tire safety first. Ask Bridgestone/Firestone —why take risks with tire safety?"

The P.A.C.E. (Paper, Allied-Industrial, Chemical & Energy) Union assisted in the dissemination of the information as a result of their union members being "locked out" of Continental Carbon, Inc. which makes carbon black, a very important component in the manufacture of tires. The members had been locked out for over three years, and as a result of using unskilled labor, defective carbon black was being sold to Bridgestone/Firestone with its knowledge and consent, resulting in the manufacture of millions of defective tires. The P.A.C.E. Union notified all 40,000 Ford and Chevy dealers in the United States of the carbon black problem with a direct mail campaign, which resulted in hundreds of dealerships looking to Firestone for indemnity from any claims. Further, consumers agreed to buy the vehicle from the dealership on condition that the dealership would agree to replace the Firestone Seeltex tires with another brand.

On December 2, 2004, the Continental Carbon Co. settled the lock-out and the P.A.C.E. Union signed a five year agreement. Finally, in August, 2005, after fourteen years on the market, producing thirty-million Steeltex tires, Bridgestone/Firestone announced that it was no longer manufacturing the Firestone Steeltex tires. This act forced by the Lisoni & Lisoni Recall Campaign cost Bridgestone/Firestone several billion dollars in future lost profits that would have resulted from the sales of the Firestone Steeltex tire line. The developments in this action were of sufficient interest to the nationwide product liability laws, consumer protections laws, the auto and rubber industry such that there were over 3,000 separate and distinct reported articles in newspapers, including but not limited to: the Wall Street Journal, the Associated Press (AP), United Press International (UPI), the Nashville Tennessean, USA Today, New York and L.A. Times, San Francisco Chronicle, Washington Post, Chicago Sun Tribune, Minnesota Star, Dallas Morning Star, and Miami Herald, and the leading international tire publication: the Rubber & Plastic News.

In fact, Rubber & Plastic News declared the safety issue of the Firestone Steeltex tires, brought to light by the Lisoni & Lisoni National Recall Campaign to be the fifth most significant rubber story in all of 2003, in its December year-end issue. The alliance between the P.A.C.E. Union and Lisoni & Lisoni resulted from a chance meeting between the Unions' representative in labor disputes, Joe Drexler, and Joe, the night before the first Press Conference at the National Press Club in Washington, DC.

In the early 1900's, the union workers in Trinidad, Colorado waged the largest and most violent labor strike in U.S. history. Pinkerton guards were hired to stop the strike and its public demonstrations. Pinkerton employed life-threatening tactics in an attempt to end the strike. Joe's maternal grandfather, Joseph Minna, was one of the strikers. He shot and killed a Pinkerton guard in self-defense, and Joe still had the rifle, a Winchester 73. Joe related this story to Joe Drexler in the lobby of the hotel in Washington DC, where the participants in the upcoming Press Conference and meeting with NHTSA were staying. When Joe Drexler, Chairman of the Trinidad Strike Memorial Organization, heard about Joe's maternal grandfather, Joseph Minna, an instant bond was formed between the two Joes.

Continental Carbon manufactured the "carbon black" material used in the manufacturing process of rubber tires. Carbon black was the most important element in causing the rubber in the tires to bond with the steel belted cords. Joe Drexler represented the P.A.C.E. Union, whose members worked at Continental Carbon and were locked out of their jobs. The P.A.C.E. Union decided to support the Steeltex Recall Campaign and appear at the planned Press Conference the next day. It was at this meeting that Joe Drexler agreed to use union employees to picket NHTSA while the Lisoni & Lisoni Press Conference was being held at the National Press Club.

During the course of the National Recall Campaign, Lisoni & Lisoni issued a news release predicting failures of Firestone tires manufactured in Akron, Ohio for use in the Indianapolis 500 Race held each Memorial Day weekend in Indiana. They were validated when failures actually occurred when the race was run on Memorial Day, the year the press release was published nationwide.

PACE International Union • 3340 Perimeter Hill Drive • Nashville, TN 37211

FOR IMMEDIATE RELEASE

Contact:
Joe Drexler, PACE Special Projects director, (cell) 615-594-2074

PACE International Union Calls for Bridgestone Firestone Steeltex Tires To Be Recalled

The following statement is from the Paper, Allied-Industrial, Chemical & Energy Workers Intl. Union:

NASHVILLE, TENN. – February 27, 2004 - - The 300,000 member Paper, Allied-Industrial, Chemical and Energy Workers International Union is supporting a law firm's efforts to have Bridgestone/Firestone Steeltex tires recalled by the National Highway Transportation Safety Administration (NHTSA).

Lisoni and Lisoni, a Pasadena, Calif., law firm that is heading this effort, has questioned the components used to manufacture the tires. Carbon black, one of the components, is a bonding material, and defective carbon black can cause tread separation.

Goodyear filed suit against Continental Carbon, one of Bridgestone/Firestone's chief suppliers, in May 2003 for the alleged delivery of defective carbon black. Goodyear discovered the alleged defective carbon black through its own independent testing, and severed its business relationship with Continental Carbon. Not all of Continental Carbon's customers conduct separate testing, and many rely on Continental Carbon to provide carbon black that meets customers' specifications.

PACE believes that both Bridgestone/Firestone and Cooper Tire received shipments of defective carbon black from Continental Carbon, but have continued their business relationship. According to PACE, this may be putting their customers and shareholders at risk.

PACE represents workers in Ponca City, Okla., who have been locked-out for nearly three years by Taiwanese-owned Continental Carbon Company, one of Bridgestone/Firestone's main carbon black suppliers. The union has charged that Continental Carbon replaced experienced workers with a cut-rate work force, resulting in high turnover at the Ponca City plant, the company's largest manufacturing facility.

Recently, a Cooper Tire representative, when questioned by PACE, stated that Continental Carbon had addressed its quality issues when it terminated two disgruntled temporary employees responsible for the production and shipment of defective carbon black. However, PACE believes that turnover and production problems at the Ponca City plant may still plague the company.

In a news release issued on January 29, Lisoni stated, "The number of people being injured or suffering property damage is growing daily as we receive new reports of alleged defective tires from consumers. As there are still nearly 30 million Steeltex tires out there on the road, it is imperative they be recalled."

CBS Evening News has been conducting its own investigation of Steeltex tires, and its most recent investigatory report appeared on its February 6 national broadcast.

"Many Steeltex tires are on emergency vehicles such as ambulances, and it is disturbing that persons already in peril may suffer a double jeopardy on their way to the hospital," said Dr. Joseph Drexler, PACE director of special projects, "It's time that NHTSA stops listening to Bridgestone/Firestone and does its job to protect the public by taking Steeltex tires off the road.

PACE sent notices last week to 40,000 tire dealers about the Steeltex tire and potential tire defects that could result from use of substandard carbon black. A recent article in *The Advocate*, a California legal journal, suggested that tire dealers had a duty to warn customers of potential unsafe tires or could be held liable for damages resulting from accidents.

According to PACE, yesterday's voluntary recall by Bridgestone/Firestone of 490,000 Canadian-manufactured Steeltex tires linked to SUV crashes that killed five people should prompt further investigation by NHTSA of U.S. manufactured Steeltex tires which have been linked to scores of other deaths and injuries.

PACE represents 300,000 workers in the paper, oil, chemical, automotive parts, industrial minerals, atomic energy and cement industries. More information on Steeltex tires and carbon black can be found at www.firestonesteeltexclassaction.com and www.fightbackonline.org

###

/2018 Class action attorneys write UN members about Steeltex tires | Rubber and Plastics News

10/1/2002 UPDATED 11/14/2012

Class action attorneys write UN members about Steeltex tires

Rubber & Plastics News

  News

NEW YORK (Oct. 1)—Three California attorneys leading a class action against Bridgestone/Firestone and Bridgestone Corp. for Steeltex tires have taken their discovery international. Joseph and Gail Lisoni and Steven M. Weinberger sent letters to all member countries of the United Nations, asking them for any evidence of Steeltex tire failures within their borders. "Many vehicles manufactured in the United States come equipped with these defective tires and they may have found their way into your country," they wrote. Bridgestone/Firestone, which has consistently pointed to a federal investigation of Steeltex tires that ended without finding any defect, said it doubted the letter would create much concern within the United Nations. Lisoni has said he plans to hold a news conference in Washington Nov. 14 to present evidence of alleged defects in Steeltex tires to the National Highway Traffic Safety Administration.

To All Ambulance Services

CBS Evening News has reported 82 rescue squads in 26 states had problems with Bridgestone/Firestone Steeltex tires.

This investigation occurred before Bridgestone/Firestone announced a recall on February 26, 2004 of 490,000 tires. The recall may be the tip of iceberg, considering there are over 30 million Steeltex tires still on the road.

Attorney Joseph Lisoni of Pasadena, Calif., who is seeking class action status for a lawsuit on behalf of plaintiffs, has called Steeltex tires "dangerous and lethal lemons," responsible for more than a dozen deaths and over 100 injuries.

Lisoni charges that Bridgestone/Firestone used substandard materials for Steeltex tires. He said 175 ambulance services around the nation have replaced Steeltex tires with competing brands after tread separations and accidents.

In May 2003, Goodyear Tire sued Continental Carbon, also a major supplier of Bridgestone/Firestone, for delivery of alleged defective carbon black, which is a major bonding material used in the manufacture of tires. Defective carbon black can cause tread separation.

<u>There is evidence that Continental Carbon also shipped alleged defective carbon black to Bridgestone/Firestone. However, Bridgestone/Firestone continues to purhase carbon black from this supplier.</u> Why? Does Goodyear care more about tire safety?

Regular safety checks on your Steeltex tires are highly recommended. If you notice defects, call your tire dealer and ask for a replacement.

If your dealer did not give you a warning about Steeltex tires when you purchased the tires or your vehicle, your dealer may also be liable for property damage and injuries caused by defective tires according to an article in *The Advocate*, a California legal journal.

Put the safety of your ambulance personnel and patients first. For further information on Steeltex tires, see *www.firestonesteeltexclassaction.com*

This is a public service message of PACE International Union representing 300,000 workers in the oil, chemical and paper industries.

615-831-6722

CBS EVENING NEWS

· Section Front
E-mail This Story Printable Version

More Rescue Squad Tire Troubles

WASHINGTON, Nov. 7, 2003

Faulty Ambulance Tires

(Photo: AP)

The 28 states where failures of Firestone Steeltex tires on rescue vehicles have been reported, according to our CBS News investigation, are: AL, AZ, CA, CT, FL, GA, IA, IL, IN, KY, KS, MD, MI, MO, MN, NJ, NY, OH, OK, PA, SC, SD, TN, TX, UT, WI.

Other facts:
- 83 rescue squads in 28 states have reported unusual failures of their Firestone Steeltex tires in recent years.
- 25 rescue squads in 15 states reported unusual failures of their Firestone Steeltex tires this year alone.
- Some squads had repeated failures for a total of at least 172 Firestone Steeltex tire failures on rescue vehicles.
- A total of at least 34 patients were aboard the rescue vehicles when the tire failures happened.
- At least 34 of the rescue squads changed brands of tires after their Firestone Steeltex tires.
- Steeltex tires aren't just used on rescue vehicles, but also on millions of RV's, light trucks, and SUV's

(CBS) Days before the birth of her grandson, Joyce Hardisty recorded a message for him, reports CBS News Correspondent Sharyl Attkisson.

"Hi, I just want to say we can't wait for you to arrive!" said Hardisty.

But soon after, she had a heart attack. A frantic situation got worse when her ambulance blew a tire and ended up on the side of the road. Amid the confusion, her breathing tube came loose. She didn't survive.

"It wouldn've have fell out if they didn't have to transfer her from one ambulance to another," says her son Mike Newton. "And she wouldn't have obviously died because of lack of oxygen to her brain."

When that accident happened, Firestone Steeltex tires were already blamed for many unusual failures on rescue vehicles – when seconds count. Now, a CBS News investigation has found 82 rescue squads in 28 states reporting problems.

The federal government has twice investigated Steeltex tires and found no defect – even saying their failure rate is lower than competitors. But consumer groups lambasted that decision. And now a class action suit is being fought for owners of Steeltex tires on millions of rescue vehicles, light trucks and RV's.

Under the lawsuit, Firestone must preserve certain damaged Steeltex tires for experts to inspect.

But experts will never get a look at some of these tires, judging by pictures obtained by CBS News. They were in line for shredding at a different company's facility, which happens to be next door to Firestone's plant in LaVergne, Tenn.

So what is Firestone saving? Only damaged tires that customers themselves ship directly to headquarters. The problem is, most customers don't know to do that.

Joe Olmsted of North Syracuse, N.Y., had no idea there was a lawsuit. So when his ambulance had two tread separations in one night with patients aboard, he didn't send the tires to Firestone headquarters. He scrapped them.

"The tread separated approximately right here, this all came apart," Olmsted said, showing Attkisson a tire.

Consumer advocate Joan Claybrook of the group Public Citizen says not collecting all the damaged Steeltex tires is a missed opportunity to get to the bottom of any problem.

"Our view is that these lawsuits are very important to the American public. They could get a lot of information they don't otherwise have access to quite easily," says Claybrook.

Matthew Newton won't ever get to know his grandmother; he was born just a few days after she died. And his parents can't help but wonder if things might have been different if only the ambulance had different tires.

"She definitely could be alive right now," said Mike Newton.

© MMIII, CBS Broadcasting Inc All Rights Reserved.

Chapter XI
LOBBY THE HOUSE & SENATE, ATTORNEYS GENERAL AND GOVERNORS FOR A CONGRESSIONAL INVESTIGATION

"Not Influence Peddling, but Peddling Influence"

From August, 2002 to 2007, Lisoni & Lisoni lobbied the House of Representatives and the United States Senate for a Congressional investigation, including but not limited to, meeting with staff members of Congressman William Tauzin (Chairman/House Commerce & Energy Committee) including his lead researcher on the Firestone Wilderness Congressional Investigation, Ann Washington, and provided her with a demonstration of the consequences of "C-95" on the Steeltex tires, through a question and answer process with William Orr, completed at Congressman Tauzin's office in Washington, DC. Each and every member of the U.S. House of Representatives and the U.S. Senate received letters from Lisoni & Lisoni each month, warning of the dangers in these Firestone Steeltex tires. Also, a letter was sent to every state's Attorney General in the United States. The letter stated:

"RE: DEFECTIVELY DANGEROUS FIRESTONE STEELTEX TIRE SERIES

Dear Attorney General:

Please find enclosed for your review copies of letters from the Office of the National Association of Attorneys General and the State of New York Office of the Attorney General, encouraging communication with your office concerning a defective series of Firestone tires known as the Steeltex line. In conjunction with a class action lawsuit, our office petitioned the NHTSA to Re-open its Defect Investigation that the NHTSA suspended in April of 2002. Attached for your review is the NHTSA response to our Petition. Thank you for your cooperation. More information on this subject may be viewed at www.firestonesteeltexclassaction.com."

On November 27, 2002, Lisoni & Lisoni sent a "Second Notice" to all fifty United States Senators, which stated:

"We previously notified you (by letter dated 8-13-02) about the grossly defective and dangerous Firestone Steeltex R4S, R4SII and AT tire line. Similar to the Firestone Wilderness product line, the Steeltex product line suffers from a lamination defect, which causes catastrophic tread separations.

These catastrophic tread separations occur without warning often while driving at highway speeds, causing the driver to lose control of the vehicle. To date, our law office has documented over seven-thousand Steeltex tread separations, having caused a minimum of eleven fatalities, and multiple incidents of life-threatening personal injuries. Our law office alone represents three individuals with fractured necks as a result of these grossly defective tires. Moreover, eleven states have removed Steeltex tires from their respective ambulance transport vehicles after at least one patient died in an ambulance due to a Steeltex tread separation, and numerous ambulance vehicles suffered multiple instances of tread separations while transporting patients. These same multiple instances of Steeltex catastrophic failures have occurred on both school and church vehicles.

On November 15, 2002, our law office filed a Petition with the National Highway Traffic & Safety Administration (NHTSA) requesting that they re-open their Defect Investigation into the Firestone Steeltex tire line as a preparatory step to a formal recall. We reiterate our request that you utilize the powers of your office to ensure that the motoring public is protected from these grossly defective tires, and that your constituents do not suffer from additional loss of life and/or life altering injuries.

More information regarding this subject may be found at www.firestonesteeltexclassaction.com."

Detailed document packages were provided to Senators Diane Feinstein (D. Calif.), Barbara Boxer (D. Calif.), John McCain, (R. Arizona) Joseph Liberman (D. Ct.) and Adam Schiff (D. Calif.). The evidence was provided, but nothing was done—more acts of concealment in furtherance of the Bridgestone/Firestone Conspiracy of Death & Destruction. Lisoni & Lisoni never learned why we received no response. Monthly status report letters were sent to each Attorney General and each Governor for each of the fifty states, warning of the dangers associated with the Firestone Steeltex tires. This information campaign resulted in tremendous cooperation from their offices in getting defective tires replaced. Many offices of Attorneys General started sending Lisoni & Lisoni information about Steeltex failures in their state: A sample letter stated:

"Honorable David Samson, Attorney General, State of New Jersey, Department of Law and Public Safety, Richard J. Hughes, Justice Complex

RE: Defectively Dangerous Firestone Steeltex R4S, R4SII & A/T Tire Series

Dear Mr. Lisoni:

By letter dated January 8, 2003, the Office of the Governor for the State of New Jersey (letter attached) referred investigation of the defective Firestone Steeltex R4S, R4SII and A/T tire series to your attention. Our office wishes to alert you of two deaths and injuries of New Jersey citizens, resulting from the aforementioned defective tires.

We reiterate that the Firestone Steeltex tire series is a lethally defective product, and that the danger of this product is being actively concealed from the motoring public. This is a public safety and welfare issue which we urge your office to pursue to prevent further tragedy and loss of life.

Our office is more than willing to share any information regarding this defective tire series and is available to communicate with you and/or members of your staff. Please feel free to contact us at (626) 440-1333. More information on this subject is available at www.firestonesteeltexclassaction.com."

Rubber & Plastic News reported on October 1, 2002:

"Three California attorneys leading a class action against Bridgestone/Firestone and Bridgestone Corporation for Steeltex tires have taken their discovery international... to all member countries of the United Nations, asking them for any evidence of Steeltex tire failures within their borders. 'Many vehicles manufactured in the United States come equipped with these defective tires and they may have found their way into your country,' they wrote. Bridgestone/Firestone, has consistently pointed to a federal investigation of Steeltex tires that ended without finding any defect, said it doubted the letter would create much concern within the United States."

Chapter XII

FILE PERSONAL INJURY CASES NATIONWIDE TO COMPENSATE VICTIMS OF STEELTEX FAILURES

"Eat the Elephant One Bite at a Time"

There had been documented 57 deaths and 162 serious injuries resulting from the defective Firestone Steeltex tires. Bridgestone/Firestone employed many law firms across the United States to defend them, forcing the plaintiffs to file lawsuits, and then they were settled as the case got close to trial, and always under the secrecy of a Confidential Settlement. Dan Rather at CBS Evening News took serious exception to Bridgestone/Firestone requiring confidentiality in settlements. Lisoni & Lisoni monitored and assisted in many other actions for damages brought by plaintiffs' lawyers across the U.S. for deaths and serious injury lawsuits against Bridgestone/Firestone as a result of failures of the Firestone Steeltex tires.

Lisoni & Lisoni had a website that published all of the damaging evidence. (www.firestonesteeltexclassaction.com) One such plaintiff was Lela Helms, an eighty-three-year old grandmother, who broke her neck due to the tread separation on her son's truck. The tire was inspected by several experts and determined to be defective.

File Personal Injury Cases Nationwide to Compensate...

Bridgestone/Firestone, Inc. challenged Mr. Bill Orr as an expert, so Gail Lisoni had to argue a "Daubert" motion, in Federal Court in Denver, Colorado. Attorneys for Bridgestone Firestone filed a motion in federal court asking the court to declare that Bill Orr was not a "qualified expert". Gail argued in support of the credentials Bill Orr had as an expert, and he was determined by the court to be a credible expert. However, as the case got close to trial, Bridgestone/Firestone then refused to settle the case if Lisoni & Lisoni continued on the case, because Bridgestone/Firestone would not contribute to any attorney fees going to Lisoni & Lisoni. Lela Helms was in failing health, and probably would not have been able to go through the trial, so Lisoni & Lisoni had to give up all rights to attorneys' fees in order to allow the client a settlement of her case. A local Denver attorney processed the settlement for no fee.

In furtherance of the Conspiracy of Death & Destruction, Holland & Knight, defense attorneys for Bridgestone/Firestone, threatened several other plaintiffs' attorneys that Bridgestone/Firestone would not settle their claims unless they agreed that Lisoni & Lisoni would not share in the contingency fee because that would help fund the class action.

In another action, John Carr vs. Bridgestone Firestone, Inc. involving a defective Firestone Steeltex tire, the court ruled incorrectly against Mr. Carr. Rubber & Plastic News reported: Dec 15, 2003: John Carr case,

"According to Lisoni, however, (Judge) Hancook erred on three different points. Lisoni said. 'First, he should never have excluded Sanderson's testimony. Second, he had no grounds on which to deny our motion to replace Sanderson with Orr. Third, he clearly disregarded the record from the Alabama Supreme Court, which has ruled a product defect case may be proven on circumstantial evidence alone, and we have tons of circumstantial evidence in this case. We also filed personal injury actions on behalf of Robert Harrington who was involved in an accident, in California, when his truck suffered a catastrophic tread separation, causing him to fracture his back. Lisoni & Lisoni also filed a lawsuit on behalf of Francis O'Brien, for injuries sustained in a car accident resulting from a tread separation, but he passed away, and his case died with him. We also filed a lawsuit on behalf of Linda Featherstone against Bridgestone/Firestone.'"

Chapter XIII

FILE INSURANCE COMPANY PROPERTY DAMAGE AND PERSONAL INJURY SUBROGATION CASES

"The Enemy of My Enemy is My Friend"

Many thousands of insurance subrogation claims existed from the 300 plus companies that honored personal injury and property damage claims that resulted from defective Firestone Steeltex tires.

These insurance companies insured the 71 model vehicles which came from the factory with defective Firestone Steeltex tires installed as original equipment.

Lisoni & Lisoni presented these insurance companies three options for recovering their damages:

1) Become a member of the National Class Action;
2) File individual subrogation lawsuits against Bridgestone/Firestone, Inc.;
3) File their own Class Actions.

Farmers Insurance Group, on behalf of the 300 plus insurance companies elected to file a Class Action of their own against Bridgestone/Firestone for claims they paid to their insured's for damages caused by defective Firestone Steeltex tire tread separations. The class action was settled – confidentially, of course!

Chapter XIV

LOBBY THE UNITED NATIONS REGARDING THE DESIGNED-IN DEFECTS OF STEELTEX TIRES

"International Cooperation Equals International Safety"

"All Points Bulletins" and letters were sent to each member of the United Nations, each member of the U. S. House of Representatives and the U.S. Senate, warning of the dangers associated with the Firestone Steeltex tires.

On September 29, 2002, Lisoni & Lisoni sent an Important Notice to all member countries of the United Nations. It stated:

"Dear Member Country of the United Nations:
The National Highway Traffic & Safety Administration (NHTSA) began a Defect Investigation into Steeltex R4S tires on September 29, 2000, as a preparatory step to a formal recall of the Steeltex R4S, R$SII and A/T tires and was done less than two months after the recall of 6.5 million Firestone ATX, ATXII and Wilderness AT tires.

On April 9, 2002, the National Highway Traffic & Safety Administration closed its investigation into the Firestone

Steeltex R4S, R4SII and A/T tires, finding no defect trend. The agency said it found the evidence does not support a defect finding against the tires, but <u>also that it would re-open the investigation if new evidence becomes available</u>. We have information that these tires are failing all over the United States and in some foreign countries, and that most failures have not been reported to NHTSA. Further, we believe that many more failures of these subject tires will fail in the future.

PLEASE NOTE THAT MANY VEHICLES MANUFACTURED IN THE UNITED STATES COME EQUIPPED WITH THESE DEFECTIVE TIRES AND THEY MAY HAVE FOUND THEIR WAY INTO YOUR COUNTRY. PLEASE ALERT YOUR NATION'S VEHICLE SAFETY DEPARTMENT OF THE POTENTIAL RISK ASSOCIATED WITH THE FIRESTONE STEELTEX R4S, R4SII, AND A/T TIRES.

We have filed a nationwide class action in the United States Court system demanding that the entire Firestone Steeltex line be recalled in the interest of worldwide public health and safety. If you have any reports of tire failures of the Firestone Steeltex tires in question on vehicles in your country, we would very much appreciate hearing from you about your experience."

An "All-Points Bulletin" was sent to all ambulance companies in the United States, which resulted in ambulance companies in thirty-six states removing the tires from their ambulances at their own cost.

It stated: "**ALL POINTS BULLETIN**Summer, 2003

RE: DANGEROUSLY DEFECTIVE FIRESTONE STEELTEX TIRES ON AMBULANCE & EMERGENCY TRANSPORT VEHICLES

This letter serves to inform you and your department about the safety hazards associated with the Firestone Steeltex (R4S, R4SII & A/T) tire series often equipped on ambulance and emergency transport vehicles. Similar to the now-infamous Firestone Wilderness tire, which experienced sudden and catastrophic tread separations, the Firestone Steeltex tire also suffers from sudden and catastrophic tread separations. Ambulance services in at least twelve states (Kansas, Illinois, Idaho, Indiana, Arizona, Georgia, South Carolina, Kentucky, Texas, Utah, New York, and Pennsylvania) have removed Firestone Steeltex tires from their fleets after experiencing catastrophic tread separations. CBS Evening News has featured six stories questioning the safety of the Firestone Steeltex tires over the last three years, and discussed the alarming Firestone Steeltex tire failures on ambulance vehicles (see www.CBSnews.com May 2, 2003; November 16, 2002; May 30, 2001).

Our firm is handling a nationwide class action lawsuit involving Firestone Steeltex (R4S, R4SII and A/T) tires, which have caused accidents, injuries, deaths and damages all across the United States.

If you or your department colleagues have had a problem with any of your Firestone Steeltex tires, please contact us at (626) 440-1333. If you want additional information regarding the status of our investigation and class action litigation, please contact us or view our website at www.firestonesteeltexclassaction.com.

Thank you for your courtesy and cooperation in this matter."

The Canadian mission at the United Nations ignored several written warnings from Lisoni & Lisoni regarding the defective Steeltex tires until the news reports on February 26, 2004, that 490,000 Steeltex tires that had been manufactured at the Bridgestone/Firestone factory in Jolliette, Quebec, Canada were being recalled.

Chapter XV

COOPERATE WITH THE ILLINOIS FEDERAL GRAND JURY INVESTIGATION

"Best Intentions Do Not Always Produce the Best Results"

Lisoni & Lisoni discussed with James Pederle, the federal grand jury investigation of the executives of Bridgestone/Firestone, regarding the Firestone Wilderness scandal, and the additional evidence involved in the Firestone Steeltex investigation; including

1) 5000 NHTSA website defect reports;
2) 177 declarations under penalty of perjury from individual class members documenting the facts of their tire failure(s);
3) Declarations under penalty of perjury from multiple Bridgestone/Firestone "whistle-blowers";
4) A copy of the "C-95" Cost Reduction Program document;
5) Copies of the Lisoni & Lisoni NHTSA Petitions to recall 11 million Firestone Steeltex tires'
6) Proof of over 60 deaths caused by defective Firestone Steeltex tires; and
7) A transcript of Firestone's CEO, John Lampe, lying under the penalty of perjury to Congress about the existence of a dangerous cost cutting custom and practice of Bridgestone/

Firestone dictating the use of sub-standard component parts in the production of Steeltex tires.

However, due to the political climate, the Federal Grand Jury Investigation of the Firestone corporate executives was secretly closed and did not result in any T.R.E.A.D. Act criminal findings. More acts in furtherance of the Bridgestone/Firestone Conspiracy of Death & Destruction.

Chapter XVI

PROMOTE DIALOGUE WITH STOCK ANALYSTS AND ENCOURAGE INSTITUTIONAL SHAREHOLDERS TO LIQUIDATE BRIDGESTONE/ FIRESTONE HOLDINGS

"Buy Low, Sell High – Damage Control"

The stock of the parent company, Bridgestone Corporation, dropped significantly due to its announcement that the prices for Firestone tires would increase, due to the rise in the cost of the raw materials. Lisoni & Lisoni consistently alleged that the Steeltex tires were defective because Bridgestone/Firestone was using substandard components and implementing unreasonable cost-cutting procedures, leading to the manufacture of millions of dangerous and defective Firestone Steeltex R4S, R4SII and A/T tires.

Bridgestone stock dropped 5.7% on the day the National Class Action was filed and announced to the public at a news conference at Golden Hands Auto Body in Pasadena, California, on August 12, 2002.

The largest institutional investor of Bridgestone Corporation stock (traded in Japan) planned to sell its Bridgestone stock after a detailed discussion of the merits of the National Recall Campaign of Lisoni & Lisoni. They called Lisoni & Lisoni because Bridgestone and Bridgestone/Firestone would not talk to them. This discussion took place a few days before the Lisoni & Lisoni Press Conference at the National Press Club to announce "C-95".

The institutional investor lobbied Lisoni & Lisoni not to announce its intent to sell their Bridgestone stock. Such an announcement would drive the price of the preferred stock down and seriously injure thousands of small investors they worked with on retirement plans. They begged Lisoni & Lisoni to delay the announcement because it would create a firestorm regarding the stock.

Lisoni & Lisoni took the "high road" and agreed not to announce the plan to sell off the stock until later, despite the fact that such an announcement would have given great credibility to the case. It was the goal of Lisoni & Lisoni to remove these defective Firestone Steeltex R4S, R4SII and A/T tires from the roads and highways of the United States and foreign countries. The National Class Action was only one means of accomplishing the goal of making the roads and highways safer for the motoring public and it was overwhelmingly successful in that regard.

In 2003, Bridgestone/Firestone added a nylon cap over the steel belts in an unsuccessful attempt to prevent tread separations; 490,000 Firestone Steeltex A/T tires were recalled in February, 2004, ambulance companies in thirty-six states removed Firestone Steeltex tires from their ambulances, a fifty-state public information campaign was started, including several CBS Evening News stories by Dan Rather and Sharyl Atkkisson.

Bridgestone/Firestone finally ceased manufacture of all of the Steeltex tires in 2005, after fourteen years on the market and a total production of thirty million, of which eleven million were still on the roads in the United States, Canada, Mexico, and several countries of Western Europe. Brazil and Saudi Arabia banned the entire line of Firestone Steeltex tires from being sold in their countries.

Bridgestone Shares Tumble After U.S. Lawsuit Filed (Update2)

By Ryoko Imaizumi and Ian Messer

Tokyo, Aug. 14 (Bloomberg) -- Bridgestone Corp. shares fell 5.7 percent after a California man yesterday sued the U.S. unit of Asia's biggest tiremaker, claiming its Steeltex tires used on Ford Motor Co. and General Motors Corp. vehicles were defective.

Shares of Tokyo-based Bridgestone fell 94 yen to 1,555 yen in trading today. It was the fourth-most actively traded stock by value on Japan's equity markets, with shares worth 10.96 billion yen ($93.6 million) changing hands.

Roger Littell's suit, filed in a state court in Riverside, California, seeks a recall of the tires, which he claims contain a lamination defect that can cause the tread to separate, and class-action status on behalf of Steeltex owners.

``There maybe some panic selling. There is no way of saying how this case may go,'' said Takeshi Ogura, an analyst at Shinko Securities Co., who has a ``neutral plus'' rating on Bridgestone.

Bridgestone/Firestone Inc. has made more than 27.5 million Steeltex R4S, R4SII and A/T tires, said Joseph Lisoni, a Pasadena, California, lawyer who represents Littell. U.S. regulators in April closed an 18-month investigation into the tires, saying there was no evidence of a defect.

The National Highway Traffic Safety Administration opened its Steeltex tire inquiry in September 2000, about two months after Bridgestone/Firestone recalled 6.5 million Firestone ATX, ATX II and Wilderness AT tires. Firestone later recalled another 3.5 million tires.

Bridgestone's Tokyo headquarters were shut for Japan's Obon summer holiday and officials were not immediately available for comment.

Chapter XVII

BRIDGESTONE/FIRESTONE CONCEALED THE DEFECTIVE TIRES AND THEN DESTROYED THEM

"If You Can't Hide the Damning Evidence, You Must Destroy It"

On October 28, 2002, Lisoni & Lisoni received an anonymous letter, from a person of superior knowledge regarding the inner workings of Bridgestone/Firestone, which stated:

> "Bridgestone/Firestone owns a chain of company-owned retail stores that do not submit warranty claims for adjustments made to consumers in the same way that their independent dealers do. Many years ago, the company decided to issue the retail group a discount off its buying price that represented the costs associated with absorbing these claims, paying the customer, and processing the tires through the normal warranty adjustment process. This was done in an effort to streamline the process and reduce cost. Unfortunately, because well over 50% of adjustment claims are handled by the company's retail chain an important base of data was lost. The only data in the warranty claims data

for Bridgestone/Firestone are those claims filed by their independent dealers, which is substantially less than half of the real amount. Bridgestone/Firestone executives knew this yet it was never disclosed in any of the proceedings with NHTSA nor the Senate subcommittees. . ."

Many of the claimants did not have the DOT (Department of Transportation) No. of their failed tire(s) because the dealership replaced the tire and destroyed the defective tire. This, in fact, concealed the number of warranty claims and, in exchange, provided large discounts to the dealerships or agents of Bridgestone/Firestone, who denied the claim and destroyed the evidence. In every denial letter, to every claimant, all signed by Norma Y. Davis, Paralegal of Bridgestone/Firestone, Inc. the letter states that if the claimant does not agree to have the tire shipped back to them C.O.D., Bridgestone/Firestone, Inc. would destroy the tire in twenty-one days.

Bridgestone/Firestone, Inc. forces the claimant to pay to have the tire shipped to Bridgestone/Firestone, Inc., and then it immediately denied their claim in writing. Most claimants felt it was a waste of money to have the tire sent back to them, so they did not sign the return tire agreement, and Bridgestone/Firestone, Inc. destroyed the tire, which was evidence of the defective nature of the Firestone Steeltex tire caused by the implementation of the "C-95" cost reduction program.

This conduct was designed to make the claims process so difficult that people would give up and not pursue their claim. It is important to note that Bridgestone/Firestone, Inc. used this denial letter consistently during the "Storage Period" between June 1, 2003 and December 31, 2003, in violation of the Case Management Order issued by Judge Christopher Sheldon in the Indio branch of the Riverside County Superior Court. Several hundred "legal claim tires" were lost as a result of Bridgestone/Firestone's unlawful conduct. The DOT Nos. were very important because they documented where the tire was manufactured and when the tire was manufactured.

At the inspection of the stored tires in Marengo, Indiana, on April 12 and 13, 2004, most of the DOT Numbers were available, although several had been purposely obliterated.

The majority of these claimants had tires that were manufactured in Decatur, Illinois, the plant that Bridgestone/Firestone admitted had manufactured most of the defective Wilderness tires, and had since been closed. The majority of the balance of tires were manufactured in Jolliette, Quebec, Canada, the plant which manufactured the 490,000 Steeltex tires which were recalled on February 26, 2004.

Larry Elkins, Senior Chemist, in Research and Development of Bridgestone/Firestone had testified that the manufacturing process of the Wilderness, Steeltex and the Truck and Bus (TBR) tires is the same process. In his deposition taken on March 15, 2004, Mr. Elkins testified:

"Q. Why would there be—and this may be a foolish layman's question—but why would there be any difference in the TBR as opposed to the Wilderness A/Ts and the Steeltex? Why would the basic manufacturing considerations not be about the same?
A. I think they were the same."

Further, after the inspection of the failed tires in Marengo, Indiana, our experts concluded that almost every tire they inspected was defective and the defects were consistent with the Cost Reduction Program C-95.

The Firestone experts, John Gardner, Brian Queser and Virginia Gregory-Kojac, were very intelligent and highly qualified and credentialed with respect to the "design" of the subject tires. However, they knew little or nothing about the manufacturing process of the subject tires. Plaintiffs' experts, William J. Orr, Micky Capley and George Rios, all were former employees of Bridgestone/Firestone, with many years' experience in the production of these subject tires. They were all involved in quality assurance, and they all documented that these subject tires were often produced without regard to the design specifications.

Further, Lisoni & Lisoni consulted with several other former employees of Bridgestone/Firestone regarding the production of these tires, and the resulting defects, including but not limited to, Alan Hogan, Jimmy Ritter, Dick Baumgardner, Sandy Trammel, Gary Kovaskitz, Rodney Martin, and an undisclosed former executive of Bridgestone/ Firestone, Inc. Many of the experts working with Lisoni & Lisoni advised us that they knew individuals who had access to "internal documents" which documented Bridgestone/Firestone's knowledge of the defects in the subject tires and the concealment of those defects from NHTSA and the consuming public, many of them made these documents available to Lisoni & Lisoni.

In the National Class Action, Bridgestone/Firestone was required to store all "claim tires" between June 1, and December 31, 2003, and it documented that it had 2,162 tires stored in a one-million square foot limestone cave in Marengo, Indiana. Lisoni & Lisoni demanded that it be allowed to have its experts examine the stored tires.

In April, 2004, Lisoni & Lisoni and their four experts - Bill Orr, Mickey Capley, George Rios and Bill Hagerty, went to Marengo, Indiana, examined, photographed and video-taped many of these tires and determined that the tires all suffered from the same defect, tread separation due to weak skim stock, as a result of the cost cutting program, "C95". Armed guards hired by Bridgestone/Firestone guarded the tires during the examinations. We were given a very limited time to examine the tires, and a single light for our viewing. Fortunately, we had brought along a videographer, and he had additional lights.

The tires were stored in huge cardboard boxes with metal straps, making the boxes extremely difficult to open. The guards and representatives from Bridgestone/Firestone, Inc. were less than helpful, and the sight of the guns was unsettling to say the least.

In July, 2004, Lisoni & Lisoni and its team of experts traveled to Bridgestone/Firestone's Research and Development plant in Akron, Ohio to inspect 400-plus tires stored there pursuant to Court Order. After inspecting a large number of failed Steeltex tires, the team determined again that the tires all suffered from the same defects, tread separation, due to using weak skim stock as a result of the "C-95" cost reduction program.

After the Marengo, Indiana tire inspection, the Lisoni & Lisoni team of experts travelled to Greenman Technologies in Lavergne, Tennessee, directly behind Bridgestone/Firestone on Bill Orr's discovery that Greenman Technologies was shredding failed Steeltex tires that were supposed to be stored in Marengo, Indiana or Akron, Ohio pursuant to Court Order.

While the members of the inspection team stayed in a van in the parking lot of Greenman Technologies, Joe entered the facility without permission and unannounced and witnessed hundreds of failed Steeltex tires being shredded. CBS Evening News was informed of Bridgestone/Firestone's conduct, which constituted "destruction of evidence", which was a contempt of court. Lisoni & Lisoni's discovery of these wrongful acts earned them a great deal of credibility with CBS Evening News and other news agencies throughout the United States. Bill Orr had discovered and video-taped this conduct on two prior occasions. The video was given to CBS Evening News.

In an attempt to destroy all evidence regarding the defective Steeltex tires, Bridgestone/Firestone hired Greenman Technologies to run an advertisement nationwide, offering to shred failed Steeltex tires without charge (it usually charged for this service). Joe witnessed this when he went to a Greenman Technologies location in Southern California with a failed Steeltex tire that had suffered a tread separation in order to document the efforts of Bridgestone/Firestone, Inc. to destroy all evidence relating to the "C-95" cost reduction program.

Norma Y. Davis, was a paralegal with Bridgestone/Firestone, and was the only person at Bridgestone/Firestone that had sent several thousand denial letters to claimants on behalf of Bridgestone/Firestone. We always believed that Norma Y. Davis was a "phantom" and did not actually exist. We attempted on numerous occasions to take her deposition so we could ask her directly about her "letters" but Bridgestone/Firestone refused to produce her. The letters were *form letters* and they all, without exception, stated that the responsibility for the failed tire rested with the consumer/claimant and not Bridgestone/Firestone.

The common theories were over-inflation, under-inflation or outside blunt force trauma, and nothing was ever mentioned about the warranty. The warranty misrepresented that Bridgestone/Firestone designed the tires with the vehicle manufacturer for the specific vehicle and its intended applications, and that Bridgestone/Firestone would warrant that the tires were safe and durable, all of which were untrue. We demanded that Norma Y. Davis submit to a deposition, however, the defense attorneys continued to refuse to produce her.

On October 1, 2003, Joe contacted Bridgestone/Firestone's defense attorney, Richard Williams, Esq. to advise him that he had information that Bridgestone/Firestone was shredding Steeltex tires and was spoiling evidence, at Greenman Technologies, Inc., which is directly behind the Bridgestone/Firestone plant in Lavergne, Tennessee—in violation of a court order. We had a videotape of the loaded trucks and piles of shredded Firestone Steeltex tires taken by Bill Orr on a previous occasion.

On October 2, 2003, Mr. Williams contacted Bridgestone/Firestone immediately and followed up with a letter to Lisoni & Lisoni, stating: "BFNT informed me that some Steeltex tires produced at the Lavergne plant, but never delivered or sold to customers, were shredded recently. These tires were never subject to the Case Management Order."

Mr. Williams had deniability because he was "told by executives of BFNT," but we all knew that executives of Bridgestone/Firestone lied and misrepresented facts whenever they moved their lips—to Congress, to NHTSA and to the motoring public.

On September 8, 2003, Bill Orr had shipped one of the Steeltex tires that he found at Greenman Technologies, prior to the shredding to Lisoni & Lisoni. The Steeltex tire was clearly a "used" tire which had suffered a tread separation, and should never have been shredded. He also sent a video tape he took of the several 16 wheel trucks loaded with defective, "used" Steeltex tires to Lisoni & Lisoni, yet Bridgestone/Firestone claimed that these tires were never sold to the public. Lisoni & Lisoni sent the tape to Dan Rather and Sharyl Atkkisson at CBS Evening News for use in another one of their news stories. More lies in furtherance of the Bridgestone/Firestone Conspiracy of Death & Destruction.

Rubber & Plastic News reported: Nov. 11, 2003:

> "'Bridgestone/Firestone is not destroying Firestone Steeltex tires intended as evidence in a California class-action lawsuit,' the Nashville-based tire maker said, in a response to a CBS Evening News report accusing them of doing just that. The report showed pictures of Steeltex tires waiting to be shredded at a recycling facility near the BFS plant in Lavergne, Tennessee 'under the case management order from California, Firestone is required to preserve (Steeltex) tires that are the subject of a legal claim,' the tire maker said in a prepared statement. 'All of these tires have been preserved.' The order specifically states that Bridgestone/Firestone can continue its tire disposal practices at all other facilities.'"

Bill Orr, in his declaration under penalty of perjury, in December, 2003, stated:

> "In my search for failed Firestone tires, I was unable to find any failed Firestone 16-inch Steeltex tires at any of the dealerships in the area. I then went to the Rutherford County Landfill, and again I was unable to find any failed Firestone 16-inch Steeltex tires at the landfill. The Supervisor of Rutherford County Landfill led me to Greenman Technologies, a tire shredding company, which is about 900 yards from the Bridgestone/Firestone plant in Lavergne, Tennessee. He told me I could probably find what I was looking for at the plant there.
>
> On Sunday, September 7, 2003, I went to Greenman Technologies, a short distance from my home, and I counted nine semi-trailers in the parking lot of Greenman Technologies. My curiosity was challenged and I opened the door to one of the trailers, which was unlocked, and found it completely full of *failed and worn* truck tires. I opened up approximately four other trailers. In the second trailer,

I immediately found three *failed* Steeltex tires, as soon as I opened the door. Because of my extensive background and experience at Bridgestone/Firestone, for twenty-five years in the research & development lab, I could recognize the different types of tires, and I saw numerous Steeltex tires, most of which I could see had suffered tread separations.

I checked the other semi-trailers in the parking lot which were unlocked, and found a similar condition—full of tires, many of which were Steeltex tires that had suffered tread separations. I took one of the three Steeltex tires out of the second trailer. I contacted Joseph & Gail Lisoni by telephone and advised them of what I had found. On October 3, 2003, I was contacted by Alison Taylor, a Producer of CBS Evening News. On October 6, 2003, I spoke to Alison Taylor, and she asked me questions about what I had found at the Greenman plant on that Sunday morning. I told her all that I could about the number of semi-trailers and the number of Steeltex tires which were awaiting destruction. She asked me to get my camcorder and take video tapes of the Greenman parking lot with the semi-trailers.

On October 12, 2003, at approximately 11:00 a.m., I went to the Greenman Technologies parking lot with my video camera. I filmed the parking lot with the semi-trailers full of tires—again, many of them had suffered a tread separation. I filmed a "mountain of rubber chips," which was the result of shredding at the back door of the warehouse. I checked the back door knob and it opened. It was unlocked. I went inside and was able to film the tire shredder itself, and a "mountain of rubber chips inside the warehouse and many tires being prepared to be destroyed. I sent the video tape to Sharyl Attkisson, CBS News, and a copy to Lisoni & Lisoni."

Trying to shut Lisoni & Lisoni down, Bridgestone/Firestone filed a disciplinary complaint against Joe & Gail Lisoni with the California State Bar attempting to get them disbarred. Tire Business reported the story: November 21, 2003:

"...in the complaint filed by John K. Gamauf, of Bridgestone/Firestone, Consumer Replacement Tire President, the company accused Mr. Lisoni of repeatedly exaggerating the number and content of complaints he'd received about Steeltex tires and also of repeatedly misrepresenting the company's actions. 'Some of Mr. Lisoni's communications to potential Steeltex clients, according to the complaint, violated the Rules of Professional Conduct, in that they did not clearly state they were communications offering legal services. He said the products are defective, and that just is not true,' a BFS spokesman said about the complaint. 'NHTSA (the National Highway & Traffic & Safety Administration) has looked at these tires and found no defect trend.' Meanwhile, Bridgestone/Firestone answered allegations made by a CBS News broadcast on Nov. 7 that the company was shredding Steeltex tires that a California Superior Court judge had ordered to be kept as evidence in the class action. The report showed pictures of Steeltex tires waiting to be shredded at a recycling facility near the BFS plant in Lavergne, Tennessee."

Lisoni stated, "I believe this is a political move on the part of Bridgestone/Firestone", and the charges were finally dismissed.

Rubber & Plastic News reported:

"Lisoni has answered charges levied against him by BSF to the State Bar of California. Lisoni's attorney, Michael G. Gerner, Esq. wrote in a letter to the State Bar that Lisoni 'always has performed according to the highest standards of the (legal) profession in representing his clients.' BFS has claimed that Lisoni had continually made false statements about the company and the Steeltex tire in connection with the class action."

So many of the class members were older, retired people, many of whom had spent their life's savings on a motor home to travel the country in their retirement years, only to suffer a catastrophic tread separation of their Firestone Steeltex tire(s) and ruin their dreams forever. They filed a claim based on the breach of the warranty. They paid to have the tire shipped back to Bridgestone/Firestone, ($25-$50) only to immediately receive a denial letter blaming them for the failure, and forcing them to pay for the return of the tire, (another $25-$50) or the tire(s) would be destroyed. As a mere sample, the following individuals submitted their defective tires to Bridgestone/Firestone and they <u>all</u> had received "form" denial letters from Norma Y. Davis, and they were all advised that if they did not pay to have their tire returned, it would be destroyed in twenty-one days. More lies in furtherance of the Bridgestone/Firestone Conspiracy of Death & Destruction:

1. Carl Hinsey, of South Bend, Indiana, suffered four failures of his Firestone Steeltex tires. In June, 2003, he sent one of his failed tires to Firestone requesting a replacement. His claim or reference number was 910442. His claim was denied by Norma Y. Davis.
2. Dwight Radeke, of Boise, Idaho, suffered a tread separation on June 25, 2003. He submitted his claim and tire to Bridgestone/Firestone, Claim No. 910551. On July 15, 2003, he received the same "form denial letter" from Norma Y. Davis.
3. Frank Larrango, of Palmdale, California, sent his failed tire to Bridgestone/ Firestone, Claim or Reference No. 910742 in July, 2003. He received his "form denial letter" from Norma Y. Davis, dated July 29, 2003.
4. Jack Greenwood, of Red Bluff, California, suffered a tread separation on August 3, 2003. He sent his claim tire to Bridgestone/Firestone in August, 2003, Claim or Reference No. 91208, and he received the "form denial letter", dated August 27, 2003 from Norma Y. Davis.
5. Jay Jenkins, of Lake Havasu, Arizona, suffered a tread separation on May 2, 2003, which caused property damage. He submitted the claim to his insurance carrier, 21st Century Insurance Co. who in turn sent the failed tire to Bridgestone/Firestone, Claim or Reference No. 911252. On August 28,

2003, the carrier received the same "form denial letter" from Norma Y. Davis.

6. William Robbins, of Walnut Creek, California, suffered two tread separations on June 4, 2003 and September 2, 2003. He sent his claim tires to Bridgestone/Firestone, Inc. and received the same "form denial letter" from Norma Y. Davis.

7. Paul O'Dell, of Glendale, Arizona, suffered a tread separation of his left rear tire on August 10, 2003. He sent his claim and the tire to Bridgestone/Firestone pre-paid. Claim No. 911482. On Sept 12, 2003, Norma Y. Davis denied his claim with her "form denial letter".

8. Joseph Caringella, of Lake Havasu, Arizona, suffered a tread separation of his left front tire on August 19, 2003. He sent the claim tire to Bridgestone/Firestone, Claim No. 911450. On September 11, 2003, Mr. Caringella received the "form denial letter" from Norma Y. Davis.

2100 defective Firestone Steeltex tires stored one-mile inside the Marengo Indiana Limestone cave, pursuant to Court Order obtained by Lisoni & Lisoni

The Marengo Indiana Tire Inspection Team: (Left to right) Gail, Greg Landtbom, Joe, George Rios, Bill Hagerty, Mickey Capely and Bill Orr

An example of a catastrophic Firestone Steeltex tire tread separation failure as discovered at the Marengo tire Inspection

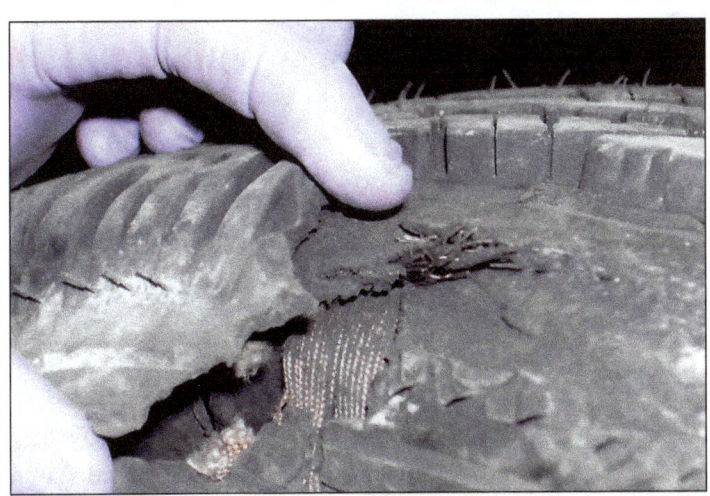

Photo of "shiny brass" discovered at the Marengo Tire Inspection demonstrating the failure of the steel cord lamination process which caused a tragic tread separation of the subject tire

Upon leaving the Marengo cave the Inspection team was surprised by an unexpected snow storm in mid-April - without snow chains!

Joe & Gail celebrating a most informative and successful Inspection of hundreds of defective Firestone Steeltex tires shipped from its warranty claim department in Lavergne, Tennesse, pursuant to Court Order

The Firestone "top secret" research and development facility in Akron, Ohio where over 400 defective Firestone Steeltex tires were stored pursuant to Court Order that were submitted by customers to Firestone's warranty department

From left to righ: Greg Mango (NHTSA engineer), Greg Landtbom, Bill Orr, Mickey Capley and Gail at the Firestone Akron, Ohio research and development plant (Notice the bright yellow security badges required to be worn by anyone on the premises). What is not shown in this picture are the armed Firestone guards observing every action taken by the Inspection team

A classic example of a Firestone Steeltex tire catastrophic tread separation observed at the Akron, Ohio Inspection

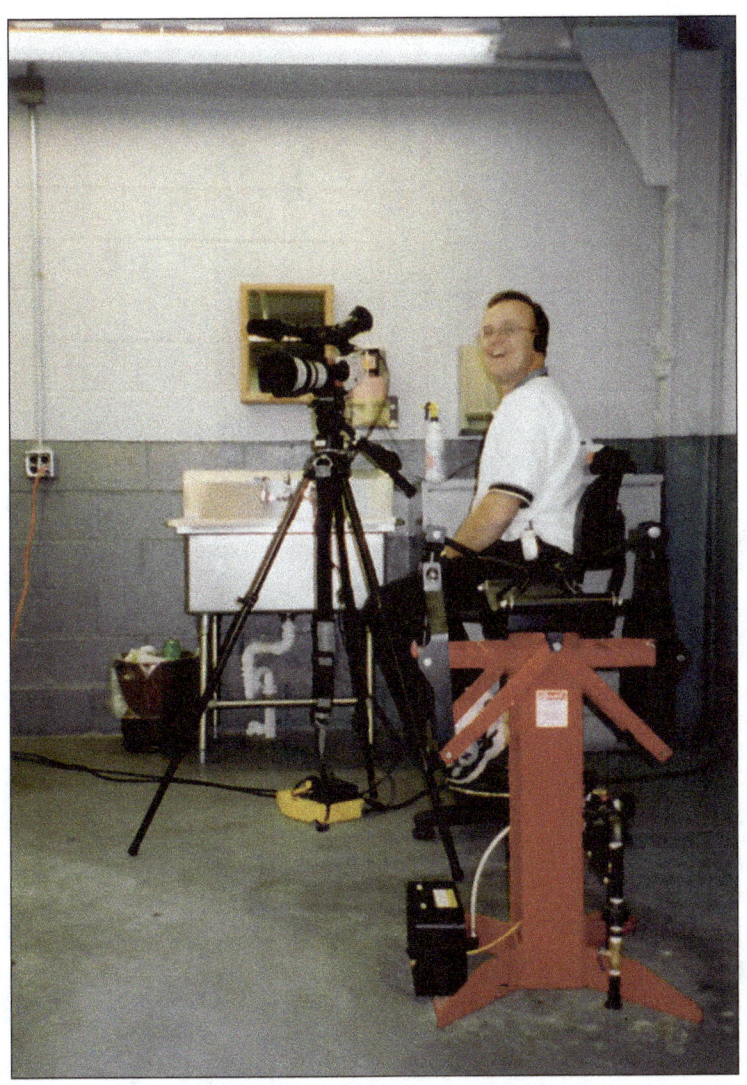

Paul Kalpheke, video-photographer filming
the Akron, Ohio Tire Inspection event

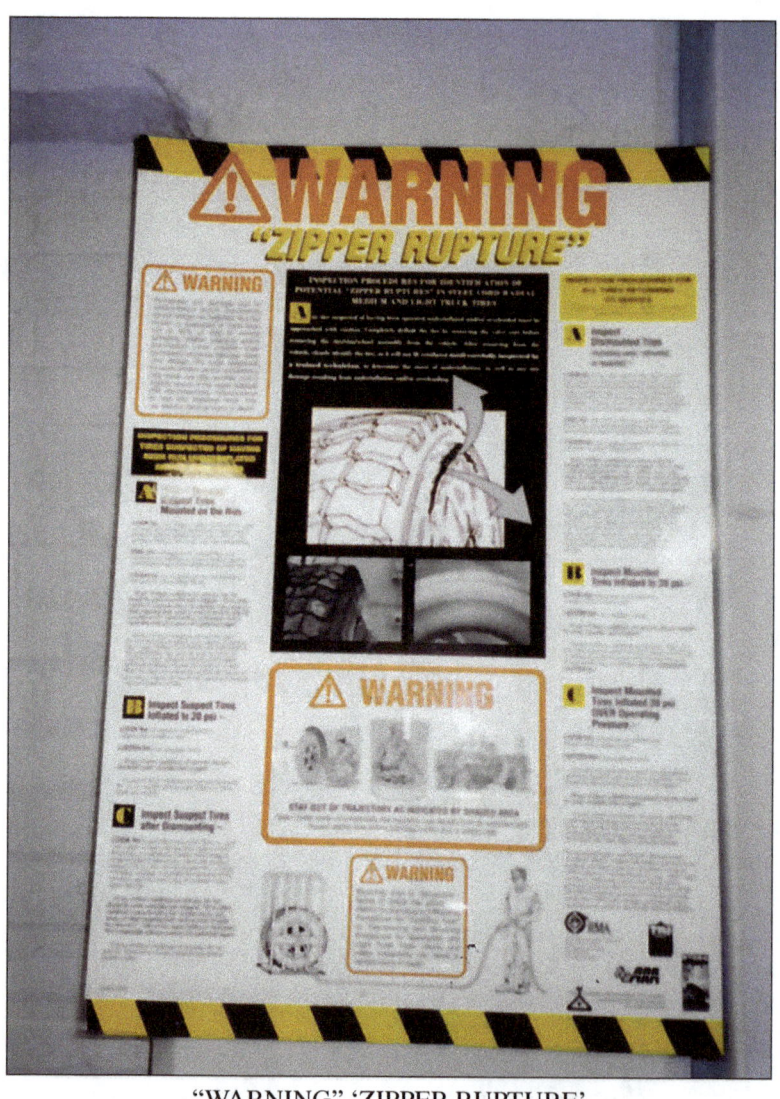

"WARNING" 'ZIPPER RUPTURE'
the warning speaks for itself — see no harm, report no harm

Gail in a private inspection room at the Akron, Ohio
Research & Development facility

Photo of the "clean room" at the "top secret" section of Akron, Ohio
Research & Development facility

Front entrance to the Brigdestone/Firestone factory just up the street and around the corner from Greenman

Photo of GreenMan technologies tire shredding plant immediately adjacent to Firestone's Lavergne, Tennessee manufacturing plant

Close-up of trailer where I found the Steel Tex

Close-up of tire chips

Chapter XVIII
LISONI & LISONI LOBBIES NHTSA AND CONGRESS

"A Government of the People, by the People and for the People"

Early in the case, Joe was contacted by a plaintiff, John Carr, who had a case against Bridgestone/Firestone as a result of his defective Steeltex tire. Joe flew to Birmingham, Alabama to attend the deposition of Mr. Carr's tire expert. After the deposition, Mr. Carr put Joe in touch with Bill Orr, who had worked for Bridgestone/Firestone for over 25 years.

Bill Orr agreed to testify as a tire expert in the Lisoni & Lisoni National Class Action. Consequently, we shipped him the defective tire which had come off the motor home of Roger Littell, a named plaintiff in the National Class Action. This tire was very significant because it was the sixth tire which came as original equipment on the same motor home—the other five had failed. This sixth tire was in "failure mode". Mr. Orr was able to dissect the tire and document the defects, prior to its failure. Mr. Orr prepared a report and Lisoni & Lisoni sent it to the defense attorneys. They immediately noticed Mr. Orr's deposition and a Notice to Produce "the tire," scheduled for May 6, 2004.

Lisoni & Lisoni had scheduled a Press Conference at the National Press Club, in Washington, DC, on May 6, 2004, to announce the meeting with NHTSA and produce "the tire" dissected by Bill Orr. At the Press Conference, Joe told the press that Attorney Gail Lisoni was not present because she was in Murfreesboro, Tennessee attending Bill Orr's deposition regarding "the tire," but that she would be in Washington, DC with Bill Orr and "the tire" that night, to be present at the meeting with NHTSA the next day. At the Press Conference a copy of the secret "C-95" document was released to the media by Joe. The "C-95" document was the "smoking gun" of every plaintiff's attorney dreams of possessing.

Gail flew to Nashville, prepared Mr. Orr for his deposition, and examined "the tire" in "failure mode." She accompanied Bill Orr to the deposition in Murfreesboro, Tennessee. During the deposition, it was revealed that they were going to fly to Washington, DC that afternoon because Lisoni & Lisoni had scheduled a meeting with all of the administrators, engineers and legal counsel for NHTSA to document the "C-95" defects in the "Littell tire." The defense attorneys asked Mr. Orr many questions about the tire and the deposition dragged on and on, even though they knew they had a plane to catch to Washington, DC. Also, the weather was getting increasingly volatile and a possible tornado was predicted for later in the day.

Finally, the deposition was over, but the defense attorneys claimed that the tire was "evidence" in the deposition and Gail could not remove it, as it would be "part of the record". Consequently, there was a heated discussion, and Gail demanded to see a judge. All of the attorneys, Bill Orr, and "the tire" immediately went to court and the judge agreed with Gail that it was her tire and she could remove it. However, he ordered that the tire had to be photographed for the defense attorneys. The tire was immediately photographed and Bill and Gail took off to the airport with "the tire".

The weather was horrendous. A tornado was brewing and it was imperative that Bill and Gail get away before it arrived, if they had any chance of making the flight. The trip to the airport took about thirty minutes. We were in front of the tornado and I could see out of the back window that the sky was completely black. We had never been in such weather, and we were scared, but pushed through.

Arriving, we made the flight only by minutes and then watched from the plane as the tornado ripped through Tennessee.

The next day, on May 7, 2003, Bill Orr accompanied Lisoni & Lisoni to the National Highway Traffic & Safety Administration (NHTSA), for a meeting with its administrators, engineers and legal counsel. Present from NHTSA were Kathleen Demeter, John White, Enid Robinson, Esq., Jennifer Timian, Esq., Jeffrey Quandt, Greg Magno, and Steven Beretsky. Also present were Joan Claybrooke of *Public Citizen* and Clarence Ditlow of *Center for Auto Safety*. Both of these watch-dog agencies were founded by Ralph Nader to promote the crashworthiness of automobiles. Bill Orr used "the tire" (Roger Littell's sixth tire) and illustrated the defects to them pointing out the significance of "C-95" and the consequential defects in the entire line of Steeltex R4S, R4SII and A/T tires.

Incredibly, after the meeting, NHTSA again denied the petition to re-open the investigation on June 11, 2003, stating that there was no defect trend. The denial was more evidence documenting the Bridgestone/Firestone Conspiracy of Death & Destruction, and its accomplice - the National Highway Traffic & Safety Administration (NHTSA).

Chapter XIX

MOTION FOR CLASS CERTIFICATION

"A Commonality of Wrongs Produces an Attempt at a Single Remedy"

On May 30, 2003, Lisoni & Lisoni filed a Motion for Class Certification, which was scheduled to be heard on February 25, 2004, in the Riverside County Superior Court in Indio, California, before Judge Christopher Sheldon. The moving papers included Declarations from 177 putative class members across the U. S. documenting their failure(s) of the subject tires, and produced Declarations from five former Bridgestone/Firestone employees, documenting the nature and extent of the defects in the "Steeltex" tires, and their similarity to the defects in the "Wilderness" tires.

Plaintiffs' Common Questions of Fact Predominated, as follows:

1. Was the member of the class an owner of a vehicle which came equipped with Firestone Steeltex tires as original equipment?
2. Did the class member suffer a failure of their Firestone Steeltex tire?
3. Was the failure caused by the defective de-engineering of the Firestone Steeltex tire?
4. Did the class member sustain property damage?
5. Did the class member replace all of the Firestone Steeltex tire(s) on their vehicle after the failure due to safety concerns?

Plaintiffs' Common Facts Supported Class Certification, as follows: The following list of facts were documented in 177 declarations under penalty of perjury submitted in support of Plaintiffs' Motion for Class Certification: They documented the common facts that,

1) Each individual owned a vehicle which came equipped from the factory with Firestone Steeltlex R4S, R4SII or A/T tires;
2) Each individual documented the type of vehicle, the tire type, the date of failure(s); and
3) Whether the individual suffered property damage as a result of the failure.

Almost all Declarations document one or multiple incidents of "tread separation", and almost all Declarations documented proper maintenance of the tires. The overwhelming majority of the subject tires were manufactured in Decatur, Illinois and Jolliette, Quebec, Canada.

Name	State	Vehicle	Tire Type	Date of Failure	Property Damage	Reference
Paul Zahorik,	AK	1999 F-350	A/T	10-02	PD	CT:92
John D. Carr	AL	1995 F-350	R4S	5-00	PD	CT:93
Connie Templeton	AZ	2000-M/H	R4S	7-02	PD	CT:94
Donald Woodward	AZ	2000-F-250	R4S	4-16-02		CT:96
Donald Supper	AZ	2000-F-Exc	A/T	12-8-01	PD	CT:98
Thomas Murphy	AZ	1995 F-350	R4S	8-25-02	PD	CT:100
Joe Cannizzaro	AZ	2000 M/H	R4S	02 (2)	PD	CT:101
Wayne Smith	AZ	1995 3500	R4SII	5-03		CT:103
John Hibbert	CA	2000 F-Exc	A/T	6-8-01	PD	CT:104
Gary Hoyle	CA	1999 M/H	R4S	01(1)-03(2)	PD	CT:106
Douglas Lee	CA	2000 GMC	R4S	9-2-02	PD	CT:108
Leroy Dubrall	CA	2000 M/H	R4S	01(1)-02(2)	PD	CT:110
Roger Littell	CA	2000 M/H	R4S	5 failures	PD	CT:111
Luann Pleasant	CA	2000 F-250	A/T	02 (2)	PD	CT:112
John Foster	CA	2000 M/H	R4S	02(1)-03(2)	PD	CT:113
S. St.Leger-Barter	CA	1999 M/H	R4S	01(1)-02(2)	PD	CT:114
Joe Lindenstein	CO	2002 F-250	R4S	4-20-03		CT:115

Motion for Class Certification

Name	State	Vehicle	Tire Type	Date of Failure	Property Damage	Reference
Douglas Timmons	CO	1997 M/H	A/T	99(1)-00(2)	PD	CT:117
Julius Miller	FL	1998 M/H	R4S	8-01(2)	PD	CT:118
Lee Warrick	FL	2000 M/H	R4S	03(2)	PD	CT:120
John Simone	FL	2000 M/H	R4S	02(1)-03(1)	PD	CT:122
David Stevens	FL	2000 M/H	R4S	8-25-01	PD	CT:124
Donald Talbert	GA	1999 M/H	R4S	6-29-02	PD	CT:125
Robert Bemis	GA	2001 F-250	A/T	12-30-02	PD	CT:127
Albert Jeyte	HI	2001 F-350	R4S	8-1-02	PD	CT:128
Rebecca Tisdelll	ID	2002 F-350	A/T	7-02(2)		CT:129
John Spira	IL	2000 F-Exc	A/T	4-23-02	PD	CT:130
Mark Lendman	IN	1997 Sub	R4S	7-02 (3)		CT:132
Kathy Muckey	IA	2002 Chevy	A/T	8-31-02	PD	CT:133
Bill Montgomery	KS	1997 M/H	R4S	8-00	PD	CT:134
D. Gregory Jones	KY	2001 F-Exc.	A/T	7-02	PD	CT:135
William Dezendorf	LA	1999 F-350	R4S	8-19-02	PD	CT:136
Leonard Beard	LA	2001 F-250	A/T	8-02		CT:138
Robert Misner	MD	2000 M/H	R4S	03 (3)	PD	CT:139
Raymond Battani	MI	1997 M/H	R4S	02 (3)	PD	CT:140
Jerry Campbell	MI	1999 M/H	R4S	6-99 (3)		CT:142
Rory Tate	MN	1996 M/H	R4S	6-00	PD	CT:143
Chris Williams	MS	2001 F-250	A/T	11-01		CT:144
William Reid	MS	19955 M/H	R4S	5-6-02	PD	CT:145
Gary McNeely	MO	1999 M/H	R4S	2-28-03	PD	CT:146
Tim Ralston	MO	2000 F-Exc	R4S	3-02		CT:147
Alan Ashton	NV	1999 1500	A/T	11-01	PD	CT:148
Milton Matthews	NV	2000 F-350	R4S	7-02	PD	CT:149
Dan Dube	NH	2000 M/H	R4S	4-03 (2)		CT:150
Glenn Bontly	NM	1999 M/H	R4S	7-02	PD	CT:151
George Dunlap	NY	1999 M/H	R4S	8-02 (3)	PD	CT:152
Bruno Klang	NY	2000 M/H	R4SII	9-02 (2)	PD	CT:154
Mark Wescott	NC	1999 M/H	R4S	7-02 (4)		CT:155
Arthur Menard	NC	2000 Chevy	R4S	6-02/8-02		CT:156
Clarence Stewart	ND	2000 Chevy	R4S	1-02		CT:157
Gary Scantlin	OK	1981 3500	R4S	4-3-03	PD	CT:158
Herbert McConn	OH	2000 2500	R4S	3-19-01		CT:159

When The Rubber Meets The Road

Name	State	Vehicle	Tire Type	Date of Failure	Property Damage	Reference
Perry Colao	PA	2001 F-250	A/T	8-26-02	PD	CT:164
Joseph Menkevich	PA	2002 F-250	A/T	poor wear	PD	CT:166
Jonathan Bartley	TN	2000 M/H	R4S	01-03 (5)	PD	CT:167
Malta Smith	TN	1999 F-350	R4SII	9-02/10-02		CT:169
Daniel Alva	TX	2000 2500	R4S	7-99	PD	CT:170
Graham Ross	TX	2000 3500	R4SII	02 (3)	PD	CT:171
Jay Heiselt	UT	2000 F-250	A/T	7-9-02		CT:173
Joe Tugaw	UT	2000 F-Exc	A/T	02 (2)	PD	CT:175
Stanley Parmentier	VA	1997 M/H	R4S	5-26-03	PD	CT:177
David Sudtell	WA	2001 F-350	A/T	10-7-02		CT:179
John Noble	WA	1999 M/H	R4S	5-7-03		CT:180
Delores Steele	WV	2000 F-350	A/T	8-18-00	PD	CT:181
Jim Morris	AL	1999 M/H	R4S	7-02	PD	CT:585
William Arnold	AZ	1999 M/H	R4S	5-26-03	PD	CT:586
Joseph Caringella	AZ	2001 F-Exc	A/T	8-19-03	PD	CT:587
Norman Chappell	AZ	2000 F-Exc	A/T	5-03		CT:589
Eric Church	AZ	2000 F-Exc	A/T	03 (3)	PD	CT:590
Virgil Cole	AZ	1997 M/H	R4S	10-8-00		CT:591
Nelson Daley	AZ	2002 F-Exc	A/T	9-20-02	PD	CT:592
Glenn Garrison	AZ	2000 F-350	A/T	5-23-03	PD	CT:594
Jay Robert Jenkins	AZ	1999 F-350	A/T	5-2-03	PD	CT:595
Cody Lann	AZ	2001 F-250	A/T	03 (2)	PD	CT:596
Eric Mace	AZ	2001 F-350	R4S	03 (2)	PD	CT:599
Chris Mavrolas	AZ	2001 Sub	A/T	03 (2)	PD	CT:600
Connie Templeton	AZ	2000 M/H	R4S	7-02/7-03	PD	CT:601
Robert Balfe	AR	2000 F-Exc	A/T	03 (2)		CT:603
James Baswell	CA	1998 M/H	R4S	02(1)-03(2)	PD	CT:604
James Cantwell	CA	2000 Sierra	R4SII	5-13-03		CT:607
Richard Church	CA	1991 M/H	R4S	8-19-01	PD	CT:609
Robert Cole	CA	1999 Sub	A/T	7-15-02	PD	CT:611
Brian Cornick	CA	2000 M/H	R4S	01(1)-02(1)	PD	CT:612
Jack Greenwood	CA	2003 M/H	R4S	8-3-03		CT:614
Richard Jones	CA	2001 F-350	R4SII	8-29-03		CT:615
Jack Greenwood	CA	2003 M/H	R4S	8-3-03		CT:614
Richard Jones	CA	2001 F-350	R4SII	8-29-03		CT:615

Motion for Class Certification

Name	State	Vehicle	Tire Type	Date of Failure	Property Damage	Reference
Walter Cleighton	LA	2000 M/H	R4S	03 (4)	PD	CT:659
T.J. Karch	MD	2000 van	R4S	03 (2)		CT:660
James Reisner	MN	2001 F-250	A/T	1-16-02		CT:661
Jennifer Isdell	MO	2002 F-Exc	A/T	7-18-03	PD	CT:662
Scott Manzer	MO	2000 M/H	R4S	6-27-03 (6)		CT:663
Bruce McAllister	MO	2000 M/H	R4S	01 (3)	PD	CT:665
David Waters	NE	1996 Sub	R4S	6-28-03	PD	CT:666
Geneva Hadnot	NE	1999 Sub	R4SII	7-03	PD	CT:668
Sigurd Nicolaysen	NJ	1998 Sub	A/T	8-01		CT:669
Raymond Lucero	NM	2000 F-Exc	A/T	8-22-03	PD	CT:670
D. Shoemaker	NM	2000 F-Exc	A/T	8-30-03	PD	CT:672
Dennis Alabaugh	NY	1999 M/H	R4S	03 (1)		CT:673
Ed Worthington	NY	1999 M/H	R4S	03 (3)	PD	CT:674
Mark Cooley	NC	2001 F-250	A/T	03 (2)	PD	CT:676
Robert Ridgeway	NC	2001 F-250	A/T	10-4-02		CT:678
Charles Baxley	OH	2000 M/H	R4S	8-1-02	PD	CT:679
Terri Valentine	OH	2000 F-350	R4S	5-30-03	PD	CT:680
George Haugen	OK	1993 M/H	R4S	10-29-03	PD	CT:681
Clarence Parsons	OR	2000 M/H	R4S	03 (2)	PD	CT:682
David Scarfani	OR	1999 F-350	A/T	02(1) - 03(2)	PD	CT:683
Hugh Buffham	PA	2001 F-250	A/T	6-30-02	PD	CT:685
Ray Lynch	PA	1999 M/H	R4S	02(1) - 03(1)		CT:686
Thomas Kennedy	SC	1999 M/H	R4S	02(1) – 03(1)	PD	CT:689
Michael Shilling	SC	1999 E-350	R4S	03 (2)		CT:691
Doug Mayhew	TN	2000 F-350	A/T	8-01		CT:692
R. Kirk Anderson	TX	GMC Sav	R4S	02(1) - 03(1)		CT:693
Jennifer Clift	TX	2001 F-350	A/T	1-03	PD	CT:694
Dale Olson	TX	1999 M/H	R4S	02 (2)	PD	CT:696
Harold Renninger	TX	1998 M/H	R4S	01(1) - 02(1)		CT:698
Paul Southerland	TX	2000 F-350	A/T	8-2-03	PD	CT:699
Elke Firth	UT	1998 M/H	R4S	03 (2)	PD	CT:700
Michael Gourley	UT	1999 F-350	A/T	02(2) - 03(1)		CT:701
Joseph Lewis	WV	2000 M/H	R4S	7-22-02	PD	CT:702
Carl Voigtsberger	WY	1999 F-250	A/T	8-1-03	PD	CT:703

When The Rubber Meets The Road

AMBULANCES

Name	State	Vehicle	Tire Type	Date of Failure	Property Damage	Reference
James Barnard	CT	3- F-350	R4SII	4-17-02	PD	CT:704
Paul Genest	GA	2002 F-250	R4S	03 (3)	PD	CT:705
Jeff Stringer	IL	1999 E-450	R4S	9-15-03	PD	CT:706
Jeff Troutman	IL	2000 E-450	R4S	02(2) - 03(4)		CT:707
David Kleis	IA	2000 E-450	R4S	00 (6)		CT:708
Larry Tedrow	IA	1999 E-350	R4S	02 (1) - 03(1)		CT:709
Fred Bouc	IA	1997 E-350	R4S	03 (3)		CT:710
Cindy Small	IA	2002 E-350	A/T	03 (6)		CT:711
James Osborne	KS	2001 F-350	R4S	7-02		CT:712
Art Groux	MA	1999 E-450	R4S	7-16-01	PD	CT:713
Rob Deuel	NJ	1998 E-350	R4SII	03 (2)		CT:715
Rob Deuel	NJ	2002 E-350	R4SII	03 (1)		CT:715
Ed Wisowarty	NJ	1997 E-450	R4S	6-00	PD	CT:716
Gregg Bedell	NY	2000 E-350	R4S	8-22-03		CT:717
K. Heistermann	OH	1993 F-350	R4S	4-25-03	PD	CT:718
Doug LaRue	OH	2001 E–350	R4SII	01 (2)		CT:719
Brad Lancaster	OK	E-450	R4S	2-3 failures	PD	CT:720
Jeff Zimmerman	PA	1998 E-350	A/T	00 (2)	PD	CT:721
Gus Lutjens	SD	1996 E-350	R4S	02 (2)		CT:722
Penny Gray	TX	2 ambulances	00 (several)			CT:723
Tim Wolf	TX	2001 E-450	R4SII	3-01 (2)		CT:725
William Watson	TX	1999 E-450	R4S	00 (6)		CT:726
William Watson	TX	2002 E-450	R4S	03 (1)		CT:726

Plaintiffs documented their common questions of law and fact as follows:

1. Whether Steeltex R4S, R4SII and A/T tire brands are defectively designed and/or manufactured;
2. Whether Bridgestone/Firestone was aware of the propensities for de-lamination and tread separation of the Steeltex R4S, R4SII and A/T tire brands while vehicles are in motion;

3. Whether Bridgestone/Firestone could modify the Steeltex R4S, R4SII or A/T tire brands, if not cure it completely;
4. Whether the Steeltex R4S, R4SII or A/T tires brands defect are limited to certain vehicles and light trucks;
5. Whether the Steeltex R4S, R4SII or A/T tire brands defects constitute a safety-related defect;
6. Whether Bridgestone/Firestone wrongfully profited from the distribution and sale of defective Steeltex R4S, R4SII or A/T tire brands intended for installation, under false pretenses by actively concealing the Steeltex R4S, R4SII or A/T tire brand defect;
7. Whether Bridgestone/Firestone's conduct as alleged in this Complaint constitutes fraudulent concealment;
8. Whether Bridgestone/Firestone's conduct as alleged in this Complaint led to its unjust enrichment; and
9. Whether each and every Steeltex R4S, R4SII and A/T brand tire should be recalled and replaced in a manner that will correct their inordinate propensity for failure."

William J. Orr, Micky Capley, Alan Hogan, Robert Skeans, and George Rios provided expert opinions in Declarations under Penalty of Perjury. Plaintiffs documented the commonality of the facts of all the claimants, as follows:

A. "All declarants owned a vehicle which came with Steeltex tires as original factory equipment on their vehicle;
B. The 177 declarants come from 46 out of the 50 United States;
C. 27 out of 177 declarants are from California, clearly the greatest number from any state;
D. 66 of the declarants had multiple failures of their Steeltex tires.
E. 66 of the declarants owned motor homes with a Ford F-450 chassis.
F. 15 declarants owned Ford Excursions which are the subject of the recall.
G. 26 of the declarant owned a Ford F-350 pick-up truck.

H. 25 of the declarants owned a Ford F-250 pick-up truck.
I. 21 of the declarants are employees of ambulance companies who had suffered tread separations and failures of their Firestone Steeltex tires which came as original equipment on their ambulances.

All these facts documented the commonality of the claims. Defendants argued that there were so many different kinds of vehicles, which made it impossible to have a common question of law or fact. This argument was not supported by the facts. Bridgestone/Firestone Inc. designed the tires for the specific vehicle, which came from the factory—equipped with the Firestone Steeltex tires. All of the vehicles had Steeltex tires as original factory equipment.

Regarding the motor homes, there were approximately thirty different models of motor homes, however, defendants failed to admit that ALL of the motor homes came with a Ford F-450 chassis and Steeltex tires as original factory equipment. All of the ambulances also came with a Ford F-450 or F-350 chassis with Steeltex tires as original factory equipment.

In the Lisoni & Lisoni National Class Action, plaintiffs were seeking damages for the replacement of their Firestone Steeltex tires as a result of their defective condition, and for any property damage resulting from the failure of their Firestone Steeltex tire(s).

On February 23, 2004, Judge Sheldon, inexplicably, on his own motion, continued the hearing of the Motion for Class Certification to March 17, 2004. On February 26, 2004, Bridgestone/Firestone, Inc. was ordered by NHTSA to recall 490,000 Steeltex tires. Judge Sheldon's conduct in continuing the motion on his own initiative was viewed by Lisoni & Lisoni to be unlawful, illegal and improper conduct to allow Bridgestone/Firestone, Inc. an opportunity to prepare an argument as to why class certification should not be granted to the Lisoni & Lisoni National Class Action that demanded the recall of eleven million Firestone Steeltex tires still in service on the seventy-one models of vehicles that came factory equipped with the defective Firestone Steeltex tires.

Motion for Class Certification

Rubber & Plastic News reported: February 25, 2004:

"A California Superior Court judge has postponed until March 17 a hearing to determine whether to grant certification to a class action lawsuit on behalf of owners of Firestone Steeltex tires. There was no immediate reason available as to why Judge Christopher Sheldon moved the certification hearing from its original date of February 25. A Bridgestone/Firestone spokesman said only, 'We'll just present our case on March 17.'"

Further, on March 16, 2004, Judge Christopher Sheldon received a letter from Joseph Drexler, of the P.A.C.E. International Union which stated:

"As a labor union representing 300,000 members, we are writing you to urge support for the class certification of the lawsuit filed against Bridgestone/Firestone concerning the Steeltex tire. We represent workers who manufacture components used in the production of Bridgestone Firestone tires. We are concerned that use of defective materials by Bridgestone Firestone may contribute to tread separation in Steeltex tires. We believe that a broad class of plaintiffs and public safety will be served by allowing this lawsuit to go forward. We have strongly advocated that Steeltex tires should be recalled by the National Highway Transportation Safety Administration, and we believe that there is sufficient community of interest such that the facts in this case will serve not only the plaintiffs but the broadest public interest."

On March 17, 2004, the court denied Plaintiffs Motion for Class Certification, without prejudice. Judge Christopher Sheldon's statements show a complete lack of understanding of the facts of the class action when he stated,

"Well, the J.P. Morgan case is a DCA case, and those people have already reversed me once in this case. I don't want to do it again, and I don't think there's been a factual showing that there is a common question of fact in this case. We don't know what the causation for the failures are. For example—and I'm not going to dwell on everything, but the class of everybody who bought Bridgestone tires or Firestone tires is huge and the basic reason for having a class action suit allowed is because it's more economically reasonable to do so. And in this case I've got people in thirty-eight states, states with different sets of facts regarding why the tires failed, what kind of vehicles they were on, what the history of the tire is, and the history of the manufacturer of the tire. We have one hundred three or eight different... Counsel, Counsel, I'm sorry. We're in two different universes right now; and I've issued my ruling. And I'll ask counsel for the prevailing party to prepare the order; and you know, its without prejudice. And if sometime, somewhere down the line that this becomes clear that this is a proper class action situation, you can bring the motion again. Court's adjourned."

On March 17, 2004, Judge Christopher Sheldon, unbelievably, denied class action status and did not even mention the February 26, 2004, Recall of 490,000 Firestone Steeltex tires by NHTSA, later stating that the "recall tires" were not part of the class action – which was demonstrably false.

After the denial of class certification on March 17, 2004, plaintiffs filed their Renewed Motion for Class Certification, on June 1, 2004. Plaintiffs modified their definition of the class to include: "those persons residing in the United States who currently own or owned a vehicle which came factory equipped with Firestone Steeltex R4S, R4SII, or A/T tires, which were manufactured in Decatur, Illinois, Jolliette, Quebec, Canada, Mexico, Lavergne, Tennessee, and Aiken, South Carolina, between 1995 and the present. Subclasses were defined as follows:

1. Those persons residing in the United States who currently own or owned a vehicle which came factory equipped with Firestone Steeltex R4S, R4SII or A/T tires, and who

sustained property damage to their vehicle as a result of the failure of the Firestone Steeltex R4S, R4SII or A/T tire(s);
2. All class members who are "consumers" as that term is defined in California Civil Code Section 1760(d), and who have not suffered monetary damages;
3. Those individuals who received a "'replacement tire(s)" after their original Steeltex tire(s) failed, and who suffered a failure of the "replacement tire."

Lisoni & Lisoni filed charges against the judge for bias in favor of Bridgestone/Firestone, however, these charges were dismissed by the California Judicial Council. We always believed that there was collusion between Bridgestone/Firestone and Judge Christopher Sheldon. In fact, in 2009, he was removed from the bench by the Council on Judicial Performance, due to many improprieties.

On April 12 and 13, 2004, in preparation for their Renewed Motion for Class Certification, plaintiffs' counsel, Joseph and Gail, and their experts, Bill Hagerty, William J. Orr, George Rios and Micky Capley went to a limestone cave in Marengo, Indiana, where 1,706 Firestone Steeltex tires were being stored pursuant to the Case Management Order in the class action. The Plaintiffs' team examined, photographed, and videotaped in excess of 112 defective tires. The Inspection Report was submitted to the court. All of the experts agreed that almost every tire we inspected was defective and suffered from defects which were consistent with the consequences of Project "C-95". We only found one tire with a puncture and one tire with a nail. Further, the Marengo Inspection Report tire survey documented that the failed BFS tires were manufactured in Decatur, Illinois, Jolliette, Quebec, Canada, Mexico and the "replacement tires" in South Carolina.

The commonality of all the failed tires was that their failure mode, the most frequent cause of failure, was "B1LB2" (belt number one leaving belt number two). This type of failure is identical to the Wilderness, Dueler and Steeltex recalled tires. Most of the tires were manufactured between 1998 and 2002.

The Marengo survey also identified abundant failures caused by "BLC" (belt leaving casing). BLC was also a cause of failure in the most recent recall tires. Approximately thirty-two percent (32%), of the inspected failed tires exposed shiny brass, which is a defect directly related to the curing of the tire and the quality of sulfur used in the tire.

There was class-wide proof of the defect, as documented in the Marengo Indiana Tire Inspection Report. William J. Orr, Micky Capley and George Rios all documented that almost every "stored tire" in Marengo, Indiana was defective and that the defects were consistent with the cost cutting program, "C-95".

Firestone's "defective design" could have be determined on a class-wide basis, due to the lack of an additional nylon/synthetic band or layer to reduce the frictional-flex heat build-up and de-lamination tendency between the woven-steel belts of the tread and the rubber compounds and sidewall that have been vulcanized to bond together. The tread to sidewall integrity was too weak to accommodate the differing flex patterns between the tread and the sidewall, especially with varying factors of inflation pressure, heat build-up, speed of travel, and dynamic vehicle loads.

The "defective design" issues were supported by poor quality control during production, due to the "C-95" cost reduction program, which allows moisture and solvents to adversely affect the steel belt to rubber bonding initially and during road usage over time, and also the poor quality of the rubber compounds, also as a result of the "C-95" cost cutting program. Rushing the tires through production, without adequate time and temperature for the rubber "vulcanization" process to bond all the layers completely and permanently, was yet another problem with these tires.

The causation of the failure of the subject tires is a legal argument to be determined by the experts. An individual class member cannot determine the causation of the failure. The individual class member can only state the "facts of the failure". The overwhelming majority of declarants stated in their Declarations that their Firestone Steeltex tire "suddenly and unexpected suffered a tread/sidewall separation." Further, they all stated that they properly maintained their tires, and most of the claimants stated that they had either personally checked their tires, or had them professionally checked prior to leaving on their trip.

It was clear to the experts at the inspection in Marengo, Indiana, on April 12 and 13, 2004, that the failed tires were defective, and that the defects in the tires were consistent with the consequences of the cost-cutting program, "C-95".

Bill Orr stated in his Declaration under Penalty of Perjury,

"For the last thirteen years with Firestone, I was a Senior Lab Technician, in Research and Development at the Technical Center, and one of my main functions was to analyze customer complaint tires, which had been returned to the Technical Center. I was trained, and considered one of the best in failure mode identification and cutting analysis by engineers, Japanese advisors, corporate quality assurance executives, sales engineers, technicians and my department manager... The BFS executives discuss at considerable length the differences in the different models of the Steeltex tires, however, it is all irrelevant, because, while there are different models for different vehicles, the manufacturing process is the same, and it is the manufacturing process which results in these defective tires."

Micky Capley, stated in his Declaration Under Penalty of Perjury,

"Throughout my career with Bridgestone/Firestone, I learned that management had ignored my rejections, and often times removed the reject tags, returning the same material that was out of tolerance to another shift to be used without disposition."

George Rios stated in his Declaration Under Penalty of Perjury,

"I am familiar with the Cost Cutting Program, C-95, and more importantly, I am familiar with the consequences of this program on the tires manufactured by Bridgestone/Firestone, Inc...I witnessed many instances where they "cut corners" and ignored safety standards and concealed defective compounds by allowing bad components to be "worked into" good components which then contaminates the tire, which can lead to premature and unexpected failure."

On April 16, 2009, the Metropolitan News-Enterprise published a story about the removal of Christopher Sheldon from the bench, written by Sherri Okamoto, which stated:

"Riverside Superior Court Judge Christopher Sheldon has agreed to accept censure, resign from the bench, and never seek judicial office or sit on assignment, the Commission on Judicial Performance disclosed yesterday...A three judge panel was appointed to hear the case, and a stipulation was executed on March 18, 2009, whereby Sheldon agreed to tender his irrevocable resignation effective May 12...In addition to violating the California Rules of Court, Sheldon agreed that he failed to observe the standards of conduct for judicial officers, failed to act in a manner that promoted public confidence in the judiciary, and failed to diligently discharge his administrative responsibilities."

Christopher Sheldon was allowed to go on leave until October 23, 2009, when he would complete his twentieth year of service and be eligible to retire with maximum benefits.

On April 9, 2004, Lisoni & Lisoni filed Plaintiffs' Objections to Proposed Order Denying Class Certification. However, Judge Christopher Sheldon signed the Proposed Order without any changes, or explanations, even though the Proposed Order had many "additions" which were never discussed in writing or at the hearing.

The Court ordered:
"The Court finds that plaintiffs have failed to present evidence to satisfy the prerequisites for class certification despite their burden to do so. Plaintiffs fail to refute with evidence, the substantial evidence submitted by Firestone. Accordingly, plaintiffs Motion is denied without prejudice.

1. Plaintiffs failed to establish that common questions of fact predominate:
   A. "The undisputed Declarations of Firestone's witnesses James Gardner, Brian Quieser and Virginia Gregory-Kocaj establish that because of variations in type, size load capacity, vehicle application, materials, rubber compounds, internal construction, weight and tread depth, the Steeltex tires at issue constitute not a single product, but 103 distinct products."
   B. "Evaluations of each tire must take into account the design and characteristics of the tire itself, the details of the vehicle on which it is mounted, and the history of its purchase, use and service conditions—all of which are unique and individual, and not susceptible to class-wide proof;"
   C. "Tires differ in various respects as to type, size, load capacity, vehicle application, materials, component configurations, compound placement, and as a result, the forces and stresses imposed on each are different and differently imposed, causing the tires to perform differently, including in their durability and resistance to tread/belt separation or other failures."
   D. "Plaintiffs have failed to identify any correlation between the Steeltex tires at issue and any injury to the putative class members."
   E. "Firestone's Declarations of Brian Queiser and James Gardner also note the necessity for individual analysis tire by tire to determine a cause of failure. Plaintiffs fail to present any class-wide evidence that could be fairly applied to the claims of all proposed class members to contradict the foregoing."
   F. The Firestone Tire Warranty Maintenance & Safety Manual, which was attached to Plaintiffs' Reply Brief, is only a "Point of purchase" marketing flyer from 2001. Only a portion of putative class members could have been exposed to the point of sale flyer; it does not provide class wide evidence of representations to purchasers."

G. "The same failure of plaintiffs to provide evidence is fatal to these classes as well.

Because every member of the alleged class would be required to litigate numerous and substantial questions determining his individual right to recover, no class action is permissible for the California claims."

2. "Plaintiffs Failed to Demonstrate Commons Questions of Law Predominate."
3. "Plaintiffs Failed to Identify an Ascertainable Class."
4. "The purported Class, as defined by plaintiffs, impermissibly creates Conflicts of Interest amongst its Putative Class Members."
5. "Plaintiffs Fail to Establish the Typicality and Adequacy of its Class Representatives"
6. "Plaintiffs have not provided evidence nor demonstrated that a class action would be superior alternative in this case, nor that it would provide substantial benefits to the parties and to the judicial system. It appears that individual actions by persons suffering personal injuries and regulatory oversight by the National Highway Traffic & Safety Administration provide better paths for evaluating and remedying potential defects in vehicle tires, based on the evidence before this Court."

To re-iterate, this Order was written by counsel for Bridgestone/Firestone, Inc. and "rubber-stamped" by Judge Sheldon. His conduct violated his oath of office to properly enforce the law, which further fueled Lisoni & Lisoni's suspicion that he was in collusion with Bridgestone/Firestone, Inc.

It is incredible that Bridgestone/Firestone recalled almost 500,000 Firestone Steeltex A/T tires on February 26, 2004, which is the third largest tire recall in U.S. history, and they did so the day after our scheduled hearing on our Motion for Class Certification. Yet, there is not a single mention of the recall in the 14 page Order Denying Plaintiffs Motion for Class Certification.

Joseph L. Lisoni, a Pasadena California plaintiffs' attorney, seeks a court-ordered recall of approximately thirty million Steeltex tires. At the hearing requesting class certification on March 17, 2004, in a courtroom packed with reporters from virtually all of the major news outlets in the U.S., Judge Sheldon unbelievably denied certification of the class. In ruling that the class would not be certified, he made the outrageous comment that the 490,000 tires that were recalled by NHTSA on February 26, 2004 were not part of the National Class Action. He made this ruling with full knowledge of the 177 declarations from victims of the Steeltex tire failures - fifteen of which were owners of Ford Excursions which were at the heart of the NHTSA Recall of 490,000 Steeltex tires on February 26, 2004.

He added insult to injury by stating from the bench in articulating the rationale of his ruling, that his court was "very small and not capable of handling a national class action."

When Lisoni & Lisoni responded by saying he could transfer the case to the Superior Court in Riverside, California, which handled major, complex litigation cases, he ignored the request to transfer the case and retired from the bench into the safety of his private chambers.

Lisoni & Lisoni filed charges against Judge Christopher Sheldon for bias in favor of Bridgestone/Firestone, Inc., however, the charges were dismissed by the California Judicial Council. We always believed that there was criminal collusion between Bridgestone/Firestone, Inc., and Judge Christopher Sheldon.

On September 10, 2004, defendant Bridgestone/Firestone filed its Memorandum of Points and Authorities in Opposition to Plaintiffs' Renewed Motion for Class Certification. On September 27, 2004, plaintiffs filed the Plaintiffs' Reply Brief to Motion for Class Certification and Supporting Declarations and Exhibits. On October 1, 2004, Defendant filed its Sur-reply Memorandum of Points and Authorities in Opposition to Plaintiffs' Renewed Motion for Class Certification. On October 14, 2004, Plaintiffs filed their Sur-Reply Brief to Renewed Motion for Class Certification.

The hearing on the Renewed Motion for Class Certification was held on October 20, 2004, and Judge Sheldon took the matter under submission and allowed plaintiffs to file a supplemental brief to discuss the case of *Quacchia vs. Daimler Chrysler Corp*, and other related cases.

On November 4, 2004, Plaintiffs filed Plaintiffs' Supplemental Brief Pursuant to Order of Court re Class Certification. On November 12, 2004, defendant filed its <u>unauthorized</u> Supplemental Memorandum of Points and Authorities in Opposition to Plaintiffs Renewed Motion for Class Certification.

The Declarations of William J. Orr, Micky Capley and George Rios, documented that all of the Steeltex tires were manufactured by the same manufacturing process. Almost all of the Steeltex tires at issue in this class action were designed to be installed on the particular vehicle on which they were installed at the factory. The Declarations of William J. Orr, Micky Capley and George Rios established sufficient causation of the failure of these Steeltex tires to justify certifying the class as to both liability and damages. These three individuals had extensive expertise involving the production of these Firestone Steeltex tires after the implementation of the cost cutting program "C-95". William J. Orr had extensive expertise in documenting the defects found as a consequence of the "C-95" cost-cutting program.

The matter was submitted and all supplemental briefs were filed by November 12, 2005. Finally, on January 28, 2005, Judge Christopher J. Sheldon issued his Notice of Ruling denying Plaintiffs Renewed Motion for Class Certification.

The Notice of Ruling was prepared by the court, which was short, while the Order Denying Plaintiffs Renewed Motion for Class Certification was prepared by defense counsel, Richard D. Williams, Esq. of Holland & Knight, and included items that were not even discussed at the hearing, but was "rubber stamped" by Judge Christopher Sheldon on February 18, 2005, all in furtherance of the Conspiracy of Death & Destruction, which then included Judge Christopher Sheldon.

Plaintiffs submitted substantial evidence documenting the failures of some of the 490,000 Firestone Steeltex A/T tires, manufactured in Jolliette, Canada and installed on Ford Excursions, for issues involving tread separations, including but not limited to fifteen declarations from owners of the subject Ford Excursions which had failures of the Steeltex A/T tires, which were recalled on February 26, 2004 for tread separations. Again, there is not a single mention of the recall of the Steeltex A/T tires in either the Notice of Ruling or the Order Denying Renewed Motion for Class Certification.

The Notice of Ruling provided the following grounds for denial of plaintiffs renewed motion:

1. "The Court concludes that it cannot identify one single design defect common to all members of the purported class;"
2. "The thrust of plaintiffs' argument is that because of a cost saving program C-95, BFS 'de-engineered its manufacturing process so as to produce defective tires and concealed knowledge of the same from its consumers;"
3. "Unfortunately for plaintiffs, nowhere in their moving papers is a coherent Definition of de-engineering provided. Nowhere is the 'de-engineering' linked to any particular tire failure."
4. "In the present case, there are up to 103 listed populations of tires differing in design, size and capabilities. Over a ten-year period, the tires were used on any number of distinct vehicles including but not limited to light trucks, SUV's, motor homes and ambulances. The tires were subjected to normal wear and tear under various road conditions, distinct care and service histories, maintenance and inflations requirements. The trier of fact would have to take into account all of the above factors in determining whether a particular tire failure was the result of a BFS design flaw;"
5. "Questions of law would, contrary to plaintiffs assertions, have to be determined under several states statues as delineated in defendant's Exhibit A to their opposition. California has no interest in litigating claims of citizens of the 38 states contemplated in this action. Many individual histories show no contact with California whatsoever. Additionally, plaintiffs' acquiescence to a California forum does not affect defendants' due process rights as to proper venue.

Lisoni & Lisoni suspected judicial irregularities because on February 23, 2004, the court on its own motion continued the hearing until March 17, 2004.

On Feb. 26, 2004, Bridgestone Firestone was required by NHTSA to recall 490,000 Firestone Steeltex A/T tires, manufactured in Joliette, Quebec, Canada, which were included in the class action, resulting in the third largest recall in U.S. history.

After the Renewed Motion for Class Certification was denied by Judge Christopher Sheldon, Plaintiffs appealed. The California Court of Appeal ruled against plaintiffs stating that there could be no nationwide class action, because the laws of the fifty states regarding product liability were different. Lisoni & Lisoni took serious exception to the decision because the product liability laws of the fifty states were not relevant in the certification of the class action. The issue was, was there a common question of "fact" among the victims of Steeltex tire failures in each of the fifty states.

Undeterred by the Appellate Court's adverse decision, Lisoni & Lisoni took advantage of the recent federal legislation, the *Class Action Fairness Act of 2005*, and filed a new federal court class action in Los Angeles, before the Honorable Christina A. Snyder, alleging totally different theories—breach of warranty involving all of the tires, whether or not they have failed.

This second class action was also denied certification in the federal court for the Central District of California by Judge Christina Snyder. The Court ignored the fact that the National media coverage of the class action was instrumental in forcing Bridgestone/Firestone into adding a nylon cap in 2003 over the steel belts in the Firestone Steeltex tires in an attempt to avoid tread separations on all of the Steeltex tire models.

Despite the denials of class certification in the state and federal class actions, Lisoni & Lisoni was successful in getting 3,500 independent tire dealers in the United States to stop selling Firestone Steeltex tires. Finally, in mid-2005, Bridgestone/Firestone ceased manufacturing the Firestone Steeltex R4S, R4SII and A/T tire brands, after fourteen years. Eleven-million defective Steeltex tires continued to fail causing property damage, injuries and claiming the lives of innocent victims.

The result of the Lisoni & Lisoni Public Information Campaign resulted in thousands of owners of vehicles that were equipped with Firestone Steeltex tires as original factory equipment to remove the defective tires from their vehicles and replace them with tires manufactured by other tire makers. Further, the Lisoni & Lisoni "All Points Bulletin" mailed to every ambulance company in the United States that had ambulance units equipped with Firestone Steeltex tires, was very effective.

The mailing list of the ambulance companies was purchased from Hugo Dunhill in New York City, New York. Although NHTSA denied Lisoni & Lisoni's Third Recall Petition which demanded the recall of the ambulance tires, Joe & Gail caused all the ambulance companies in 36 states of the U.S. to remove the Firestone Steeltex tires from their ambulance units voluntarily. Bridgestone/Firestone, Inc. executives went "ballistic" when they started receiving thousands of telephone calls from the affected ambulance companies demanding that it reimburse them for the cost of the tires they purchased to replace the defective Steeltex tires.

Further, a company named "Tire Rack" was used by Bridgestone/Firestone to sell the defective Firestone Steeltex tires which had been removed from automobiles by all of the Ford and Chevrolet auto dealerships in the U.S., to unsuspecting consumers in the U.S. Its' unconscionable conduct in selling defective Steeltex tires was another step in the furtherance of the Bridgestone/Firestone Conspiracy of Death and Destruction.

Metropolitan News-Enterprise

Thursday, April 16, 2009

Page 1

Riverside's 'Jogging Judge' Sheldon Agrees to Resignation, Censure

By SHERRI M. OKAMOTO, Staff Writer

Riverside Superior Court Judge Christopher Sheldon has agreed to accept censure, resign from the bench, and never seek judicial office or sit on assignment, the Commission on Judicial Performance disclosed yesterday.

Sheldon, 60, was dubbed the "Jogging Judge" after being publicly admonished in 1998 for leaving his courtroom clerks to sign off on negotiated criminal dispositions while he ran up and down the courthouse stairs for exercise.

The commission yesterday issued a public decision approving the stipulation reached between its staff and Sheldon. Commission Chair and Fourth District Court of Appeal Justice Judith D. McConnell said that "[u]nfortunately the issuance of a public admonishment did not deter Judge Sheldon from abandoning his judicial responsibilities in the future."

She said that Sheldon's continued routine of "working part-time while being paid a full-time salary" was "utterly unacceptable and casts disrepute upon the judicial office."

Formal Proceedings

The commission filed a notice of formal proceedings against the judge in January, charging him with misconduct in routinely leaving the courthouse for the day before noon, after concluding his dependency calendar, without informing his supervising judge or receiving authorization for his half-day absence.

In his Jan. 29 response to the commission, Sheldon acknowledged that he used to leave the Indo courthouse after completing the dependency calendar, which usually occurred before noon, but denied that his superiors were unaware of this practice.

"In fact, no superior raised any issue with me regarding my hours until September 12, 2008, and when it was raised, I conformed my hours to their expectations, he said. He also denied, without elaboration, that he was unavailable to do other judicial work in the afternoons.

A three-judge panel was appointed to hear evidence in the case before Sheldon, his counsel—San Diego attorneys Reginald A. Vitek and Heather L. Rosing—and commission lawyer Andrew S. Blum proposed a stipulated resolution of the inquiry.

The stipulation was executed on March 18, pursuant to which Sheldon has agreed to tender his irrevocable resignation from judicial office, and to not preside over any judicial proceedings after May 12.

He will then go on leave, approved by his presiding judge, until Oct. 23, when he will complete his 20th year of service and be eligible to retire with maximum benefits.

Sheldon admitted that between early 2007 and late 2008, he routinely left the courthouse early and did not seek to make himself available to other judicial work during these absences.

Judge's Admissions

In addition to violating the California Rules of Court, Sheldon agreed that he failed to observe the standards of conduct for judicial officers, failed to act in a manner that promoted public confidence in the judiciary, and failed to diligently discharge his administrative responsibilities.

McConnell said that Sheldon "demonstrated a flagrant disregard for his obligations to his fellow judges, the public and the reputation of the judiciary," explaining that his responsibilities were not limited to the completion of his daily calendar.

"Judges who conclude their calendars early in the day may be assigned other duties, including presiding over cases other courts are unable to handle," she wrote, emphasizing that unapproved absences "can have a significant impact on the operation of the court, especially in a county such as Riverside with as longstanding and well-publicized backlog of court cases."

Prior Discipline

Sheldon was previously disciplined for running a misdemeanor pretrial calendar by having the attorneys negotiate dispositions, generally involving negotiated pleas in exchange for probation, with or without jail time, and leaving it to the court clerks to stamp his name on the orders.

In that case, the commission found that Sheldon was derelict in not personally taking the bench and making certain that the defendants were entering their pleas knowingly and voluntarily, in not imposing sentences in open court, and in leaving the courthouse during the calendar on one occasion without arranging for another judicial officer to cover.

It also found that he engaged in improper extrajudicial activity by exercising on the stairs while his courtroom was in session, and that he had undermined confidence in the judiciary.

Sheldon has been a judge since October 1989, when then-Gov. George Deukmejian named him to the now-defunct Desert Municipal Court. He had been a sole practitioner in Blythe for more than six years before that, and was a Riverside County deputy district attorney earlier in his career.

He was elevated to the Riverside Superior Court by then-Gov. Pete Wilson in 1992 and assigned to the juvenile dependency department in Indio in 2005. He did not return a call seeking comment on his resignation.

Copyright 2009, Metropolitan News Company

Chapter XX

BRIDGESTONE/FIRESTONE, INC AND BRIDGESTONE CORPORATION

"They Were Corporations with Splendid Abilities But Were Absolutely Corrupt"

Bridgestone/Firestone Inc.'s CEO, John Lampe lied to Congress about the existence of any cost reduction program, as well as what he knew, and when he knew it, regarding the defective Wilderness scandal. He misrepresented facts to the investigators involved in the NHTSA Wilderness tire investigation in 2000. Mr. Lampe was forced to resign during the pendency of the Firestone Steeltex National Recall Campaign, on March 31, 2004. His resignation was predicted by Lisoni & Lisoni in letters to Firestone dealers throughout the United States. When Congressional investigations revealed that Bridgestone/Firestone failed to disclose its knowledge of the widespread tread separation problems to the public and to the Senate Sub-committees, Congress enacted, the *Transportation Recall Enhancement, Accountability and Documentation* (T.R.E.A.D) Act of 2000, which authorizes criminal prosecution for concealment of facts relating to defects in tires.

The United States, foreign countries and consumers stated their distrust for Bridgestone/Firestone and Bridgestone Corporation regarding their business practices which constituted the foundation of the "Bridgestone/Firestone Conspiracy of Death and Destruction". The Lisoni & Lisoni National Steeltex Recall Campaign caused serious damage to the brand name integrity of both companies and resulted in the Bridgestone Corporation suffering a 69% decline in profits as of November 1, 2006.

With the passage of time, large numbers of consumers made claims for damages suffered as a result of Steeltex tire tread separations. They demanded reimbursement for damages done to their light trucks, recreational vehicles and ambulance units. Instead of an apologetic reimbursement, the victims of Steeltex tire tread separations received letters from Bridgestone/ Firestone, Inc, a wholly owned subsidiary of Bridgestone Corporation of Japan, blaming them for the tread separations and denying their claims. These denial letters were all signed by the same individual, Norma Y. Davis, Paralegal at Bridgestone/Firestone, and were often mailed out the same day the customers' defective tires had arrived at the Bridgestone/Firestone plant in Lavergne, Tennessee for inspection and forensic analysis.

Lisoni & Lisoni provided detailed evidence of the Steeltex tire defects to CBS Investigative Correspondent, Sharyl Attkisson and the evidence was shown to the nation in a lead story by Dan Rather, Anchor of CBS Evening News, and presented by Investigative Reporter, Sharyl Attkisson. Their continuing investigation into the increasing number of failures of Steeltex tires and serious tread separations on ambulances equipped with Firestone "Steeltex" tires, resulted in ambulance companies in thirty-six states, to voluntarily "change off" their Firestone "Steeltex" tires due to safety concerns. These "Steeltex" tires for ambulances were manufactured at the same time as the admittedly defective "Wilderness" tires, using the same "C-95" Cost Reduction Program in their manufacturing process.

It defies reality that Bridgestone/Firestone, Inc. and Bridgestone Corporation continually claimed there was absolutely nothing wrong with the Steeltex tires used on ambulances, especially, given the fact that the state of Ohio, home of Bridgestone Firestone, Inc. removed all Firestone Steeltex tires from their ambulances. The Ohio State Ambulance Association published a front page article in their monthly newsletter, informing its members of the dangers associated with the use of the seriously flawed Steeltex tires on their ambulance units. Bridgestone/Firestone, Inc. did everything in its power to deny the allegations made by Lisoni & Lisoni to the Ohio State Ambulance Association.

The best they could do with this attempt to mitigate the damage caused it by the article was a statement by the publication summarizing Bridgestone/Firestone's response. The article identified the name and telephone number of a Bridgestone/Firestone employee in charge of damage control. The employee was charged with the job of responding to several thousand telephone requests they'd received from ambulance companies in thirty-six states demanding cost reimbursement for replacement tires purchased from other tire manufacturers used to replace their "changed-off" Steeltex tires.

CBS Evening News did a major story on these defective Steeltex tires on ambulances in several states. The story featured Alan Hogan, a former Bridgestone/Firestone, Inc. employee, who had a full unabridged copy of the "C-95" Cost Reduction Program, detailing the cause of the defects in the Firestone Steeltex tires on ambulance units. The frightening fact was that many of the failures of ambulance tires occurred while transporting patients to hospitals. In fact, a grandmother died on the way to the hospital due to a Steeltex tire tread separation suffered by the ambulance unit transporting her at a high rate of speed to her local hospital emergency room. These replacement tires were paid for by the ambulance company, since Bridgestone/Firestone had consistently stated that there was nothing wrong with its "Steeltex" tires and denied the ambulance companies monetary compensation for the cost of the replacement tires.

William Orr, the Lisoni & Lisoni "whistle-blower" and former Bridgestone/Firestone tire failure analyst, was featured in the CBS Evening News in a Dan Rather/Sharyl Attkisson story, which focused on the dangerous ambulances driving on defective Firestone Steeltex tires with patients aboard.

The "Steeltex" tires, which came as original equipment on ambulances built by Ford Motor Company, were manufactured at the Decatur, Illinois Bridgestone/Firestone plant, which also made the majority of the defective "Wilderness" tires. After the Decatur plant closed, it was reported by CBS Evening News in a Dan Rather/

Sharyl Attkisson story that after a four-month internal investigation, Bridgestone/Firestone said a "faulty design and a unique manufacturing process at the Decatur plant caused some tires to suddenly lose their tread or suffer other failures."

The Decatur plant used a process known as "pelletizing," in which rubber pellets were blended with a lubricant that caused the rubber to bond with the steel belts in the tire manufacturing process. However, the more lubricant used, the more problems it created with adhesion of the rubber to the steel cords, resulting in catastrophic tread separations. Other Bridgestone/Firestone plants used rubber slabs, which required less lubricant.

Bridgestone/Firestone, Inc. and Bridgestone Corporation both knew that the lubricant would cause a serious tire breakdown. Nonetheless, both corporations concealed these facts from NHTSA and the individual state automotive safety agencies. This is just another step taken by the two corrupt corporations in furtherance of the criminal Bridgestone/Firestone Conspiracy of Death & Destruction.

The false denials by Bridgestone/Firestone regarding any problems associated with the "Steeltex" tire when used on ambulances, light duty trucks, and motor homes eventually caused the NHTSA recall of 490,000 "Steeltex A/T, Load Range D" tires, on February 26, 2004, manufactured at the Bridgestone/Firestone plant in Joliette, Quebec, Canada. These tires generally were installed as original factory equipment on Ford Excursions (1999-2002). These "Steeltex" tires caused five deaths and two injuries in Canada, serious problems in the United States and were installed on vehicles in several Western European countries.

Dan McDonald, spokesperson for Bridgestone/Firestone, lied to the media and stated in the announcement of the recall, "We have not identified a specific defect in these tires, but we thought that rather than go through an investigation, we would just step up and replace the tires." NHTSA, a co-conspirator, with Bridgestone/Firestone, Inc. and Bridgestone Corporation, supported McDonald's false statement and refused to release the data it had on the defective tires. Bridgestone/Firestone said it was a "voluntary recall" but the official 2004 Recall List of the National Highway Traffic & Safety

Administration clearly states it was a "government recall" – the only recall in 2004.

In the second Petition to the National Highway Traffic & Safety Administration (NHTSA), Lisoni & Lisoni documented 57 deaths and 162 serious injuries since 1999, as a result of the defective Firestone Steeltex tires. NHTSA did nothing, because of their loyalties to Bridgestone/Firestone, Inc. and Bridgestone Corporation in favor of the tire manufacturers and made it a co-conspirator in the Bridgestone/Firestone Conspiracy of Death and Destruction. Bridgestone/Firestone wrote to NHTSA and asked that the recall data not be released to the motoring public. NHTSA, in violation of its duties, set forth in the federal law that established its existence, granted the request.

An article by Safety Research & Strategies in July, 2004, entitled *"What is behind the Ford Excursion Tire Recall?"* made the following observation:

"In February 2004 Firestone found itself in the headlines again when it agreed to recall 497,000 Steeltex tires that were predominantly installed as original equipment on 2000 through early model 2003 Ford Excursions (Recall No. 04T-003). While no specific defect pattern was noted, the tires experienced sidewall failures, tread separations, blow-outs and unexplained loss of pressure and caused at least six crashes involving five deaths.

The Steeltex line covers a number of different tire types and sizes, those subject to the recall include only the Radial AT size LT265/75R16, Load Range D, manufactured in the Joliette, Quebec plant during March 1999 through December 2002 and installed on Ford Excursions.

The Steeltex recall is unusual on two fronts: NHTSA, Bridgestone/Firestone and Ford all credited the recall to the use of the Early Warning Reporting data that was required by Congress following the Ford/Firestone controversy in 2000. This is the first recall to result from the use of the EWR data and is widely being touted as a successful test of the system even by agency critics. According to NHTSA personnel and published reports, the agency examined the EWR data it received from Ford and Firestone and determined that the AT version of the Steeltex in a Load Range D fitted on Excursions, Ford's largest SUV, showed a failure rate that raised 'concern.' The agency's initial evaluation of the EWR led to direct communications with Ford and Firestone and a suggestion a recall was in order. In what appears to have been successful negotiations Firestone agreed to recall the allegedly defective tires. However, the nature of the negotiations, the lack of a formal investigation, and EWR data that is still not (and may never be) available for public scrutiny leads to a healthy dose of skepticism by some NHTSA-watchers. If the Steeltex recall represents a success, the data and rationale should be made available for review. Keeping the data and analysis secret, information that is normally included in defect investigations, makes the process a closed one. Public access to this information is rendered more important because there are no specific guidelines for recalls and there are often conflicting precedents. A review of the Steeltex recall also reveals what appears to be a Ford problem that under NHTSA statute forced the entire burden on Firestone. Tires, even those that are specified by a vehicle manufacturer of OE application, unlike other component parts are the sole responsibility of the tire manufacturer. Thus the recall burden fell on Firestone, despite what appears to be tires that were specified with too low a margin of safety. The recalled tires are being replaced with a higher load range (Load Range E)—the same tire used on the Ford F250/350, which shares its platform with the Excursion. The lack of a specific failure pattern, a higher failure rate on a size used almost exclusively on Ford Excursions, and statements from Firestone that many of the failures occurred due to overloading all suggest Ford's specification of an inadequate load range. Tire experts familiar with the situation concur that this is likely. The use of a lower load range left the Excursion with a margin of safety that was too low, harkening back to Ford's decisions for the Wilderness and ATX on the Explorer. The Steeltex tire has been under scrutiny following the ATX/Wilderness investigation by NHTSA and lawyers. While there is an inherent discomfort to stand behind the safety of any Firestone tire, particularly those made during the 1990's when the company instituted major cost cutting programs, the claims data reviewed by NHTSA did not raise to the level at which an investigation or recall appeared warranted."

Firestone "Steeltex" Load Range E tires manufactured at the same time, at the same plant and by the same manufacturing process failed at a much greater volume. However, Bridgestone/Firestone, Inc., despite Lisoni & Lisoni's documented inventory of over 5,500 claims, consistently denied there was any problem with any of the "Steeltex" tires still on the roads and highways of the United States. Prior to the recall on February 26, 2004, senior management individuals and corporate quality assurance experts of Bridgestone/Firestone, Inc. stated under oath that there were no known problems with the "Steeltex" tires, yet Bridgestone/Firestone, Inc. was forced to recall 490,000 "Steeltex" tires at a cost of at least one billion dollars proving that Bridgestone/Firestone, Inc. was lying about the defects in the Firestone Steeltex tires, reiterating, "BFS executives lie whenever their lips are moving."

With regard to the NHTSA recall order of 490,000 Firestone Steeltex tires and with full knowledge of the millions of defective Steeltex tires still in use, U. S. Transportation Secretary Norman Y. Maneta was quoted in the publication *"Professional Ethics"* as saying,   "It is a good example of showing that 'our system of safety standards is working.'" Secretary Maneta, in making this statement, totally ignored the decision of the U.S. Secret Service and President George W. Bush to remove the Firestone Steeltex tires on the President's light duty trucks at his ranch in Texas and on the Chevrolet Suburbans used to transport him and the First Lady from the White House to Camp David.

The publication, *"Professional Ethics,"* made the following observation with regard to the Bridgestone/Firestone and Bridgestone Corporation NHTSA recall order: ". . .Amazing, it cost this company over one-billion dollars to do this and they are willing to without fully investigating it and fighting it. . ."

In the article, published by *"Professional Ethics"*, after the recall of 490,000 Steeltex tires, the author, goes on to state:

"One final note that I would like to point out is that they are doing this recent recall 'voluntarily', is not necessarily out of kindness. The following is a reference to the 2000 recall that carries the same idea. Firestone and Ford officials tried to characterize the recall as 'voluntary,' but over the last weeks the company has come under increased pressure to respond as the number of complaints continued to rise. . .(i) anyway, how are we, the public, supposed to judge if it was voluntary or not? For the most part it really just shows us that they are trying to cover their butts so they don't get an avalanche of lawsuits again. . ."

The subject article goes on to state:

"Proper tire care should be number one on the dealerships lists. Just as the Firestone Wilderness and ATX tires were pulled off the shelf, the Steeltex tires should be pulled off the shelf too. The best way to deal with the situation is by the companies taking more precautions on SUV vehicles and making the citizens feel safer when they are deciding to purchase one of their vehicles."

Bridgestone/Firestone continued to identify its action as a "customer satisfaction program," yet the National Highway and Traffic Safety Administration (NHTSA) continued to identify it as an "agency recall". Although the Steeltex recall at the time was the third largest in U.S. history, millions of Firestone "Steeltex" tires remained in operation on the roads and highways of the United States and foreign countries. This action on the part of the two corporations was responsible for creating the risk of thousands of motorists in the U.S. suffering a catastrophic tread separation, at any time—"*where the rubber meets the road*"—in furtherance of the Bridgestone/Firestone Conspiracy of Death & Destruction.

Bridgestone/Firestone stopped manufacturing the Steeltex tires in 2005 after thirteen years and selling over thirty-million Firestone Steeltex tires. Lisoni & Lisoni argued that Bridgestone/Firestone, Inc. and Bridgestone Corporation were guilty of criminal violations of the federal legislation known as the T.R.E.A.D. Act.

In an action, defying all reason, the executives at Bridgestone/Firestone, Inc. were not indicted by the U.S. Department of Justice for violating the T.R.E.A.D. Act. More proof of the conspiracy between Bridgestone/Firestone, NHTSA and the Secretary of Transportation, Norman Manetta.

Bridgestone Corporation's Annual Report for December 31, 2003-2005 states:

"In fiscal years 2003 and 2002, BSA has paid $96 million and $245 million respectively, for the direct cost of voluntary tire recall and for product liability suits and claims, class actions, and the Attorneys General settlement, net of proceeds from product liability insurance recoveries. As a result of the payments, as of December 31, 2003 and 2002, BSA has recorded liabilities for matters related to the voluntary tire recall and resulting litigation amounting to $140 million and $285 million, respectively. In both the individual product liability personal injury case and the class action litigation, BSA's approach has been to offer reasonable settlements and to defend its position aggressively where such settlements are not possible. There can be no assurance that product liability suits and claims and class action lawsuits will be resolved as currently envisioned and, accordingly, the ultimate liability could be higher that the recorded liability. However, in the opinion of BSA management, the ultimate disposition of these product liability suits and claims and class action lawsuits could possibly be material to the results of the operations in any one accounting period but will not have a material adverse effect on the financial position or liquidity of the Company's Americas operation. In November 2002, an attorney who had filed a purported class action suit alleging that all the BSA Steeltex tires (fourteen million of which are estimated to be in service as of December 31, 2003) were defective, petitioned the NHTSA to reopen an investigation of such tires which that agency had closed in April 2002. The NHTSA denied that petition in June 2003 and on March 17, 2004, the court denied plaintiffs' motion for class certification. Plaintiffs have indicated that they will pursue other remedies, including appeal. BSA management has thoroughly investigated this issue, and continues to monitor the performance of the tires in question. However, except with regard to the February 26, 2004 voluntary safety campaign addressed below, BSA (i) does not believe that a recall or similar action of its Steeltex tires is necessary or appropriate, (ii) strongly believes that the related litigation is without merit; and (iii) plans to vigorously defend its position. Accordingly, BSA has made no provision for any related contingent liability. On February 26, 2004, BSA announced a U.S. voluntary safety campaign to replace, free of any charge to consumers, approximately 297,000 tires. The tires are Firestone-brand Steeltex Radial A/T tires in size LT265/75R16, and in Load Range D, which are on 2000-2002 and some early model year 2003 Ford Excursion vehicles. All the affected tires were made between March 1999 and December 2002 at BSA's plant in Joliette, Quebec, Canada and none are presently being manufactured by BSA. BSA will also replace approximately 20,000 exported tires meeting the same criteria. BSA estimates that the total direct costs of the voluntary safety campaign will approximate $30 million and believes the voluntary safety campaign will be completed by September, 2004, however, no amounts relating to the voluntary safety campaign have been recorded in the Company's consolidated financial statements as of December 31, 2003."

The statement made in paragraph one, in the subject Annual Report of Bridgestone Corporation that its "recorded liabilities for matters related to the voluntary tire recall and resulting litigation amounting to $140 million dollars and $285 million dollars, respectively," was absolutely false. The publication (*Professional Ethics*) in an article dated March 6, 2004, documented that the NHTSA Steeltex recall order cost Bridgestone Corporation one billion dollars. Further, the cost of reimbursing ambulance companies in thirty-six states cost the world's largest tire manufacturer many millions of dollars. In addition, Bridgestone/Firestone, Inc. and Bridgestone Corporation were forced to reimburse and take back thousands of Steeltex tires from all Ford and Chevrolet automotive dealerships in the U.S. The price tag for this reimbursement program cost Bridgestone Corporation many millions of dollars. These expenditures resulted in Bridgestone Corporation's profits to drop 69% by 2006.

> An Associated Press story, by Carl Friere and released, November 1, 2006, states: "Japanese tire maker Bridgestone Corporation reported a 69% drop in profits for the first three quarters, Wednesday, blaming expenses from the surging cost of rubber and other raw materials as well as closures of two plants in the U.S."

The Bridgestone Corporation's statement blaming the huge loss of profits to the "surging cost of rubber and other raw materials" is entirely false. Bridgestone Corporation owns the largest rubber plantation in the world, located in Liberia, Africa. It does not need to buy rubber from independent sources. The subject plantation in Africa is guilty of gross violations of human rights for the manner in which it treats the workers and family members that live and work on the plantation.

Paragraph three of the subject Annual Report states:

> "However, except with regard to the February 26, 2004 voluntary safety campaign addressed below, BSA (i) does not believe that a recall or similar action of its Steeltex tires is necessary or appropriate, (ii) strongly believes that the related litigation is without merit and (iii) plans to vigorously

defend its position. Accordingly, BSA has made no provisions for any related contingent liability."

This opinion of the Bridgestone auditors (Deliotte) was proven to be false in the following particulars:

1) Bridgestone/Firestone, Inc. was forced to pay the Ford and Chevrolet dealerships millions of dollars to reimburse them for the Steeltex tires their customers refused to accept as original factory equipment on all of the Chevrolet Suburbans and the Ford fifteen- passenger vans at the time of purchase;
2) Bridgestone/Firestone had to pay ambulance companies in thirty-six states as compensation for the tires they purchased from other tire manufacturers to replace the Steeltex tires on their ambulance units that were original factory equipment or to replace at no cost the Steeltex tires with other Bridgestone/Firestone brand tires;
3) Bridgestone/Firestone, Inc. lost hundreds of millions of dollars when numerous members of the motoring public of the United States replaced their Steeltex tires on their vehicles with tires manufactured by other corporations, i.e. Goodyear, Cooper, Michelin.

    Bridgestone/Firestone, Inc. and Bridgestone Corporation's profits in the tire replacement markets suffered huge losses when individual motorists failed to replace their Steeltex tires after their period of usefulness, with additional Steeltex tires.

    Consequently, Bridgestone/Firestone, Inc. and Bridgestone Corporation lost hundreds of millions of dollars due to the fact that they lost the sales income that would normally occur when original Steeltex tires reach the end of their projected life;
4) Bridgestone/Firestone, Inc. ceased manufacturing all models of the Firestone Steeltex brand of tires in 2005 after having manufactured thirty million of them over a thirteen-year period of time.

Also, paragraph four of the subject Annual Report falsely states that 297,000 Steeltex tires were recalled. In fact, the official recall number of tires totaled 490,000;
5. In 2006, Bridgestone Corporation reported a 69% loss of profits which began with the February 26, 2004 recall.

The Bridgestone Corporation either lied to its auditors or grossly underestimated the foreseeable consequences of the Lisoni & Lisoni National Tire Recall Campaign that destroyed the Bridgestone brand name integrity in the worldwide tire market.

AP Wire | 11/01/2006 | Bridgestone reports 69 pct. profit drop

Business

Posted on Wed, Nov. 01, 2006

Bridgestone reports 69 pct. profit drop

CARL FREIRE
Associated Press

TOKYO - Japanese tire maker Bridgestone Corp. reported a 69 percent drop in profits for the first three quarters Wednesday, blaming expenses from the surging cost of rubber and other raw materials as well as the closures of two plants in the U.S.

Profit at Bridgestone for the nine months ended Sept. 30 slid to 50.0 billion yen ($427.4 million), from 159.3 billion yen for the same period the previous year.

Bridgestone said the drop in profit came amid increased sales in Japan, the U.S., Europe and other regions. Sales during the nine months rose 13 percent to 2.163 trillion yen ($18.49 billion), from 1.921 trillion yen the year before.

Sales in overseas markets were lifted in part by a weaker yen, strong bus and truck tire sales in the U.S. and increased sales of passenger car and light truck tires in Europe, it said in a statement.

The company left unchanged its fiscal year forecast for a profit of 62.0 billion yen ($530 million) on sales of 2.95 trillion yen ($25.22 billion).

Bridgestone's results have only in recent years recovered from losses related to a massive tire-recall scandal at its U.S. subsidiary, Bridgestone Firestone North American Tire, six years ago.

Last year, Bridgestone paid $240 million to Ford Motor Co. to settle its dispute with the U.S. automaker in lawsuits related to the 2000-2001 recalls of Firestone tires on Ford vehicles.

At least 271 people were reported killed and hundreds more injured in accidents involving Firestone ATX and AT tires, and the manufacturer recalled 6.5 million tires.

The settlement ended the dispute between Bridgestone and Ford, which saw the reputation of its Explorer sport-utility vehicle damaged because that model was involved in most of the accidents. Bridgestone blamed the accidents on defects in some Ford vehicles, while Ford maintains the tires were entirely at fault.

http://www.centredaily.com/mld/centredaily/business/15899685.htm   11/8/2006

Lawsuit could cost Firestone nearly $3 billion | Trailer/Body Builders

MENU TRAILER BODY BUILDERS. SEARCH LOG IN REGISTER

WELCOME TO OUR NEW SITE: To navigate to each section, click on the icon at the top left to see the drop-down X

ARCHIVE

Lawsuit could cost Firestone nearly $3 billion

Aug 13, 2002

can cause the tread to separate from the rest of the tire, "in a matter of seconds, leading to the tire's total destruction," the attorney's said in a statement. "Without question, millions of people are currently at risk who are riding the roads on Steeltex tires," Lisoni said. Lisoni said the tires are designed for trucks, and many are fitted onto municipal vehicles such as school buses, ambulances and fire engines. Lisoni said his law firm, Lisoni & Lisoni, in Pasadena has approached Firestone about recalling the tires, but the company has refused to meet with him. The firm recently handled another lawsuit against Firestone relating to a Steeltex tire blowout and resulting in multiple deaths and injuries. That suit was settled, Lisoni said. This new suit was filed on behalf of Roger Littell of Riverside, California, who has seen four Steeltex tires on his 1999 motorhome disintegrate, according to the lawyers. Littell is a racing car enthusiast and was involved in road testing Firestone tires between 1955 and 1974, the lawyers said. Two years ago, Firestone recalled 6.5 million tires, most of them installed on Ford Motor Co. Explorer SUVs, after officials linked the tires to a series of fatal accidents. The recall ended a 94-year relationship between Firestone and Ford, and placed the future of the Firestone brand in doubt.

LISONI & LISONI
225 S. Lake Avenue, 9th Floor
Pasadena, CA 91101
PH 626-440-1333
FAX (626) 577-0310

GAIL MARIE LISONI, ESQ.   JOSEPH LOUIS LISONI, ESQ.

FOR IMMEDIATE RELEASE
ALL POINTS BULLETIN

April 4, 2006, Pasadena, California.

BRIDGESTONE FIRESTONE'S DEFENSE THEORY SUFFERS WHEN FEDERAL COURT RECENTLY RULED NHTSA REPORT "UNTRUSTWORTHY" AND INADMISSIBLE

Bridgestone Firestone's Steeltex tire defense suffered a major setback when the Federal Court in Washington DC, ruled its major defense theory is not admissible in evidence as rebutable proof to discredit evidence of the continuous trend of catastrophic tread separations suffered by the Bridgestone Firestone Steeltex R4S, R4SII and A/T tires.

The National Highway Traffic & Safety Administration has fallen to an unprecedented level of disrespect when in a product liability case the federal court in Washington, D.C., held that the NHTSA reports have been deemed "untrustworthy" because the manufacturers are allowed to submit "confidential" information, and are able to decide "what" information they will provide to NHTSA as "confidential". The court held "Defendant engaged in a "cherry picking" strategy of the type of data to submit to NHTSA...NHTSA's resulting report, therefore, is not an accurate product, and within the realm of this litigation is untrustworthy...." See Jones v. Ford Motor Company, 230 F. Supp2nd 480 (E.D. Va 2004). In 2004, NHTSA was found to be over-budget and under-performing in the early warning system of identifying defect trends.

NHTSA has known about the Bridgestone Firestone Tire Tread Separation problem for years. Lisoni & Lisoni, in association with the consumer advocacy group, Tires Across America, has petitioned NHTSA in November, 2002 and May 26, 2004 to recall the Firestone Steeltex R4S, R4SII and A/T tire lines. Both Petitions were denied by NHTSA. In so doing, NHTSA misrepresented the number of claims and many critical facts such as the number of deaths and serious injuries resulting from the Firestone Steeltex tires.

In February, 2004, NHTSA forced Bridgestone Firestone to recall 497,000 Firestone Steeltex A/T tires manufactured in Jolliete, Quebec, Canada, which came as original equipment on Ford Excursions. Many more dangerous tires within the Firestone Steeltex tire line must also be recalled. The Firestone Steeltex tires need to be recalled immediately to prevent the sudden and unexpected tread separations resulting from Bridgestone Firestone's cost cutting programs. An immediate recall of the 30 million Bridgestone Firestone Steeltex tries would prevent certain deaths, injuries and property damage claims occurring in the United States and foreign nations.

Seven people have died as a result of these defective Firestone Steeltex tires in California in August, 2005, including an outstanding female soccer player on the United States national team. The injuries and deaths are not limited to those drivers who suffer a catastrophic tread separation of the Firestone Steeltex tire. In November, 2005, a husband and wife were killed in Tennessee when a Ford F-250 suffered a tread separation, lost control and crossed over the yellow line and hit the vehicle head-on, killing both occupants. Finally, the injuries and deaths can also occur after the tread separation of the Firestone Steeltex tire, while waiting for roadside assistance, which is the second largest cause of injury or death involving motor vehicles.

Bridgestone Firestone has consistently grossly misrepresented the truth about the quality and safety of its tires. Bridgestone Firestone has misrepresented material facts about these tires to NHTSA, to Congress, to the American public, and to each owner of a Firestone Steeltex tire which came with the Bridgestone Firestone Tire Warranty. The public must be warned about the danger of a sudden and unexpected catastrophic tread separation of the Firestone Steeltex R4S, R4SII or A/T tires, through no fault of the consumer, as a result of the cost cutting efforts of Bridgestone Firestone and Bridgestone Firestone's concealment of material information form the public.

For more information, visit our website: www.firestonesteeltexclassaction.com

Chapter XXI
NHTSA

"Absolute Power Corrupts Absolutely"

The National Highway Traffic & Safety Administration (NHTSA) is an agency of the executive branch of the U.S., government, part of the Department of Transportation. It describes its mission as "saves lives, prevent injuries, and reduce vehicle related crashes."

As part of its activities, NHTSA is charged with writing and enforcing federal motor vehicle safety standards to protect the U.S. motoring public from deaths, injuries and property damage resulting from defective vehicles and their component parts.

NHTSA was formed December 31, 1970, after the book entitled *Unsafe at Any Speed - The Designed-in Defects of Motor Vehicles*, by Ralph Nader. Nader's book was a comprehensive indictment of the U.S. automotive industry and resulted in Congressional legislation, known as the *Highway Safety Act of 1970* and was signed into law by President Lyndon Johnson. This New York Times bestseller resulted in the creation of the doctrine of "crashworthiness," which forced the U.S. automotive industry to implement numerous safety related components in their vehicles offered for sale to the U.S. consumer, i.e. seat belts, head restraint devices, collapsible steering wheels, and padded dashboards.

NHTSA replaced the federal agency known as "National Highway Safety Bureau."It has jurisdiction over all automotive manufacturers that produce motor vehicles in the United States, and is headquartered in Washington, DC. Its motto, in addition to its mission statement, is *"People saving people."* In 2004, it had an annual budget of over $800 million dollars.

From the date of its inception up until 1993, its activities in promoting Ralph Nader's doctrine of "crashworthiness" resulted in safety regulations that protected the drivers and occupants of motor vehicles that were victims of serious motor vehicle accidents. However, in the last twenty-one years, its investigations of automobile crashes have become difficult to understand, extremely controversial, with numerous automotive component industry experts debating the veracity and statistical validity of its investigations.

NHTSA failed to meet its constitutional duty to protect the motoring public from the millions of dangerously defective Firestone Steeltex tires. NHTSA's closure of four investigations of the Steeltex tire documents its corruption, ineptness and incompetency. The four closed investigations documented its secret conspiracy of death and destruction with Bridgestone/Firestone, Inc. and Bridgestone Corporation in avoiding the financial failure of the largest tire manufacturers in the world because of their callous disregard for human life by placing profits ahead of safety.

On May 12, 2000, Bridgestone/Firestone, Inc. issued the following press release:

> "We at Bridgestone/Firestone take great pride in the quality and durability of the Radial ATX and Wilderness tire lines and believe a dialogue with the National Highway Traffic Safety Administration (NHTSA) will give us an opportunity to provide the agency with the facts regarding our products. We look forward to working with the NHTSA and we will cooperate fully with the agency's requests. We are confident that the agency will proceed to evaluate the available data in a fair and objective manner, and once it has had an opportunity to assess the relevant information, the NHTSA will confirm what we believe. Our tires are safe products."

Subsequent to this press release, NHTSA closed its investigation of the Firestone Wilderness tire line and did not issue a recall order. The Wilderness tire line suffered thousands of failures, resulting in hundreds of deaths and injuries and thousands of property damage accidents, yet, NHTSA refused to recall the Wilderness tire line. The public outcry for an investigation of NHTSA's wrongful conduct resulted in a Congressional investigation which ordered the recall of 6.5 million Firestone Wilderness tires in 2000.

On January 9, 2002, Rubber & Plastic News reported:

"The National Highway Traffic & Safety Administration's Office of Defects Investigation has a 'flawed' process for identifying potential auto and tire defects, according to a new report from the Transportation Department's Office of the Inspector General. ODI's data 'significantly underestimates the number of potential safety defects', the report said." A peer review panel to examine safety data would help the office's consistency in instigating defect investigations. It said as would timely completion of regulations required by the Transportation Recall Efficiency Accountability and Documentation (TREAD) Act."

On January 10, 2002, Caroline E. Mayer, of the Washington Post, reported in an article entitled "*Highway Safety Agency Faulted on Probes*,"

"Federal highway safety regulators need to make major improvements in collecting and analyzing data about potential auto defects to avoid another debacle like the Firestone tire episode, the Transportation Department's internal watchdog unit said yesterday.

A report by the department's inspector general's office faulted the National Highway Traffic & Safety Administration (NHTSA) for using what it called a 'seriously flawed system' of incomplete and often inaccurate data in deciding whether to open an investigation. Hundreds of people were killed and injured before ten million Firestone tires were recalled starting in August 2000.

The report also questioned whether the agency is equipped to carry out a new law passed in response to the Firestone recall. The report said NHTSA 'still faces several challenges in fully implementing [the new law] and improving its ability to identify potential safety defects.'...NHTSA Administrator Jeffrey W. Runge defended the agency's past actions. 'We believe that the process currently used by the ODI to identify potential safety defects... [has]worked well,' he wrote to the inspector general. 'We do believe that very few, if any significant safety defects have escaped detection. Runge's comments drew a sharp dissent from the inspector general's office. 'We strongly disagree with this statement,' the report said. 'The Firestone Incident... and the case examples in our report clearly illustrate that ODI's process and procedures need major improvements. 'The report echoes criticism safety advocates have made for years about weaknesses at NHTSA. Clarence M. Ditlow, executive director of the *Center for Auto Safety*, said the report 'shows the ODI program over the years has been at best, haphazard.' He added: 'We're glad someone looked under the hood, and we need continued oversight to bring NHTSA up to speed on auto defects. Ken Johnson, spokesman for Rep. W.J. "Billy" Tauzin, (R-LA) chairman of the House Commerce Committee, which also held hearings, said 'the report verified our suspicions that NHTSA's process for reviewing data was fundamentally flawed.'

Even though the new law provides new resources to NHTSA, the agency has already fallen behind in drafting new regulations, and the new information system for identifying defects 'is at risk because of poor project planning and management,' the report said."

On February 28, 2002, at the Hearing before the Subcommittee on Commerce, Trade and Consumer Protection of the Committee on Energy and Commerce House of Representatives, John Lampe lied under oath when he answered questions from Representative, David Dingell:

> "Mr. Dingell: ...Did Bridgestone Firestone launch some sort of cost-cutting effort in the early and mid-1990's to deal with its profit and loss and debt situation?
>
> Mr. Lampe: Congressman Dingell, I'm not-could you be a little bit more specific? We're always-certainly we're always trying to improve our productivity and keep our expenses under control.
>
> Mr. Dingell: The journal quotes Mr. Ono, who is a man I gather of some importance in the company, who said that last year's results show the improvement of cost-cutting in the five-year period. My question: Was there a cost-cutting program which went on at Firestone or not?
>
> Mr. Lampe: Congressman Dingell, there are always measures in our company to keep our expenses under control.
>
> Mr. Dingell: Was there a name for this cost-cutting program?
>
> Mr. Lampe: I'm not sure what the Congressman is referring to.
>
> Mr. Dingell: Well, all I know is that you had a cost-cutting program going on according to Mr. Ono. Have you ever talked to him about this?
>
> Mr. Lampe: Mr. Ono has returned to Japan, sir. Again, if you could be more specific, I'll certainly try to address it...
>
> Mr. Dingell: Were any of these changes made for cost-cutting reasons?
>
> Mr. Lampe: Not that I know of, Congressman. I don't know of any – again, we make a number of changes. We try to

improve our tires. We try to make our tires better all the time. I was not in manufacturing at the time, so I know of-I know of none.

Mr. Dingell: Does any of these result in the use of less-expensive materials and compounds and production processes?

Mr. Lampe: Again, Congressman, I cannot-I cannot state to that. I will tell you that we're always looking to be able to use better materials at a better price if we can improve the quality of our tires.

Mr. Dingell: Would you please submit to this committee a list of all changes in materials, compounds, in production processes, and in structure of the tires made during this period?

Mr. Lampe: Of course we will, Congressman. . .

Mr. Dingell: Would you submit a list of materials, structure, changes in manufacturing processes, please, to this committee that occurred during that period of time?

Mr. Lampe: I said I would, sir, yes, sir."

<u>Lampe said he would, but he never did</u>. He adhered to the custom and practice of Bridgestone executives to *"lie whenever their lips are moving"*. He committed the crime of Contempt of Congress, but was not charged because he resigned from Bridgestone/Firestone, Inc. on March 31, 2004.

On the same day, February 28, 2002, the NHTSA Administrator, Jeffrey W. Runge, M.D. testified before the Subcommittee on Commerce, Trade and Consumer Protection Committee on Energy and Commerce U.S. House of Representatives regarding NHTSA's implementation of the Transportation, Recall, Enhancement, Accountability and Documentation (T.R.E.A.D.) Act. He testified:

"The TREAD Act was enacted on November 1, 2000, as a direct consequence of hearings before the Committee on Energy and Commerce on the safety of Firestone tires and related matters. In the course of the hearings, the Committee determined that NHTSA could have detected the problems with the tires sooner if it had obtained reports about the tires' problems in a timelier manner. The T.R.E.A.D. Act therefore contains provisions requiring vehicle and equipment manufacturers to report periodically to NHTSA on a wide variety of information that could indicate the existence of a potential safety defect and to advise NHTSA of <u>foreign</u> safety recalls and other safety campaigns. The Act increases civil penalties for violations of the vehicle safety law and provides criminal penalties for misleading the Secretary about safety defects that have caused death or injury. It authorizes the Secretary to require a manufacturer to accelerate its program for remedying a defect or noncompliance if there is a risk of serious injury or death, and requires that manufacturers must have a plan for reimbursing owners who incur the cost of a remedy before being notified by the manufacturer. It also prohibits the sale of motor vehicle equipment, including a tire, for installation on a motor vehicle if the equipment is the subject of a defect or noncompliance recall. In a remedy program involving tires, the manufacturer must include a plan that prevents replaced tires from being resold for use on motor vehicles. The Act also directs the Secretary to undertake a comprehensive review of the way in which NHTSA determines whether to open a defect or noncompliance investigation.

Thanks to the additional resources the T.R.E.A.D. Act gave us, we are well on our way to accomplishing all of the goals of the Act's requirements. First, I will report on the actions we are taking that relate to the defects investigation program, and then our actions to end and adopt safety standards and regulations.

On our actions to improve safety defect investigations, we have met all the rulemaking deadlines in the T.R.E.A.D.

Act and are in the final stages of implementing other provisions that do not contain such deadlines. Within the defects program, the key T.R.E.A.D. Act provisions gives us the authority to issue a final rule that establishes an Early Warning Reporting System. When this rule is final, motor vehicle and motor vehicle equipment manufacturers would be required to report a wide variety of information and to submit relevant documents to us periodically. In the past, our decisions on whether to open defect investigations have primarily been based on complaints we receive from consumers. Our efforts to identify potential defects in a timely manner have been hampered by an inability to obtain relevant information in the possession of the manufacturers. Experience has shown that manufacturers often obtain information suggesting the existence of a safety-related problem months, and sometimes years, before consumer complaints to NHTSA indicate a potential problem...We have proposed to require all manufacturers of motor vehicles and motor vehicle equipment to submit information about claims and notices they receive about deaths and injuries that are allegedly due to defects in their products..."

Lisoni & Lisoni filed its first Petition with NHTSA to re-open its investigation and demanding that the eleven million Firestone Steeltex tires still on the roads of the U.S. be recalled. The Petition was denied by NHTSA.

Miles Moore from Rubber & Plastic News reported: April 15, 2002:

"The National Highway Traffic & Safety Administration has closed its investigation into Firestone Steeltex R4S, R4SII and A/T light truck tires, finding no defect trend. NHTSA began the investigation into Steeltex tires, Sep. 29, 2000, less than two months after the recall of 6.5 million Firestone ATX, ATXII and Wilderness AT tires. Noting that the complaint patterns against the Steeltex tires seemed to be affected by media coverage of the recall, the agency said it found the evidence does not support a defect finding against the tires, but also that it would re-open the investigation if new evidence becomes available. 'With the closing of this issue, we are now in an even better position to focus our efforts and resources on the forward-looking work of rebuilding our company and the Firestone brand.'"

CCN reported on May 5, 2003, before the recall of 490,000 Steeltex tires:

"Bridgestone Firestone spokesman, Dan McDonald, told CNN that the Steeltex tires perform 'excellent on the roads,' and that their failure rate is 'extremely low.' He added that only the National Highway & Traffic & Safety Administration has the authority to order a recall. NHTSA declined to recall the Steeltex line last June, noting in its report that the failure rate on the tires was 'low when compared to some competitor tires of the same load rating.' McDonald said the internal document (C-95) summarized a 'brainstorming session' designed to 'improve efficiency and quality.' He said many of the proposed initiatives were never implemented.

Lisoni added that William Orr, a senior lab technician at Firestone's plant in Lavergne, Tennessee, plans to meet with NHTSA officials Wednesday. Orr contends he was fired after he complained to management that poor workmanship and inferior materials were producing dangerous tires. Bridgestone/Firestone says Orr was fired because he stole $7,000, and he didn't raise his quality complaints until after he was dismissed. The Tennessee Department of Labor cleared Mr. Orr of all alleged wrongdoing after a full evidentiary hearing.

Lisoni says he expects to eventually represent over eight-million Steeltex tire owners, calling this is "the largest single product liability class action in U.S. history."

After NHTSA's denial of the Lisoni & Lisoni Petition to re-open the Investigation, and the recall of 490,000 Steeltex tires cemented their role as a co-conspirator in the Bridgestone/Firestone

Conspiracy of Death and Destruction. This was the second revelation that NHTSA was a facilitator with Bridgestone/Firestone Inc. and Bridgestone Corporation in their conspiracy of death and destruction.

Miles Moore of Rubber & Plastic News reported: June 23, 2003:

"NHTSA denied Lisoni's petition to re-open investigation. 'We're pleased that NHTSA denied the petition,' a Bridgestone/Firestone spokesman said June 16, 'But we're not surprised because it reaffirms what we've been saying all along that Steeltex tires are performing well. We believe this should answer all questions about Steeltex tires.'"

This statement was proven to be entirely false by the NHTSA official Order of Recall of 490,000 Firestone Steeltex tires.

Lisoni & Lisoni responded, stating:

"In denying the Petition to re-open, NHTSA refused to recognize any claim that was not on its website, and stated that it only had knowledge of 872 complaints. This statement was made, despite the fact that in a Press Conference held at the National Press Club in Washington DC on the day Lisoni & Lisoni filed its First Petition, it documented over 2,000 Firestone Steeltex tire complaints on the NHTSA website and produced documentation copied from the NHTSA website. Lisoni & Lisoni proved that NHTSA had concealed a huge number of complaints on different websites, such as 'Ford', 'Chevy', 'SUV's and light 'trucks'."

It should be noted that the fact that NHTSA denied the Lisoni's Petition to re-open is of little merit because Steven Beretsky, of NHTSA, whose incompetent investigation was responsible for the denial of the Wilderness recall Petition was also the investigator of the Firestone Steeltex Petition.

In response to Bridgestone's comments that the denial of the First Petition would answer all questions about the Steeltex tire, Rubber & Plastic News reported:

"December 8, 2003: Lisoni said he will file a second petition in January with NHTSA to open a defect investigation of the tire. He also got the California Superior Court in Indio – where his class action lawsuit against Bridgestone Firestone is filed – to schedule a Dec. 31 hearing to consider his accusation the tire maker destroyed scrap Steeltex tires the court had ordered kept as evidence in the suit. . .

A BFS spokesman called Lisoni's charges of destruction of evidence 'unfounded' and 'malicious'. He also noted NHTSA twice has given the Steeltex 'a clean bill of health.' It is irresponsible for Lisoni to make that charge of destroying evidence, the BFS spokesman said. His accusation is just false, not supported by the facts. He said the record on Steeltex is clear. 'The tires are performing very well in the field, and NHTSA has twice found no defect trend. . .'

In his new petition to NHTSA, Lisoni said, he will focus on complaints of alleged Steeltex failures on ambulances. He claims he now has affidavits from emergency squads in thirty-three states, and predicted he will have them from 40 states by January."

Lisoni & Lisoni filed new petitions – the second petition addressed the problems with recreational vehicles, SUV's and light trucks, and the third petition addressed the problems with ambulances equipped with the Firestone Steeltex tires. The second and third petitions were summarily denied by NHTSA, stating there was no defect trend sufficient enough to warrant re-opening its investigation. The denial decisions were illogical, incompetent, and totally failed to recognize the mountain of evidence provided by Lisoni & Lisoni which clearly proved that the Firestone Steeltex tire was suffering catastrophic tread separations across the entire United States and its territories, resulting from a defective condition of manufacturing which rendered these tires unreasonably dangerous.

NHTSA's denials of the three Steeltex tire Petitions filed by Lisoni & Lisoni, proving the need to recall the eleven million Steeltex tires still in use across the United States, cemented its role as a secret co-conspirator in the Bridgestone/Firestone, Inc. and Bridgestone Corporation Conspiracy of Death and Destruction.

Further, NHTSA's conduct in protecting the top executives of the two corporations from criminal prosecutions by the U.S. Department of Justice for violations of the T.R.E.A.D. Act spoke volumes about its role as a facilitator of the corrupt and unethical conduct of Bridgestone/Firestone, Inc. and Bridgestone Corporation, in implementing the "C-95" Cost Reduction Program company-wide.

These three denial reports, produced by NHTSA, did not state that the Firestone Steeltex tire was not defective. But, rather stated, "After a review of the petition and other information, NHTSA has concluded that further expenditure of the agency's investigative resources on the issues raised by the petition does not appear warranted. The agency accordingly has denied the petition."

The Lisoni & Lisoni investigation of the NHTSA website containing consumer complaints of defective Firestone Steeltex tires revealed that it refused to recognize any claim that related to the Firestone Steeltex tire that was not on its website. In closing its first investigation of the Steeltex tire, it claimed to only have knowledge of 872 complaints regarding the Firestone Steeltex tires. It is important to note that the first Lisoni & Lisoni petition to re-open the Investigation of the eleven-million Steeltex tires still on the road documented in excess of 2,900 complaints on their own website. They hid them on other websites, such as "Ford", "Chevy", "SUV's", pickup "trucks", "ambulances", and other model vehicles.

In truth and fact, the denial of the three petitions filed by Lisoni & Lisoni in an attempt to obtain a recall of the remaining eleven-million Steeltex tires still on the road, is of little merit. Its Office of Defects Investigation, in particular, Steve Beretsky, who denied the three petitions to re-open the Investigation into the Firestone Steeltex R4S, R4SII and AT tires was also the NHTSA investigator responsible for the denial of the Petition to Recall fourteen-million defective Firestone Wilderness tires. Millions of Firestone Wilderness tires were recalled only after NHTSA was ordered to do so as a result of a comprehensive investigation by the U.S. Congress in 2000, co-chaired by Senator John McCain (R-AZ) and Congressman W.J. Billy Tauzin (R-LA).

The federal court found that a NHTSA report was not sufficiently "trustworthy" to be admitted into evidence. The court noted that since the defendant, Ford Motor Company, had selectively withheld certain information, NHTSA's report, which was based on that information, was untrustworthy.

The National Product Liability Reporter, published from Washington DC, reported on the Lisoni & Lisoni National Steeltex Recall Campaign on a regular basis as did the National Class Action Reporter. In addition, The Federal Register printed exact copies of NHTSA's official denials of the three Firestone Steeltex Recall Petitions filed by Lisoni & Lisoni:

1. The first Petition to Recall all Firestone Steeltex tires still in service at the time it was filed;
2. The second Petition requesting that NHTSA reconsider its denial of the first Petition and citing volumes of new evidence proving the defects in the Firestone Steeltex tire line caused by the "C-95" Cost Reduction Program;
3. The third petition demanding a recall order of all ambulance units equipped with Firestone Steeltex tires across the United States.

In an article published by *"Safety Research & Strategies"*, in 2004, entitled "Inspector General Finds NHTSA is Over Budget and Underperforming in Early Warning System," the safety firm revealed:

"The office of Inspector General (OIG) released a second audit report related to NHTSA performance and cited the agency's poor implementation and cost over-runs associated with Advanced Retrieval Tire, Equipment, Motor Vehicle Inspection system (ARTEMIS). ARTEMIS is the NHTSA system developed to analyze and identify trends in the early warning reporting data required from manufacturers (following the TREAD Act) that includes reports on deaths and injuries, property damage and warranty data...

Despite public claims by NHTSA it would make the data available on the public record, NHTSA back-tracked on its promise claiming they would wait to see the outcome of a lawsuit filed by the rubber manufacturers association (RMA) which seeks to keep the data confidential. The RMA claims the data won't help consumers that there is plenty of data available to the public and the data should be used by trained federal investigators only-something agency officials are symptomatic to as they are concerned that they will be inundated with Petitions for Defect Investigations from those who don't know how to use the data. Public Citizen filed suit to obtain release of EWR data – including warranty claims. In the meantime, NHTSA claims it will wait for the courts to decide before any data are released."

Despite the fact that NHTSA denied all three Petitions filed by Lisoni & Lisoni, it was inundated with criticism of its denials by thousands of citizens across the United States prompted by the information they possessed and which was received by them from the Lisoni & Lisoni National Steeltex Tire Recall Campaign. The extent of the damage caused to NHTSA's reputation and credibility as a result of the public information campaign forced NHTSA to reluctantly issue a recall order for 490,000 Firestone Steeltex tires on February 26, 2004.

In an article published by *"Safety Research & Strategies"*, in 2004 entitled "Early Warning Data Prompts another Bridgestone/ Firestone Recall," the organization reported:

> "For the second time BFS has recalled tires allegedly based on unfavorable early warning Data—the data that manufacturers are required to provide NHTSA following the Ford/Firestone Recalls and the subsequent TREAD Act. This time BFS is recalling 250,000 Bridgestone 'Dueller AT 693' replacement tires...made in Tsou, Japan...The company estimates 27,000 are left in service. Despite NHTSA assertion that portions of the TREAD data would be available for public scrutiny the agency reneged on this promise and is now facing litigation vying for its release. NHTSA spokesman, Rae Tyson claims, "If we let all of the

information be made public, it would have a chilling effect on the data we get. If, for example warranty data got out, manufacturers might quit offering warranties or quit handling problems via warranty...Once again, the public has no means to verify or assess the data that led to this recall. We are expected to accept the manufacturer's judgment and that of under-staffed, under-funded agency that regulates them..."

On June 30, 2015, an article authored by Drew Angerer and Jim Watson, in *"Car & Driver"* magazine entitled, *"Why NHTSA is More Defective Than the Defects it Investigates?"* In the comprehensive article, it is stated,

"The agency responsible for over-seeing the nation's vehicle safety is full of incompetent, mismanaged staff who are practically set up by their superiors to fail. According to a recent audit by the Department of Transportations' Inspector General, yes, the National Highway Traffic & Safety Administration is that bad. The eleven-month audit, coming after a scathing House report last September, was further proof that NHTSA needs to clean house before it attempts to tackle a record number of recalls and complaints from car owners...An average of 333 complaints flood NHTSA's office of Defects Investigations each day—that's 78,000 a year—and only one person screens them all. About 90% of these complaints never get a second review, which means there's an extraordinarily high likelihood for problems to slip by undetected...One employee said he uses his 'gut feeling' to determine if there is a problem or not. Top managers don't agree on what warrants an investigation, and screeners overlook vehicle defects that their managers typically demote, even if the problems are potentially serious. The NHTSA website complaint form has vehicle-part categories that aren't explained to the layman and even automakers trip up when they classify their own problems. NHTSA employees mislabel data, which is one reason they missed GM's ignition-switch problems (for example, they used 'Unknown', or 'Other' data and 'Exterior Lighting: Headlights: Switch' instead of 'Electrical systems: Ignition: Switch')"

It takes NHTSA months and years beyond its own publicly stated deadlines to investigate most defects. In a Senate hearing during the third week of June, 2015, Senator Claire McCastkill (D-Mo) stated with regard to NHTSA:

"I'm not about to give you more money until I see meaningful progress on reforming the internal processes of this organization. . . .You can't start throwing money until you have a system in place to make this agency function like it's supposed to."

After NHTSA denied its three Petitions Lisoni & Lisoni continued its national and international public information campaign. In addition to the 490,000 Steeltex tires recalled, the public information campaign resulted in massive numbers of "change-offs" of Steeltex tires from ambulance units in thirty-six states and led to the *unprecedented decision of Bridgestone/ Firestone and Bridgestone Corporation in 2005 to cease manufacturing the Firestone Steeltex tire brand*.

Prior to the decision, the Steeltex tire had a history of being installed on seventy-one model vehicles as original factory equipment. As of 2005, Bridgestone Firestone, Inc. had manufactured 30 million Steeltex tires, of which, eleven million were still in use on the roads and highways of the United States. When the eleven million Steeltex tires still on the road were voluntarily changed off or not replaced at the end of their useful life, the Lisoni & Lisoni National Steeltex Recall Campaign was described by the Nation's Consumer Advocacy Groups as "*a consumer's reverse recall program*." This development marked the end of the Firestone Steeltex tire chapter of the Bridgestone Firestone, Inc. and the Bridgestone Corporation Conspiracy of Death and Destruction.

Inspector General Finds NHTSA Over Budget and Under Performing in Early Warning System
Copyright © Safety Research & Strategies, Inc., 2004

The Office of Inspector General (OIG) released a second audit report related to NHTSA performance and cited the agency's poor implementation and cost overruns associated with the Advanced Retrieval Tire, Equipment, Motor Vehicle Information System (ARTEMIS). ARTEMIS is the NHTSA system developed to analyze and identify trends in the early warning reporting data required from manufacturers (following the TREAD Act) that includes reports on deaths and injuries, property damage and warranty data.

The OIG report (Follow-Up Audit of the Office of Defects Investigation) found the development of ARTEMIS proceeded without a development strategy, proper sequencing of events and milestones, or reliable cost and schedule estimates. As a result, development costs increased from 76 percent ($5.35 million to $9.4 million) and the schedule was extended four times. OIG also found that $17.12 million in funds needed for future operations and maintenance couldn't be verified and were reduced to $11.46 million. Adding to the problems, ARTEMIS, which was fully operational in July doesn't have the capability to perform advanced predictive analyses that can point out potential defect trends as intended. In an attempt to remedy this shortcoming, NHTSA began working with the FAA and other organizations to determine how to obtain this capability.

OIG also noted that the agency has a duty to ensure that EWR data is thoroughly and consistently analyzed, particularly because of the decision to limit public release of the data to only death, personal injury, property damage, and production numbers for light vehicles. However, even this limited data is still unavailable. Despite public claims that the data were available or would be available NHTSA backtracked on its promise claiming that they would wait to see the outcome of a lawsuit filed by the Rubber Manufacturers Association (RMA), which seeks to keep the data confidential. RMA claims the data won't help consumers, that there is already plenty of data available to the public, 1 the data should be used by trained federal investigators only—something agency officials are sympathetic to as ..y are concerned that they will be inundated with petitions for defect investigations from those who don't understand how to use the data. The vehicle manufacturers have not supported the RMA action and claim that NHTSA's position on releasing a portion of the data is acceptable. In addition to the RMA lawsuit, Public Citizen has also filed suit to obtain release of EWR data—including warranty claims. In the meantime, NHTSA claims it will wait for the courts to decide before any data are released.

ttp://www.safetyresearch.net/Library/SRS035.htm   12/28/2005

Chapter XXII

TIRES ACROSS AMERICA

"The 4th of July - Independence Day"

In June, 2005, Lisoni & Lisoni embarked on a grass-roots campaign to remove the Firestone Steeltex tires from the roads and highways of the United States, by organizing the class members to put signs on their lawns over the fourth of July weekend to bring attention to the dangers of the Firestone Steeltex tire line.

On June 22, 2005, Lisoni & Lisoni issued the following press release:

> "FOR IMMEDIATE RELEASE NEWS BULLETIN ALERT Re: JULY 4TH, 2005 WEEKEND NATIONAL DEMONSTRATION IN SUPPORT OF THE RECALL OF 30 MILLION DEFECTIVE FIRESTONE STEELTEX TIRES WHICH CAME AS STANDARD FACTORY EQUIPMENT ON FORD AND GMC LIGHT TRUCKS, SUVs, AMBULANCES & MOTOR HOMES.
>
> On February 26, 2004, NHTSA ordered the recall of 490,000 Firestone Steeltex tires which were manufactured in Joliette, Quebec, Canada, and which came as original equipment on Ford Excursions. There are still millions of defective tires manufactured at this plant which were not recalled, and we are fighting to get them recalled. Many ambulance companies in

Tires Across America

thirty-six (36) states have voluntarily removed the Firestone Steeltex tires from their ambulances due to safety concerns. Many of the failures occurred while transporting patients.

Two Petitions to the National Highway Traffic & Safety Administration have been filed demanding the recall of these allegedly defective tires.

On the fourth of July weekend, victims of Firestone Steeltex tire tread separations will display their tires on their front lawns across America with signs "Recall Defective Firestone Steeltex Tires."

The names, addresses, and telephone numbers of persons displaying defective tire recall signs will be supplied to you in the event you wish to interview them or photograph their tires.

Direct all questions to the Firestone Recall Campaign office at 626-440-1333 or check our website at www.firestonesteeltexclassaction.com."

In May, 2006, Lisoni & Lisoni issued the following press release:

"The safe tire alliance known as Tires across America exists to provide the motoring public an avenue to replace and be reimbursed for defective Firestone Steeltex R4S, R4SII and A/T tires.

On the fourth of July, Tires across America will accept claims for defective Firestone tire replacement costs and provide free assistance to all claimants who have been denied warranty replacement or reimbursement costs from Bridgestone/Firestone dealers or from the company's headquarters in Nashville, Tennessee on or before Independence Day.

For more details, just fax a request to the fourth of July Firestone Steeltex Challenge to 626-577-0310. A package will be mailed to you free immediately upon receipt of your faxed request. If you have no fax machine, just mail a request to P.O. Box 90965, Pasadena, CA 91109-0965.

Tires Across America hereby states its strong support for the Petition to Recall thirty-million Firestone Steeltex tires currently in service on 71 different model vehicles in the United States. 490,000 Firestone Steeltex A/T tires have already been recalled in Joliette, Canada and ambulance units in thirty-six states have voluntarily removed these tires after failures which caused injuries and deaths to patients and paramedics.

The Firestone Steeltex R4S, R4SII and A/T tires are no longer manufactured but those that are still on the road must be recalled so the death toll, now at 57, and the serious injuries toll, now at 161, does not continue to be a growing trend across the United States.

Hopefully, Bridgestone Firestone does the "right thing" before Independence Day so the Tires Across America volunteers in each of the 50 states can enjoy the fourth of July with their families and loved ones and no other people will become victims of the Firestone Steeltex tire failures."

On September 4, 2006, Tires Across America, through Lisoni & Lisoni, issued the following press release:

"BRIDGESTONE/FIRESTONE FACING ASIAN, CHINESE, PACIFIC RIM CUSTOMER BASE COLLAPSE-PLANTS CLOSING IN U.S. AND CHILE DROP PROFITS TO 68% IN FISCAL FIRST HALF OF 2006.

TRYING TO HIDE MASSIVE NUMBERS OF LEGAL PROBLEMS, BRIDGESTONE WAS SHOCKED WHEN A JAPANESE COPY OF THE JAPAN TIMES ON-LINE BROKE THE NEWS THAT WHAT WAS ONCE A SINGLE PERSONAL INJURY CLAIM LED TO THE RECALL OF WILDERNESS TIRES (28 MILLION), FIVE PETITIONS TO RECALL 30 MILLION STEELTEX

TIRES, THOUSANDS OF FIREHAWK AND DEULER TIRES TOGETHER WITH THE FAILED EFFORTS TO IMPROVE THE POTENZA TIRE IN ASIA, CHINA AND PACIFIC OCEAN CONSUMER BASES.

COST REDUCTION PROGRAM C-95 IS NOW PUBLIC. THIS FAILED ATTEMPT ON THE PART OF THE BRIDGESTONE CORPORATION TO SAVE TWO-BILLION DOLLARS IN MOUNTING CORPORATE DEBT LED TO THOUSANDS OF INJURIES AND DEATHS, BY REDUCING THE QUALITY OF MOST SAFETY COMPONENTS IN THEIR LINES OF TIRES.

WHEN BRIDGESTONE CORPORATION'S LABOR NEGOTIATION TACTICS FAILED WITH THE UNITED STATES STEELWORKERS REGARDING LABOR PRACTICES IN NIGERIA, THE FAILURE LED TO THE SHOCKING CLOSE OF BRIDGESTONE'S PLANT IN CHILE.

SEASONED STOCK INVESTORS ARE TRYING TO CAMOUFLAGE THEIR SELL OFF OF PORTFOLIO HOLDINGS OF BRIDGESTONE CORPORATION STOCK NOW DOWN OVER 600+ POINTS AFTER THE MAY 1, 2006 FILING OF THE PETITION TO RECALL THIRTYMILLION STEELTEX TIRES AND THE ADMISSION DURING A PLAINTIFFS' PRESS CONFERENCE THAT THOUSANDS MORE WILDERNESS TIRES MUST BE RECALLED AND THE COMPANY CANNOT MEET THE DEMAND FOR MORE REPLACEMENT TIRES.

TIRES ACROSS AMERICA RECOMMENDS STOCK ALERT!

SELL BRIDGESTONE CORPORATION STOCK IMMEDIATELY"

The Tires across America events produced thousands of complaints resulting from defective Firestone Steeltex tires suffering catastrophic tread separations which gave the Lisoni & Lisoni National Recall Campaign great credibility as a nationally recognized consumer advocacy organization.

Chapter XXIII

BRIDGESTONE/FIRESTONE: A COMPANY THAT LITERALLY HAS BLOOD ON ITS HANDS

"Slave labor equals human rights violations"

Firestone Natural Rubber Co. is a subsidiary of Bridgestone Americas, Inc. Head-quartered in Nashville, Tennessee. The company operates the largest contiguous (de facto slave labor) rubber plantation in the world, in Liberia, Africa.

In 1926, the Liberian government granted Firestone a 99 years lease for a million acres at a price of 6 cents per acre. Firestone also provided a $5 million loan at 7% interest to the government to pay the foreign debts it had, and to build a harbor needed by Firestone. The loan was given in exchange for complete authority over the government's revenues until the loan was repaid.

On June 6, 1990, during the First Liberian Civil War, the resistance group, National Patriotic Front of Liberia took over the Firestone plantation and evacuated U.S. personnel. In 1977, the company faced a number of violent protests, as its employees wanted better working conditions, better pay, and resettlement benefits.

Firestone struck up an alliance with the Liberian warlord, Charles Taylor. He used the rubber plantation as his base of operations in a civil war that ultimately killed 300,000 people.

"Frontline" producer, Marcel Gaviria, investigated Firestone's relationship with Charles Taylor and documented that between 1989 and 1992, Firestone struck a deal with the warlord and channeled millions of dollars to Taylor in exchange for being able to keep the profitable rubber plantation in operation.

The workers (de facto slave labor) accused the company of labor abuses, including exploitive child labor, which they claimed amounted to modern day slavery. Workers specifically claimed that Firestone's high daily quotas forced them to employ their own children, subjecting them to grueling and dangerous work conditions.

Eventually the chaos and the brutality of the civil war came to an end. Charles Taylor was tried in the International Court of the Hague.

The International Criminal Court (ICC) is a court of last resort for the prosecution of serious international crimes, including genocide, war crimes, and crimes against humanity. Its treaty, The Rome Statute, was adopted in July, 1998. The Court began work in 2003, following ad hoc tribunals set up in the 1990's to deal with atrocity crimes committed in the former Yugoslavia and Rwanda. Twenty years after the Rome Statute, the ICC has made significant headway in bringing global attention to accountability. Today, as human rights crisis's marked by international crimes continue to proliferate, its mandate has proven to be both more needed and more daunting. He was found "responsible for acts of terrorism, murder, rape, sexual slavery, cruel treatment, recruitment of child soldiers, enslavement and pillage". Charles Taylor is now serving a 50 year prison sentence.

The gripping PBS *Frontline* and *Pro Publico* investigation explosively exposed Firestone's secret deal making with the powerful Liberian strongman, Charles Taylor.

Its multi-year investigation which draws from de-classified diplomatic cables and court documents, paints a disturbing portrait of Firestone.

Warlord, Charles Taylor, was a charismatic figure, educated at a small American university in Massachusetts, landed a top job in the Liberian government before fleeing the country after being accused of embezzlement in the 1980's. Tracked down in the U.S., Chalres Taylor was sent to a Massachusetts jail – where he somehow escaped.

Charles Taylor went to Mexico and then to Libya, where he trained under Muammar Gaddafi. Soon, Taylor, hardened by military training and harboring mighty ambitions, was back in Liberia, raising a rebel army of his own.

In June 1990, warlord Charles Taylor's band of fighters – notoriously comprised of children, many of whom were on drugs, in costume, or wielding AK-47's – approached Firestone's plantation with demands for food, money and cars. Many of Firestone's enslaved laborers were killed but management executives fled unharmed.

With Firestone's top managers gone, Taylor and his forces assumed control of the plantation and made it an operations base. Firestone was keen to get the slave labor rubber plantation back, or at least resume operations there, according to the investigation. The site provided 40% of U.S. latex supply. Within months, Firestone began discussions with the warlord. At the time, Taylor had no formal power, but he controlled much of the country, a vast territory that many had taken to calling "Taylorland". By this time, he had also cemented his reputation as a ruthless warlord, a status that made him a controversial negotiating partner both within Firestone and beyond.

Taylor was anxious for Firestone to resume operations to: he saw the company as a source of credibility and cash. He privately (in a deal struck with Firestone executives in the jungle) welcomed Firestone back on the condition that it fire a top manager and "pay taxes" in Taylorland. Firestone paid $2.3 million dollars to the warlord, according to evidence unearthed by the *Frontline/Pro-Publico* team. The agreement for this had been typed out and signed on the guerrilla leader's stationary. During the early 90's, a period in which Firestone and warlord Taylor's rebel army co-habited the plantation, Taylor continued to use Firestone's one-million acre rubber plantation as he pleased. In October, 1992, the plantation became a staging ground for "Operation Octopus", Taylor's final bloody drive to power: the invasion of Monrovia, Liberia.

At least one U.S. diplomat who was serving in Liberia during those years of conflict comes down harshly on Firestone's secret dealings with Taylor. A former U.S. Diplomat, Gerry Rose, says he believes Firestone has <u>blood on its hands</u>. "I believe they facilitated a warlord in his insurrection and in the atrocities."

In an article authored by Christian Miller and Jonathan Jones (March 19, 2015), entititled "A Company that Literally has Blood on Its Hands" in the authoritative publication "Pacific Standard" revealed that in 1996, Firestone, one of the world's largest tire-makers, was locked in a grueling labor dispute with the United Steelworkers of America. The Union portrayed it as a struggle between blue-collar workers and a company that was aiming to slash the pay and benefits of its employees. Thousands of workers went on strike, and the Union mounted a consumer boycott of Firestone products and those of its Japanese owned corporate parent, Bridgestone. There were protest demonstrations to including "black flag" motorcycle brigade at the Nation's most famous auto race, the *Indianapolis 500*.

The Steelworkers – who had begun representing Firestone employees after a merger with another union, the United Rubber Workers, in 1995 – also began looking into the company's activities abroad, most notably its rubber operations in Liberia. With the help of private investigators, the Union uncovered evidence that in the early 1990's Firestone had been the source of money and logistical support for Charles Taylor, the notorious Liberian warlord whose violent bid for power had ensnared the country in a horrific civil war. The union then developed plans to use what it believed might have been <u>criminal conduct by Firestone</u> as leverage in the contract negotiations.

Plans were hatched to hold press conferences. A secret briefing was prepared for U.S. Vice-President, Al Gore. Importantly, there were also discussions about using the evidence of dealings with Charles Taylor to demand that Firestone permit the steelworkers to play an active role in monitoring labor standards in Liberia. The union's documents for the time suggest it saw a greater good in revealing Firestone's history with the warlord, Charles Taylor, - that doing so might make the company "accountable to the Liberian people and to the world," as the union stated in the introduction of the <u>43-page confidential report detailing their findings</u>. But the Steelworkers Union never made its findings public. Instead, it buried the investigation of Firestone's role in the Liberian civil war, and Firestone's actions remained secret for more than 20 years. It is not known if U.S. Vice-President, Al Gore, ever saw the confidential report.

Just two weeks after the union completed its inquiry, Firestone and the Steelworks met in confidential negotiations, and soon reached a deal. The Union won concessions on pay and benefits. But any formal notion of improving working conditions in Liberia was abandoned, and Firestone's dealings with warlord, Charles Taylor, would not be aired until a *Pro Publica* and PBS *Frontline* investigation in late 2014.

The Steelworkers would not comment at all – on their investigation into Firestone's activities in Liberia, what role the investigation had played in the negotiations, or why the Union had decided to keep the information secret. In an e-mail, Wayne Ranick, a spokesman for the Steelworkers, said the union could not comment on the matter because key leaders from that time period, including the Union President and General Counsel, are now dead. Other figures in the investigation had retired.

Does Bridgestone/Firestone have blood on its hands from the manner in which it ran its Liberian rubber plantation in the past and today? The Lisoni & Lisoni response is "Res ipsa loquitor" – latin for "The facts speak for themselves".

Chapter XXIV

CONCLUSION

"Never Have So Few Done So Much For So Many"

The major steps taken in furtherance of the Lisoni & Lisoni National Recall Campaign from August 12, 2002 to the present have resulted in the following:

a. A NHTSA recall of 490,000 Firestone "Steeltex" A/T tires, (third largest in U.S. history) on February 26, 2004;
b. A nationwide "All-Points Bulletin" alert to all ambulance companies in the U.S. resulting in ambulance companies in thirty-six states voluntarily replacing the Firestone "Steeltex" tires from their ambulances due to safety concerns;
c. Bridgestone/Firestone's addition of the nylon cap in 2003/2004 over the steel belts in a failed attempt to prevent the tread separations in the Firestone Steeltex tires;
d. The construction of an information website to disseminate and make available all known information about the defective Firestone "Steeltex" line of tires. http://www.firestonesteeltexclassaction.com
e. Bridgestone/Firestone no longer manufactures these Steeltex tires as of 2005, after producing 30 million of them over a 13 year period;

Conclusion

f. 3500 independent dealers no longer sell Firestone Steeltex tires;
g. The formation of a nationwide movement known as "Tires Across America" (July 4, 2005) dedicated to informing those using Firestone "Steeltex" tires on their vehicles of the propensity to suffer tread separations;
h. A state and national federal court class action complaint (class not certified) requesting the recall of eleven million Firestone "Steeltex" tire models still in service.

By BOOTIE COSGROVE-MATHER / CBS/AP / February 26, 2004, 4:55 PM

490,000 Steeltex Tires Recalled

bridgestone/firestone / AP

Bridgestone/Firestone announced a recall Thursday of about 490,000 16-inch Steeltex tires linked to sport utility vehicle crashes that killed five people. About 297,000 of the Steeltex LT265/75R16 Load Range D tires are on the road in the United States and 20,000 more internationally, the company said.

"We haven't identified a specific problem with the tires," company spokesman Dan MacDonald said. "The data suggested that there's an issue, and the decision was made that instead of having a long drawn-out investigation to figure out if there is a problem, let's just step up and replace the tires."

The tiremaker said it learned two months ago that there were six crashes involving SUVs with Steeltex tires. It said it reported the information to the National Highway Traffic Safety Administration, as required, and announced the voluntary recall.

The safety administration first noticed a pattern of crashes and blowouts with Steeltex tires, federal officials said.

CBS News Correspondent Sharyl Attkisson reports customers have complained of catastrophic tread separation and other dangers.

The tires were made in Canada for use on Ford Excursions from 2000 to 2002 and some early 2003 models.

The tires are among those that have been the subject of a **CBS News** investigation. The government has investigated them twice before, but cleared them for use.

The recall comes 3½ years after the company began a recall of 17 million ATX, ATX II and Wilderness AT tires. More than 200 people were reported killed and hundreds more injured in rollover crashes after the tread on those tires separated. The company has spent an estimated $1.5 billion on that recall, including the settlement of dozens of lawsuits.

A current lawsuit accuses the tire manufacturer of using substandard materials to make a Steeltex model not covered by the recall. A hearing is scheduled next month to determine whether the suit should become a class-action case. The lawsuit seeks at least $1 billion in reimbursement for motorists and a recall of Steeltex R4S, R4SII and A/T tires.

CBS News has documented problems in other Steeltex tires - about 41 million Steeltex tires of various models have been produced and are standard equipment on 71 types of vehicles, including pickup trucks, SUVs and recreational and emergency vehicles. However, safety officials say they see no need for a wider recall.

U.S. Transportation Secretary Norman Y. Mineta praised the company's decision to recall the tires, saying it "shows that our system of safety standards is working."

© 2004 CBS Interactive Inc. All Rights Reserved. This material may not be published, broadcast, rewritten, or redistributed. The Associated Press contributed to this report.

Share / Tweet / Reddit / Flipboard / Email

Featured in U.S.

Robert Wagner called a "person of interest" in Natalie Wood death

For the first time since reopening the investigation into the mysterious death of the legendary actress, investigators speak out to "48 Hours"

CBS News honored with duPont-Columbia Awards

"CBS This Morning" co-host Gayle King co-hosted the Alfred I. duPont-Columbia University Awards Tuesday honoring outstanding contributions to journalism

Latest from CBS News

04 Olympian's tweet says Team USA chose flagbearer "dishonorably"

05 Trump signs budget deal, ending government shutdown

From "60 Minutes"

"60 Minutes" Presents: On the "60 Minutes" Menu

50 years of "60 Minutes"

Leaning Tower of San Francisco

Ex-British spy on leading a "double life" as a famous author

Kabul under siege while America's longest war rages on

The American scientist who's seen North Korea's nuclear secrets

Is Portland still Portlandia?

RT's editor-in-chief on election meddling, being labeled Russian propaganda

Predicting crime in Chicago

Combat veterans coming home with CTE

237

Chapter XXV

AN OPEN MESSAGE TO BRIDGESTONE CORPORATION

"Those Who Do Not Learn From History Are Doomed to Repeat It"

In the years following the NHTSA recall of 490,000 Firestone Steeltex tires, Bridgestone/Firestone suffered several more tire recalls, including but not limited to:

1. On August 26, 2004, Bridgestone Corporation recalled 27,200 Dueler A/T 693 tires;
2. On November 7, 2007, Bridgestone Corporation recalled 2101 Dueler H/T 684II tires;
3. On August 22, 2008, Bridgestone Corporation recalled an additional 2100 Dueler H/T 684II tires;
4. October 24, 2008, Bridgestone/Firestone recalled 162,251 Firestone FR380 tires;
5. On June 29, 2009, Bridgestone/Firestone recalled an additional 127,183 FR380 tires;
6. On November 8, 2013, Bridgestone Corporation issued a voluntary recall of 1.2 million tires worldwide, including more than forty different types of truck and bus tires, the largest tire recall recorded in Japan's history;

An Open Message to Bridgestone Corporation

7. On January 29, 2016, Bridgestone Americas Tire Operations (BATO) recalled 35,907 Firestone FS561 tires.
8. On May 6, 2016, Bridgestone Americas Tire Operations recalled approximately 2,900 Firestone FR 710 and Firestone Champion Fuel Fighter replacement tires.
9. On September 6, 2018, Bridgestone Corporation recalled approximately 2700 certain all position, wide based radial commercial truck tires.

Bridgestone Corporation consistently violated civil and criminal laws and ignored the safety of its customers. To wit:

   a. Bridgestone Corporation, on September 15, 2011, agreed to Plead Guilty to Participating in <u>Conspiracies</u> to Rig Bids and Bribe Government Officials, and <u>agreed to pay</u> a <u>criminal fine</u> of $28 million;
   b. On February 13, 2014, Bridgestone Corporation Agreed to Plead Guilty to Price Fixing on Automobile Parts Installed in U.S. Cars and paid a fine in the amount of $425 million dollars.
   c. On July 7, 2016, the California Bureau of Automotive Repairs reached a settlement in an action where its shops were accused of a conspiracy to defraud and made untrue or misleading statements or records during undercover operations conducted by the BAR between 2013 and 2015;
   d. On May 15, 2018, a female employee, of more than thirty years, filed suit against Bridgestone/Firestone in Lavergne, Tennessee, in federal court alleging that she was sexually harassed and then fired on trumped-up charges.

<u>Absent government or judicial intervention, if Bridgestone/ Firestone Corporation does not abandon its use of substandard component parts and does not take immediate remedial measures in its tire manufacturing process, and does not terminate its unlawful business practices or cease its human rights violations at its rubber plantation in Liberia,</u>

__Africa, the end result will be a multi-national corporation with manufacturing plants all over the world, populated by thousands of employees who make millions of tires, that nobody wants to buy!__

The National Firestone Steeltex Tire Recall Campaign proved that the Firestone Steeltex tires <u>were defective</u> and did subject the American motoring public to an unreasonable risk of tire failures. Lisoni & Lisoni accomplished their goal of removing these defective tires from the roads and highways of the United States and countries of Western Europe. They made the ultimate sacrifice in that they did not get paid, but they proved that "it was not about the money, but about saving lives."

The Bridgestone/Firestone Steeltex National Recall Campaign was the largest privately funded tire recall campaign in the history of the United States. Wilderness was recalled as a result of a Congressional investigation. Steeltex was recalled as a result of the imagination, dedication, and hard work of two lawyers in California.

"Where the Rubber Meets the Road" is the story of their sacrifice and heroic acts that saved the lives of thousands of motorists using the roads and highways of the United States.

Chapter XXVI

THE PERSONAL TOLL ON LISONI & LISONI

"Great Victories Require Great Sacrifices"

The firm of Lisoni & Lisoni had always maintained a successful law practice, fighting for plaintiffs against Fortune 500 corporate defendants that manufacture defective products. After Lisoni & Lisoni filed the class action, Bridgestone/Firestone embarked on a course of conduct in furtherance of their Conspiracy of Death & Destruction, to destroy the firm of Lisoni & Lisoni.

In January, 2003, John Gamhauf, President of the Bridgestone/Firestone Replacement Division, filed several disciplinary charges against Joseph Lisoni, Esq. and Gail Lisoni, Esq., seeking their disbarment for allegedly making false statements at their first Press Conference at the National Press Club in Washington, DC.

Lisoni & Lisoni retained Michael Gerner, Esq. to represent them before the State Bar at a cost of $15,000. After providing all necessary documents and evidence to prove that the charges were unfounded, the charges were dismissed. Joseph Gamhauf of Bridgestone/Firestone attempted a second time to file more charges, by contacting Governor Arnold Schwartzenegger, and asking for his intervention. The Governor declined and those charges were never re-filed.

Lisoni & Lisoni assisted the United Steelworkers in their strike against Bridgestone Firestone, offering the whistle-blowers to them, which helped in obtaining a new contract.

The developments in this recall campaign were of sufficient interest to the nationwide product liability laws, consumer protection laws and the auto and rubber industry, such that there have been over 3,000 separate and distinct reported articles in over 300 daily newspapers, including but not limited to: the Wall Street Journal, the Associated Press, the Nashville Tennessean, USA Today, New York and Los Angeles Times, Washington Post, Chicago Sun Tribune, Minnesota Star, Dallas Morning Star, Miami Herald, and the leading international tire publication, the Rubber & Plastic News.

In fact, Rubber & Plastic News declared the Lisoni & Lisoni National Recall Campaign regarding the Firestone Steeltex tires to be the "Tenth most significant story in all of 2003" (the fifth most important story in the rubber products industry).

Although Bridgestone/Firestone had yet to take a case through trial, it acted in furtherance of the conspiracy by blocking any income to Lisoni & Lisoni. The firm was involved in several actions in Colorado, Georgia, Florida, Alabama and Texas, and had provided assistance to the lead plaintiffs' counsel and was expecting consulting fees.

Bridgestone/Firestone's counsel from Holland & Knight, Colin Smith, Esq. advised the individual law firms that Bridgestone/Firestone would not settle with them unless they agreed that Lisoni & Lisoni would not share in any attorney fees. Joe started borrowing money to finance the National Recall Campaign.

The personal toll on Lisoni & Lisoni was devastating. Joe was always responsible for the finances of the law firm, and as the pressures increased so did his bad decisions. He was "throwing good money after bad. . ." The financial pressures finally forced us to sell our two-million dollar dream home in Pasadena, California, and move to a rented townhouse in Pasadena.

Joe's physical and mental condition deteriorated substantially to the point where he could not manage his affairs, and caused him to make some bad decisions which resulted in a two-year suspension from the California State Bar, which was the only disciplinary action against him in 40 years of practicing law. He suffered from severe depression after the traumatic turn in our lives, which caused him to suffer a physical and mental breakdown. After thirty-six years together, our relationship became so compromised that we separated and were divorced in 2008.

We were forced to file for bankruptcy in 2008.

In 2009, Joe embarked on a rehabilitation campaign with the full support of Gail and used his struggles to draw attention to mental illness. He began by walking daily, increasing his walk to ten miles a day. Then he started swimming at the YMCA in Santa Ynez, California. daily. He began competing at United States Senior Swimming meets and has won six medals to date. He granted interviews to newspapers about his swimming and always stated that he was swimming to bring attention to mental illness and remove the stigma attached to it. In 2016, he competed in the World Senior Games in St. George, Utah and he won the bronze medal in the 800 meter freestyle for his age group of 65-69 years.

In the years following our divorce, we became good friends and began to re-invent our individual and inter-personal relationship – a circumstance that happily continues on today!

Chapter XXVII

THE PLAYERS – WHO THEY WERE AND WHAT ARE THEY DOING NOW

"All the World is a Stage"

The Advocate	A California legal publication that published an article informing the lawyers in California that tire dealers have a post-sale duty to warn prior purchasers of its tires and automobiles of defects, discovered after the time the vehicle and tires were purchased, currently serves over 50,000 attorneys in California—which is the largest legal market in the United States.
Anonymous	Revealed Firestone's failure to report to NHTSA Steeltex tire failures handled by company owned stores.

The Players – Who They Were and What are They Doing Now

Associated Press	News Agency that covered the Firestone Steeltex Tire Recall Campaign from the first day the national recall campaign began up until the recall of 490,000 Firestone Steeltex tires on February 26, 2004; today, it is an American Not-for-profit multi-national news agency headquartered in New York City, New York; published in more than 1700 newspapers, in addition to more than 5,000 television and radio stations. The AP operates more than 200 news bureaus in more than 100 countries.
Sharyl Attkisson	CBS Evening News Correspondent who conducted the investigation of the Firestone Steeltex tires resigned from CBS on March 10, 2014 where she held the position of Washington, DC correspondent. She was nominated for an Emmy Award for her investigative reporting of the Bridgestone/Firestone tire fiasco. She now is a five-time Emmy Award Investigative Reporter and recipient of the prestigious Edward R. Murrow Award of three books and hosts a public affairs television program – "Full Measure

	with Sheryl Attkisson" in Washington, DC, which is viewed by 45 million households in the U.S. on Sunday mornings.
Diana Becker	President, Capital Administrators Insurance Company provided proof of hundreds of Firestone Steeltex tire failures.
Charles Bennett, Esq.	General Counsel of General Motors (1971); after the deposition he returned to his office at the General Motors headquarters in Michigan.
Steve Beretsky	NHTSA employee who denied the Wilderness Recall petition; subsequently, he denied three petitions from Lisoni & Lisoni and closed all investigations without issuing any recall recommendations for Firestone Steeltex tires.
Ken Berger, Esq.,	Attorney for Bill Orr in his Wrongful termination case filed in the state of Tennessee against Bridgestone/Firestone; he continues to practice law in Murfreesboro, Tennessee.
Bush Bernard	Reporter for The Tennessean covering the Firestone Steeltex Tire national recall campaign; authored two front-page articles, which contributed to Bridgestone/Firestone

The Players – Who They Were and What are They Doing Now

	recalling 490,000 Steeltex tires manufactured in Canada; he was terminated shortly after the front page stories were published. He continued to pursue a career as an automotive industry journalist in the four years following his termination. He passed away at age 58 on August 1, 2008.
Howard Breuer	Reporter, Pasadena Star News. He published the first article announcing the filing of the national class action by Lisoni & Lisoni. He left the Pasadena Star News in 2005 and now handles media relations for Equinox Media, a multi-faceted media outlet located in Beverly Hills, California.
President George W. Bush	The United States Secret Service removed Firestone Steeltex tires from the President's Ford 250 trucks used on his ranch in Texas and the Chevrolet Suburbans used to transport him from Camp David to the White House; he lives today in the state of Texas.
Business Wire	An International News Agency that published dozens of press releases prepared by Lisoni & Lisoni regarding the Firestone Steeltex Recall Campaign; it was founded in 1961 and

	currently disseminates full text press releases from companies and organizations worldwide.
Robert Butterworth	Attorney General of the State of Florida, sued Firestone with five other states for breach of warranty and unfair business practices; currently he is in the private practiceof law in the state of Florida.
Mickey Capley	Former Firestone employee, who was our expert in the Firestone Steeltex recall Campaign; on July 26 and 27, 2004; he was part of the team who inspected damaged tires at Marengo, Indiana and Akron, Ohio to determine their failure mode; he now lives in Tennessee.
Joseph Caringella	Resident of Lake Havesu, Arizona. A Firestone Steeltex Class Action member who suffered Steeltex tread separation and his claim was denied by Bridgestone/Firestone paralegal, Norma Davis.
John Carr, Jr.	A plaintiff in personal injury action against Bridgestone Firestone, Inc.; lost in a summary judgment because he allegedly did not have a qualified expert regarding his alleged defect in the Steeltex tire that exploded on his vehicle; he continues to live

The Players – Who They Were and What are They Doing Now

	in Birmingham, Alabama and owns and operates Coastal Consulting & Products, which works in the field of oil refracting and power plant installations.
Chicago Sun Tribune	National News Print Media Company which produced several articles about the Firestone Steeltex tire recall Campaign; it was founded in 1844 and has a circulation of 470, 548 readers
Edith Chung, PhD,	Psychologist retained by Lisoni & Lisoni to travel to China to document injuries and damages suffered by the Chinese doctors; she continues to practice psychology in Los Angeles, California.
CNN	Television, all news all the time station, which covered the Lisoni & Lisoni Steeltex National Tire Recall campaign; it is owned today by its founder, Ted Turner and is available in 100 million U.S. households.
Joan Claybrooke	Director of Public Citizen, founded by Ralph Nader, and formerr head of the National Highway Transportation & Safety Administration; strongly advocated for the recall of the Firestone Steeltex line of tiresat a meeting with NHTSA;

	characterized Firestone's conduct as "criminal"; she announced her retirement from Public Citizen on December 9, 2008, after holding her position for 27 years.
Consumer Reports	Nationwide publication that rates the quality of products on the market in the United States; interviewed Joe Lisoni about the defects in the Firestone Steeltex tires; it continues to be dedicated to unbiased product testing, consumer research and advocacy with a circulation of 3,800,000 readers.
Continental Carbon Co.	Manufactured the defective carbon black, sold to Firestone, which allows the bonding between the rubber and steel cords, which resulted in the manufacture of defective Steeltex tires.
Aubert Y. Coran	Tire expert retained by P.A.C.E. to testify as to the dangers incident to using substandard carbon black in the manufacturing of automobile tires like the Firestone Steeltex tire line; currently he is an award winning American Scientist noted for his contributions to the development of rubber products.
Dallas Morning Star	National News Print Media Company which produced

The Players – Who They Were and What are They Doing Now

	several articles about the Firestone Steeltex tire recall Campaign; it is a daily newspaper serving the Dallas/ Fort Worth area of Texas with a circulation of 271,000 daily subscribers.
Norma Y. Davis	Paralegal for Bridgestone/ Firestone, Inc. who denied all warranty claims submitted to the two companies.
Kathleen C. DeMeter	Director of the National Highway Transportation & Safety Administration (NHTSA) Office of Defects Investigations, Department of Transportation; she continues in her position to the present time
Joseph Digange	President of First Los Angeles Bank in Los Angeles, California, arranged lunch for Joe Lisoni with Charles Manatt, Esq., National Democratic Party Finance Chairman; after leaving First Los Angeles Bank he continued on in the field of financial institutions.
Congressman David Dingel	Member of the Subcommittee of the U.S. House of Representatives Commerce, Trade and Consumer Protection; questioned John Lampe re "C-95" Cost Reduction Program at the T.R.E.A.D. Act Implementation hearing; he remained in the

	U.S. House of Representatives until January 3, 2015 - serving for sixty years. President Barack Obama awarded him the Presidential Medal of Freedom in 2014.
Clarence Ditlow, III	Director of *Center for Auto Safety* in Washington, DC, founded by Ralph Nader; advocated the Recall of the Firestone Sreeltex tires before NHTSA continued to be regarded as America's foremost advocate for automotive safety; until his death in November, 2016 from cancer at the age of seventy-two.
Thomas M. Dodson	Forensic tire expert hired by NHTSA to examine tires stored at Marengo, Indiana; he gained an international reputation in the field of tire forensics until his death on October 21, 2010, in Akron, Ohio.
Joseph Drexler, PhD,	P.A.C.E. Union Special projects Director re: Continental Carbon strike and major supporter of the Firestone Steeltex Tire recall Campaign; currently he is an adjunct professor of International Labor Relations and Global Economy at the Joseph Kobel School of International Studies at the University of Colorado in Denver.

The Players – Who They Were and What are They Doing Now

Larry Elkins	Plant Manager of Bridgestone/ Firestone, Inc. in Lavergne, Tennessee; introduced "C-95" Cost Reduction Program to Bridgestone Firestone employees.
Mark Emkes	Became CEO of Bridgestone Americas Holdings, Inc. when John Lampe retired; he continues as CEO and President.
Harvey Firestone	Founder of Firestone Tire & Rubber Co., 1900; died February 7, 1938 in Miami Beach, Florida.
Robert Fisher	Owner, Fisher & Associates, Public Relations expert who produced the nationwide media public information campaign against Firestone as it applied to the Steeltex tire line; he continues in the field of public relations & consulting in Westlake Village, California.
John Gamhauf	President of Bridgestone/ Firestone Replacement Division in Lavergne, Tennessee; he has left Bridgestone/ /Firestone and today is promoting a new point of sale consulting company for the tire industry in the U.S.
Michael Gerner, Esq.	Attorney retained by Lisoni & Lisoni to defend them against charges brought against them

	at the California State Bar by Joseph Gamhauf of Bridgestone/Firestone, Inc.; he continued to practice law until he retired in 2015.
Golden Hands Auto Body Shop	A shop in Pasadena, California where the subject Ford Club van with the defective tire was stored; it is still in business repairing damaged vehicles.
Alan Paul Gooding, Esq.	Attorney colleague of Joe & Gail Lisoni who participated in the strategy that produced the settlement of the case involving the 10 Chinese doctors. Currently enjoying retirement in California
Greenman Technologies	Industrial firm used by BFS to shred defective tires in violation of Court Order; as of August, 2002 it is now American Power Group Corporation.
Jack Greenwood	Resident of Red Bluff, California; Firestone Steeltex Class Action member who suffered Steeltex tread separation and claim was denied by Norma Davis.
William O. Hagerty	Independent tire expert; acted as Lisoni & Lisoni's forensic tire consultant throughout the entire Firestone Steeltex National tire recall campaign; currently he concentrates his

The Players – Who They Were and What are They Doing Now

	expertise in tire standards for retail sales outlets, recently testifying against Walmart in 2012, resulting in a $27.5 million dollar jury verdict.
Danny Hakin	New York Times Reporter covering the Firestone Steeltex National Tire Recall Campaign; currently he is in charge of the New York Times London Bureau.
Lela Helms	Victim of a tread separation of a Firestone Steeltex tire; she sued Bridgestone/Firestone, Inc. for her injuries – a fractured neck; she passed away several years ago.
Carl Hinsey	Resident of South bend, Indiana; Firestone Steeltex Class Action member who suffered Steeltex tread separation and claim was denied by Bridgestone/Firestone Paralegal, Norma Davis; he passed away in 2005.
Alan Hogan	Former employee of Bridgestone/Firestone who agreed to testify as a "whistleblower" in the Firestone Steeltex National Recall Campaign. On July 26 and 27, 2004, he was part of the team who inspected damaged tires in Akron, Ohio that suffered tread separations to determine

	the mode of failure; today he operates an auto body repair shop in Wilson, North Carolina.
Holland & Knight	Defense attorneys for Defendant Bridgestone/Firestone, Inc. in class action; 1100 attorneys in twenty-one offices throughout the United States and around the world.
Shoyico Ishibosho	Founder of Bridgestone Corporation, 1931; died December 11, 1976.
Jay Jenkins	Resident of Lake Havesu, Arizona; Firestone Steeltex National Class Action member who suffered Steeltex tread separation and claim was denied by Norma Davis, Paralegal of Bridgestone Firestone, Inc; he is an independent insurance broker in Phoenix, Arizona;
Ken Johnson	Spokesman for Rep. W. J. "Billy" Tauzin (R-La) Chairman of the House Commerce Committee investigating Firestone's Wilderness tires; after Congressman Tauzin's retirement he was employed by private industries and on April 9, 2013 he was hired by the Solar Energy Industries Association in Washington, DC.

The Players – Who They Were and What are They Doing Now

Paul Kalpheke	Videographer at the Marengo, Indiana and Akron, Ohio inspections; he also provided the necessary lighting in the Marengo cave.
Alan J. Kam, Esq.	Formerly employed by NHTSA as an in house legal expert with the office of Defects Investigations; today, he is the Director of "Highway Traffic & Safety, LLC" in Bethesda, Maryland, that acts as consultants on federal motor vehicle safety issues as they relate to NHTSA.
Christine Karbowiak	Bridgestone/Firestone, Inc. spokesperson; currently she is the Chief Administrative Officer of Bridgestone of Americas Holdings, Inc since April 1, 2010.
John Lampe	Chairman, President & C.E.O. of Bridgestone Americas Holding, Inc.; he retired on March 30, 2004, ending a thirty-year career in the tire business.
Greg Landtbom	Lisoni & Lisoni staff member, and twin brother of Gail Lisoni, who participated in the tire inspections in Marengo, Indiana and Akron, Ohio; currently he owns Greg's.

	Glass which specializes in the installation of "old glass" in San Francisco Victorian homes
Frank Larrango	Resident of Palmdale, California; Firestone Steeltex National Class Action member who suffered Steeltex tread separation and claim was denied by Bridgestone/ Firestone Paralegal, Norma Davis.
Arnold "Doug" Larson, Esq.	Attorney in the firm of Iverson, Yoakum, Papiano & Hatch, representing Bridgestone/ Firestone, Inc. in the lawsuit brought in Los Angeles by Chinese doctors; He hired Mark Pearson, Esq. to take twenty depositions taken in China in February/March, 2002;
Roger Littell	One of the two leading plaintiffs in the national class action to recall all Firestone Steeltex tires in use on vehicles in the U.S. and Canada and countries of Western Europe; he currently lives in Yucca Valley and used to transport veterans to military installations in California. He retired in 2015 and is still a steward of the SCCA racing organization.

The Players – Who They Were and What are They Doing Now

Jack H. Loar	Bridgestone/Firestone Director of Process Engineering Development; implemented "C-95 Cost Reduction Program at Bridgestone/Firestone plants in Lavergne, Tennessee.
Los Angeles Times	National News Print Media Company which produced several articles about the Firestone Steeltex National Tire Recall Campaign; it is published in Los Angeles, California with a circulation of 600,449 readers.
Greg Magno	NHTSA engineering expert in charge of processing the Lisoni & Lisoni tire recall petitions, including the three petitions filed by them; he attended the inspection of the defective Firestone Steeltex tires in Akron, Ohio.
Dan MacDonald	Spokesman for Bridgestone America's Holding Company and Bridgestone/Firestone North American Tire during the Firestone Steeltex National Tire Recall Campaign; he left Bridgestone/Firestone and is the Tennessee State Director of "Best Buddies International," the largest organization dedicated to the social isolation of millions of people with intellectual and developmental disabilities.

Charles "Chuck" Manatt, Esq.	Founder and Senior partner of the firm of Manatt, Phelps Rothenberg & Tunney (now Manatt, Phelps & Phillips), Los Angeles; Chairman of the National Democratic Finance Council; introduced Joe Lisoni to Washington, DC politics; remained in Democratic politics and became National Democratic Party Chairman. He died in July, 2001 from complications from a stroke suffered after surgery.
Caroline E. Mayer	Washington Post Reporter; wrote article 1-10-02, criticizing NHTSA for seriously flawed data system; she continues to write articles focusing on marketing scams and product safety.
Tim Morris	Author of Letter to the Editor of Rubber & Plastic News on 5-19-2003 criticizing the publication of "An Open Letter to the Industry" prepared by Lisoni & Lisoni.
Miami Herald	National News Print Media Company which produced several articles about the Firestone Steeltex tire recall Campaign; it is published in Doral, Florida with a circulation of 176,000 readers.

The Players – Who They Were and What are They Doing Now

Norman Y. Minetta	Former Secretary for the National Highway Transportation & Safety Administration; he retired in June, 2006; he now has joined L & L Energy, Inc. as Vice-Chairman, in Seattle, Washington, which operates coal mines in China.
Miles Moore	Senior correspondent for Rubber & Plastic News, the publication that covered all aspects of the Firestone Steeltex Recall Campaign; today he covers federal regulatory affairs, Congressional action, the White House and Supreme Court activities as they relate to the tire and rubber industries for Rubber & Plastic News in Washington, DC.
Minnesota Star	National News Print Media Company which produced several articles about the Firestone Steeltex tire recall Campaign; currently it has a circulation of well over 288,315 daily readers.

Ralph Nader, Esq.	Author of "*Unsafe at Any Speed*" which created the doctrine of "crashworthiness" of automobiles; Founder of the Center for Auto Safety in Washington, DC and *Public Citizen*, in Washington, DC, created to protect the consumers of America from dangerous and defective products; he continues today as a nationally renowned consumer advocate.
Richard Nagarede, Esq.	Vanderbilt Law professor consulted by Bush Bernard of The Tennessean regarding the significance of the class certification process in the national class action being litigated in Indio, California, before Judge Christopher Sheldon; he passed away in 2011.
Nan Yuan Hotel	Located in Ningbo, China. Lisoni & Lisoni conducted twenty depositions in twenty-one days in action for damages for ten Chinese doctors, Resulting from a tread separation on 7-30-00 on W/B I-115 in California; currently rated as a four-star hotel.

Nashville Tennessean	Newspaper printed front page story about Steeltex tires on 2-22-04 4 days prior to 490,000 tire recall on 2-26-04 and a front-page story the day after the recall notice on 2-27-04; it is published in Nashville, Tennessee with a circulation of 100,825 readers; known as The Tennessean.
National Class Action Reporter	A legal publication that reported all aspects of the Firestone Steeltex National Class Action filed in Superior Court in Indio, California; it continues today to enjoy a countrywide readership.
National Press Club	Professional organization and business center for journalists, founded on March 12, 1908 and located in Washington, DC; today it is the most prestigious Press Club in the U.S.
NHTSA	National Highway, Traffic & Safety Administration is an agency of the Executive Branch of the U.S. Government charged with writing and enforcing federal motor vehicle regulations, having an annual budget of $815 million dollars.
New York Times	National News Print Media Company which produced several articles about the

	Bridgestone/Firestone Steeltex National Tire Recall Campaign.
Paul O'Dell	Resident of Glendale, Arizona; Firestone Steeltex Class Action member who suffered Steeltex tread separation and whose claim was denied by Bridgestone/Firestone Paralegal, Norma Davis.
Masatoshi Ono	Chairman, President & C.E.O. of Bridgestone/Firestone, Inc.; ordered implementation of "C-95" cost reduction program in memo to Firestone V.P, John Lampe; the first perpetrator of the Bridgestone/Firestone Conspiracy of Death and Destruction; he resigned as CEO after the Wilderness tire recall.
William (Bill) Orr	A twenty-five year employee of Firestone, who was our expert in the Firestone Steeltex National Tire Recall Campaign; was terminated from Firestone when he pointed out the dangers associated with the C-95 cost reduction program as a "whistleblower" and was falsely charged with misappropriation of funds from Bridgestone/Firestone, but was eventually exonerated; he is now retired and living happily in Murfreesboro, Tennessee.

The Players – Who They Were and What are They Doing Now

P.A.C.E. Union	Plastic, Allied-Industrial, Chemical & Energy Union of 300,000 members supported the Lisoni & Lisoni national Firestone Steeltex Recall Campaign; in January, 2005 it merged with the United Steelworkers of America and it is now a part of the largest labor union in the U.S.
Mark Pearson, Esq.	Attorney in the firm of Iverson, Yoakum, Papiano & Hatch, representing Bridgestone/Firestone, Inc. in the lawsuit brought by Chinese doctors resulting from accident of 7-30-2000; he currently practices law in San Francisco, California.
James Pederle, Esq.	U.S. Government attorney in charge of State of Illinois grand jury investigation of Bridgestone/Firestone regarding violations of the T.R.E.A.D. Act; the investigation ended without any criminal charges being filed.
LouAnn Pleasant	One of two lead plaintiffs named in the class action against Bridgestone/Firestone, Inc., filed in Indio, CA
Jeffrey Quandt	Present at the Lisoni & Lisoni presentation before NHTSA in May, 2003; currently he is the

	Chief of the Vehicle Control Division in the NHTSA Office of Defects Investigations.
Dwight Radeke	Resident of Boise, Idaho; Bridgestone/Firestone Steeltex National Class Action member who suffered a Steeltex tread separation and whose claim was denied by Bridgestone/Firestone Paralegal, Norma Davis.
Dan Rather	CBS Evening News Anchor that together with Sharyl Attkisson reported on the investigation of the Steeltex tires in conjunction with Lisoni & Lisoni; remained as Anchor of CBS Evening News until March 9, 2005. He left the network entirely in 2006 after working for CBS for forty-four years. Currently, he is the anchor of the television news magazine "Dan Rather Reports."
William Robbins	Resident of Walnut Creek, California Firestone Steeltex National Class Action member who suffered Steeltex tread separation and whose claim was denied by Bridgestone/Firestone Paralegal, Norma Davis.

The Players – Who They Were and What are They Doing Now

Enid Robinson, Esq.	Attorney for the National Highway Transportation & Safety Administration (NHTSA); participated in the presentation on 5-7-03 to reveal the results of the tires manufactured pursuant to "C-95" Cost Reduction Program, in particular the Firestone Steeltex tire; she is still employed in the legal department of NHTSA.
John Rousellot	U.S. Congressman who opposed Joe Lisoni in his Campaign for Congress, 1980; he left Congress in 1982 and was a Lobbyist until his death in May, 2003.
Jeffrey W. Runge, M.D.	Administrator of the National Highway Transportation & Safety Administration (NHTSA); in 2005, he was appointed the Chief Medical Officer of the Department of Homeland Security and was confirmed again by the Senate in 2007 as the founding Assistant Secretary for Health Affairs at the Department of Homeland Security.
George Rios	A thirty-year employee of Firestone who testified as a Whistleblower against Bridgestone/Firestone with regard to the National Steeltex Tire Recall Campaign.

Keith Romig	Director of Public & International Affairs for the P.A.C.E. Union; he appeared at the Press Conference at National Press Club on Nov, 15, 2002, endorsing the Firestone Steeltex National Tire Recall Campaign; he left the P.A.C.E. Union and is now a consultant in the areas of budget appropriations and safety products.
San Francisco Chronicle	California News Print Media Company which produced several articles about the Firestone Steeltex National Tire Recall Campaign; it is published in San Francisco, California with a circulation of 164,820 readers.
Judge Christopher Sheldon	Indio, California Superior Court Judge, who presided over the Bridgestone/Firestone National Class Action designed to recall all Steeltex tires in use around the entire U.S. and Canada; On April 5, 2009, he agreed to accept a censure, resign from the bench and never seek judicial office again. Today, he is practicing law in California.
Saul Solomon	Bridgestone/Firestone, Inc. General Counsel in the United States; office in Cleveland, Ohio during the pendency of

The Players – Who They Were and What are They Doing Now

	the national recall campaign; in 2016 he joined the law firm of Klein, Bussell, PLLC, in Cleveland, Ohio.
Honorable Christina A. Snyder	Federal Court Judge, Los Angeles, California, presiding over class action; she continues to handle class action cases in the Federal Court for the Central District of California.
Squire Sanders & Dempsey	Defense attorneys for Defendant Bridgestone Corp. in class action; 1300 attorney in 40 offices around the world; it is now known as Squire Patton Boggs.
Congressman William Tauzin	Co-chairman of the Senate & House Investigation hearing regarding the failures of the Firestone Wilderness tires; remained a member of the House of Representatives until 2005 when he went to work as the head of the Pharmaceutical and Manufacturers of America until June, 2010. He is now on the Board of Directors at Louisiana Healthcare Group.
Kathy Terrazone	Lisoni & Lisoni Office Manager and Paralegal, who directed and produced the Firestone Steeltex Recall Direct Mail Campaign and assumed full oversight responsibility for the office management while

	Joe & Gail were in China for 21 days. She is now enjoying retirement in Montana.
Jennifer Timian, Esq.	Attorney for the National Highway Transportation & Safety Administration (NHTSA); participated in the presentation on 5-7-03 to reveal the results of the tires manufactured pursuant to "C-95" Cost Steeltex tire; today she is the Chief of the Recall Management Division, Office of Defects Investigations Enforcement at NHTSA.
Linda Torre, CSR	Certified Court Reporter; accompanied Lisoni & Lisoni to Ningbo, China to record 20 depositions of victims of a tread separation 7-30-2000.
Rae Tyson	National Highway Transportation & Safety Administration, (NHTSA) spokesperson regarding the Firestone Steeltex National Tire Recall Campaign Petitions.
USA Today	National News Print Media Company which produced several articles about the Firestone Steeltex National Tire Recall Campaign; it is published daily with a circulation of 1,021,638 readers.
United Press International (UPI)	National and International News Print Media Company which produced several articles

The Players – Who They Were and What are They Doing Now

	about the Firestone Steeltex National Tire Recall Campaign; today it has 6,000 media subscribers and services news organizations nationwide.
United Steelworkers Union	Located in Pittsburg, Pennsylvania; endorsed Lisoni & Lisoni's National Recall Campaign to recall Steeltex tires; it is today, the largest labor union in the U.S. with 860,294 members.
U.S. Secret Service	After being notified by Lisoni & Lisoni of the dangers to President George W. Bush resulting from the use of Steeltex tires on the trucks he used at his Texas ranch and Suburbans that were used to transport him from the White House to Camp David, it notified the President and had the tires removed; it continues today protecting the President of the United States.
Wall Street Journal	World-wide, well respected national business newspaper; today it is published 6 days a week with a circulation of 2,777,000 readers and is considered the largest newspaper in the United States.
Ann Washington	Chief Researcher for Congressman William Tauzin in the Wilderness Congressional investigation,

	which resulted in the recall of millions of Bridgestone/Firestone Wilderness tires.
Washington Post	National News Print Media Company which produced several articles about the Firestone Steeltex National Tire Recall Campaign; it is published in Washington, DC witha circulation of 474,707 readers.
Shigeo Watanabe	President & CEO of Bridgestone Corporation; stepped down on March 30, 2006.
Kenneth N. Weinstein	NHTSA Associate Administrator for Defect Enforcement; retired from NHTSA and entered the private practice of law with the Washington, DC firm of Mayer Brown and continues to work in the field of automotive defects and safety.
Richard T. Williams, Esq.	Partner in the Los Angeles office of the firm of Holland & Knight, defense attorneys for Bridgestone/Firestone, Inc. in the National Class Action; he continues at Holland & Knight, specializing in class action defense and still represents Bridgestone/Firestone.
Fred Witherspoon, Esq.	Attorney refereed to Lisoni & Lisoni the Chinese doctors that were injured by a defective

The Players – Who They Were and What are They Doing Now

	Firestone Steeltex tire; the case led to the discovery of the nationwide defect in the Steeltex tire; he passed away in 2011, from complications associated with a stroke.
Jian Ping Zhang	Chinese paralegal who acted as liaison between clients in China and Lisoni & Lisoni; she is today a Real Estate agent in Los Angeles, California.

CPSIA information can be obtained
at www.ICGtesting.com
Printed in the USA
FSHW021936181020
74834FS